D0905027

Innovation and the Pharmaceutical Industry

Innovation and the Pharmaceutical Industry

Critical Reflections on the Virtues of Profit

Edited by

H. Tristram Engelhardt, Jr.

Rice University, Houston

and

Jeremy R. Garrett

California State University, Sacramento

M&M Scrivener Press

Published by M & M Scrivener Press
3 Winter Street, Salem, MA 01970

http://www.mmscrivenerpress.com

Trends and Conflicts®: Studies in Values and Policies
Series Editor, H. Tristram Engelhardt, Jr.

Cover design by Hannus Design

Library of Congress Cataloging-In-Publication Data

Innovation and the pharmaceutical industry : critical reflections on the virtues of profit / edited by H. Tristram Engelhardt Jr. and Jeremy R. Garrett.

p. ; cm. -- (Trends and conflicts)

Includes bibliographical references and index.

ISBN-13: 978-0-9802094-4-0 (hardcover : alk. paper)

ISBN-10: 0-9802094-4-7 (hardcover : alk. paper)

1. Pharmaceutical industry. 2. Drug development. 3. Medical innovations. I. Engelhardt, H. Tristram (Hugo Tristram), 1941- II. Garrett, Jeremy R. III. Series.

[DNLM: 1. Drug Industry--economics--United States. 2. Drug Industry--ethics--United States. 3. Health Policy--United States. 4. Pharmaceutical Preparations--economics--United States. QV 736 I584 2008]

HD9665.5.I55 2008

338.4'791510973--dc22

2008010541

ISBN: 978-0-9802094-4-0 (hardcover : alk. paper)

Printed in the United States on acid-free paper.

Contents

Preface

In every area of healthcare, decisions are life and death matters. Patients, their families, their doctor, the researchers, the makers of medicines, the operators of facilities, and even the drivers of ambulances make ethical decisions every day. Ambulance drivers decide where to take patients. Nurses or even clerks decide who gets treated first. Doctors decide which tests to run and which not to run. Drug manufacturers invest in some lines of research and not others. Administrators decide which test equipment to purchase and how much to charge for its use. People decide to be organ donors or not to be. Some people get the organs and others don't. Governments decide which countries get the medical aid. Families decide how much treatment for a loved one is enough. At every turn there are opportunities to make choices badly or well. But the worst choice is any uninformed choice, one where you don't understand the issues, the big picture, and what may be at stake.

The pharmaceutical industry is beset by claims that the companies used false data, hid studies, promoted products for non-approved uses, and lied to or bought off the FDA (Food and Drug Administration) – all to improve profits. Medical device manufacturers are accused of selling inferior products. Hospitals are accused of providing good treatment only to the well-insured. People need to trust their healthcare providers, yet the entire industry is in crisis. Among healthcare recipients, there will always be a large number of people who believe they have been hurt by someone whose job was to help them. And those people file lawsuits every day.

Bioethics applies the study of ethical decision making to all areas of healthcare – pharmaceuticals, medical devices, and hospitals among them. In the world of healthcare, particularly drug development, bioethicists and the work they do are critically important. The healthcare industry does not want to make uninformed choices, nor are they in the business of hurting people. Pharmaceutical manufacturers hire bioethicists to help provide clarity on the key issues that will result in their decisions. Many companies have such people on staff, just as they have people in charge of government regulatory compliance. There are many publications and much research devoted to bioethical studies.

I write this from a defense lawyer's perspective – not necessarily the only point of view – and from my perspective, all litigation is about ethics. Defense trial lawyers are left to explain the ethical decisions already made by others. The absence of sound bioethical training in anyone involved in healthcare litigation is as dangerous as trying a healthcare case without a basic understanding of the medicine and science involved. Not all of these essays are related to the law, but in one way or another, most are. Because litigation in these industries more frequently derives from difficult questions of judgment than from violations of rules or laws, an understanding of bioethics has become a necessary and fundamental tool of drug, device, and other healthcare litigators.

This book attempts to compile some of the best thinking from a variety of perspectives. No one opinion is promoted here above others. And, clearly, these essays were not written or compiled for the specific benefit of lawyers like myself. But these essays and works like them should be required reading for attorneys whose practice touches the healthcare industry and for anyone who makes decisions regarding any aspect of healthcare.

Martin D. Beirne
Beirne, Maynard & Parsons, L.L.P.
Houston, Texas

Pharmaceutical Innovation and the Market:

The Pursuit of Profit and the Amelioration of the Human Condition

H. Tristram Engelhardt, Jr., Department of Philosophy, Rice University & Jeremy R. Garrett, Department of Philosophy, California State University, Sacramento

Profit is often a bad word in many bioethical reflections on the pharmaceutical and medical-device industry. For many, making money in health care is politically incorrect. It is as if doing things with less money in a scarcity economy would be morally preferable. This volume critically examines the central place of profit in the development of pharmaceuticals, medical devices, and health care generally. In various ways, these essays show that, in order to pursue human well-being, one ought positively to affirm profit for the pharmaceutical and medical-device industries, insofar as innovation is intimately connected to the prospect of profit. In fact, as these various contributions make clear, it would be impossible to account adequately for the range of pharmaceuticals and medical devices that have become part of everyday medicine without recognizing that the depth and scope of innovations are tied not simply to altruism, a concern for the common good, or the pursuit of knowledge for its own sake, but crucially to the pursuit of private good and of individual profit. Any account of access to new pharmaceuticals or important new medical devices will be woefully inadequate unless it

H.T. Engelhardt, Jr. and J. Garrett (eds), *Innovation and the Pharmaceutical Industry* (pp. 1–16).

positively appreciates the driving power of what many might unabashedly call greed. What erotic interest is for marriage, interest in profit is for the development of pharmaceuticals and medical devices that can effectively lower morbidity and mortality risks. Granted, as lust must be put into its proper place in marriage so that it becomes a dimension of love, so, too, greed must be put within a social context that renders it integral to the pursuit of well-being.

I. The Social Responsibility of Pursuing Profit

The volume opens with Engelhardt's examination of the central place of the market, especially in liberal, secular, pluralist, limited democracies. As is argued, the market and the pursuit of profit have their central place by default and because of their cardinal benefits. First, the market is a cardinal place for peaceable cooperation in the face of moral disagreement. As Engelhardt argues, when moral strangers meet, the market, along with limited democracies and contracts, offers one of their major means for morally authoritative collaboration. Even when persons cannot agree about anything else, they can at least agree to buy and sell goods and services. This essay explores why the market and the pursuit of profit are not only a default mechanism for collaboration in a world marked by intractable moral controversy and diversity; it is also indispensable if one is interested in securing human survival and in decreasing morbidity and mortality risks. If the allure of profit drives innovation in the pharmaceutical and medical-device industry, then one should be concerned with any policies that limit profit in these industries as compared to others. Any attempt to curtail profit will likely lead not only to slower advances in the ability to lower morbidity and mortality risks, but it may as well threaten the capacity of humans to adapt to new microbial (such as multi-drug-resistant tuberculosis) and other threats. Critical concerns for policies that limit the profitability of the pharmaceutical and medical-device industries should also include a reassessment of easily acquired, poorly grounded, and large liability judgments against the manufacturers of pharmaceuticals and medical devices. These concerns should also include a critical regard of policies that would limit profits through the breach of patents by developing countries. Such limitations will encourage virtuous stewards of investment capital to avoid investing in the cure of diseases found primarily in such countries. The very character of human finitude places money, market and profit as central elements in the project of improving the human condition.

Capaldi develops this point further by showing the need for better public understanding of the reality and economics of contemporary healthcare—a context that recommends a full commitment to a free market economy in developing and distributing its diverse goods and services. As Capaldi argues, only such a commitment can maximize innovation as well as harness efficiency and productivity in the pursuit of the Technological Project of the modern world (i.e., the sustained attempt to "control the physical universe and make it responsive and subservient to humanity"). The Technological Project, in turn, represents our greatest success thus far, as well as our best future prospect, for increasing the longevity and quality of human life—a fact that must be made very clear to the public. One must deconstruct the false view that profit in pursuit of new pharmaceuticals and medical devices is wrong.

To this end, Capaldi argues that pharmaceutical industry should learn to market ideas, not just drugs. It should take a leading role in healthcare debates and efforts to educate the public with respect to the realities, challenges, and promises of healthcare. The industry must especially highlight the ever-present chances of newly emerging fatal diseases, explain and emphasize the central role of the profit motive in medical innovation, and acknowledge and promote their social responsibility as an important social transaction cost. Capaldi regards the pharmaceutical industry as being as vital as the defense industry, insofar as world-wide health threats pose as much danger to national security as terrorist and military threats. As with the defense industry, the pharmaceutical industry should not be asked to subsidize its contributions to the national (and international) good.

In her contribution to the volume, Pepe Lee Chang analyzes and critically evaluates the oft heard claim that pharmaceutical companies are under a special obligation vis a vis other corporations or businesses to save lives in undeveloped (and even developed) countries, either by donating, drastically reducing their prices, or relaxing their intellectual property rights to allow for the production of generic versions of their products. When pharmaceutical companies have been reluctant, understandably, to be the exclusive actors (and, hence, sole bearers of cost) in such charitable enterprises, Chang argues, they are unfairly singled out as immoral and psychopathically obsessed with profit margins. What these characterizations fail to appreciate, however, is the need first to identify a morally relevant difference between pharmaceutical and other corporations or businesses that would justify imputing a special obligation *exclusively* to the former.

To demonstrate the inadequacy of such a critique of the pharmaceutical industry, Chang situates her arguments within the geography of business ethics, drawing familiar distinctions between moral and legal obligations and also between three distinct accounts of corporate moral obligation—stockholder theory, stakeholder theory, and social-responsibility theory. After arguing that none of these accounts coherently can underwrite the social deadbeat charge leveled at pharmaceutical companies, Chang focuses on the important question of whether pharmaceutical companies are "special"—that is, relevantly and sufficiently unique with respect to their status as potential life-savers or welfare-improvers. Here she articulates and responds to five important attempts to establish the special character of pharmaceutical companies. She emphasizes throughout one very simple, but often neglected, point—namely, that any successful business or corporation, whatever their product or service line, could contribute monetary funds that could be used to purchase pharmaceutical or other life-saving goods and services. Thus, even if there exists a special obligation on the part of successful corporations to assist in saving and improving the lives of the unfortunate (a matter on which Chang does not take a final position), it scarcely follows, and indeed sounds patently unfair, to expect pharmaceutical companies to bear the full cost of discharging this obligation.

At best, then, the case for thinking the pharmaceutical industry is culpable of a unique and significant moral failure has not been made, since we have as yet no adequate specification and defense of the relevant difference(s) between pharmaceutical and other industries. At worst, Chang's simple but neglected point—that *money* is always a life-saving and welfare-improving resource and, hence, *all* corporations are always potential life-savers or welfare-improvers—might be understood to entail that such a specification and defense is unavailable *in principle.* One could add that by unjustifiably singling out pharmaceutical companies and contributing to the culture of suspicion against them, these critics, however admirable their concern for the less fortunate, actually have the unintended consequence of diverting the scarce resources and energies of the industry away from saving and improving lives and instead toward the salvaging of public reputations. The critique of the moral position of the pharmaceutical industry for not having shouldered a special obligation to care for those in need of pharmaceuticals, as many of the essays in this volume show, in the long run harms those whom the critics wish to help.

II. Autonomy, Advertising, and Pharmaceutical Costs

A topic of particular salience for contemporary pharmaceutical ethics is the triangular relationship between patient autonomy, advertising, and pharmaceutical costs. Taylor picks up the problem of escalating costs in pharmaceuticals in the US and elsewhere by critically focusing attention on accounts of the negative consequences of patient choices to purchase name-brand medications over generic brands which are equally effective. Chief among these undesirable results is sharply increasing consumer expenditures without any comparable increase in healthcare benefits. This increase, in turn, fuels another—specifically, the costs of medical insurance, which get borne primarily by individuals (regardless of whether they buy their own insurance or have it covered by their employer). According to Graber and Tansey (2005), the continued rise in pharmaceutical costs is strongly linked to patient misinformation about the risks, effects, and relative costs of different pharmaceuticals. As they see the problem, consumer ignorance and confusion produces misguided preferences for more expensive name-brands, the effects of which include social and economic problems for which consumers are also not aware. The solution, they argue, lies in a commitment to practices that both respect patient autonomy while addressing wider concerns of social justice. Specifically, they propose that patients should be required to sign a formal document indicating that they have been informed of, and understand, the personal, social, and economic costs of choosing name-brands over the generic brands. Taylor argues that Graber and Tansey's analysis and solution rests on a misunderstanding both of autonomy itself and also of its relationship to informed consent. In particular, their proposal confuses a person's being autonomous with a person's acting only in ideally advisable ways and on the basis of all available facts. For Taylor, persons can be fully autonomous with respect to their choices, even if they lack information that otherwise would have influenced their choices, since it is sufficient for the exercise of autonomy that persons make their own choices in light of their belief system, free from the interference of others. Moreover, patients may not willingly forgo the name-brands, even if they are informed about their negative effects, since they might suppose that their individual forgoing will have a negligible effect on the overall amount of pharmaceutical production, distribution, and consumption.

In his positive argument, Taylor identifies the option to choose the name-brands over general brands as the "ultimate constraining option."

By this, he means that both the person making the choice and the relevant group of which they are part are unable to exercise their autonomy as they see fit. Taylor proposes a solution which, rather than demanding a change in patients' pharmaceutical preferences, instead works within the existing financial networks overlaying the distribution of healthcare. He argues that the best way to lower pharmaceutical prices is through individual medical accounts, since this would encourage patients to compare the relative costs of different brands. In this scenario, even if some patients preferred to use expensive name-brand pharmaceuticals, their choice would not affect the healthcare costs of others. Neither would it result in a curtailment or elimination of healthcare access for others.

The view that there should be more stringent government regulation of pharmaceutical advertisements is addressed by Andrew Cohen. As he sees it, pharmaceuticals are consumer products like any other. Hence, there is no reason to impose unique or more restrictive rules to regulate the advertising of these products than those that already regulate the advertising of other products. To make this case, Cohen sets out to demonstrate how inconclusive each argument for stricter regulations on pharmaceutical advertising turns out to be. Cohen begins by considering whether and to what extent pharmaceutical advertising is consistent with a concern for patient autonomy. He acknowledges that while pharmaceutical advertising promotes consumer awareness of medical problems and their treatments, it also encourages the tendency of many patients to buy advertised name-brand drugs over the roughly equivalent, but much less expensive, generic alternatives. However, as Cohen points out, this problem is not unique to pharmaceutical advertising. It extends to all advertising, insofar as marketing restricts consumer autonomy by creating needs in the consumer. The challenge to his opponents turns out to be two-headed: they must either (1) compellingly show that pharmaceutical advertising uniquely threatens patient autonomy, or (2) demonstrate that it would not do so only under strict regulation.

Cohen explores the prospects for opponents favorable to each general strategy. He considers four separate arguments for the thesis that pharmaceutical advertising uniquely compromises patient autonomy and shows, in turn, how each fails to draw a relevant distinction between pharmaceutical advertising and advertising in general. However, things do not seem more promising for those inclined to pursue the second strategy, as the curtailing or banning of pharmaceutical advertising is likely to produce greater problems than those it is put forward to solve. For example, the primary alternative vehicle for getting information to patients would almost surely become individual physicians. Rather than serving as informed and neutral conduits of medical wisdom, however, doctors would likely be "rented" out by the companies with the largest budgets (i.e., they would be guaranteed an income stream for restricting patient access to the prescription drug market). Such a scenario would distort consumer decisions in ways that would likely have worse consequences than anything attributable to current modes of disseminating information and advertising. Cohen concludes by arguing that much depends on empirical issues - strict regulation on pharmaceutical advertising might increase consumer autonomy, but there will always be potential dangers given any regulatory regime. According to him, pharmaceutical advertising stands or falls with advertising as such, and so one has to first consider the merits of all advertising, before one points fingers against pharmaceutical advertising in particular.

III. Some Criticisms of the Pharmaceutical Industry Critically Re-Examined

In his essay, Epstein argues against what one might term updated versions of socialist arguments against the pharmaceutical industry, such as those advanced by Public Citizen (2002), as well as Relman and Angell (2002). The latter argue that the pharmaceutical industry holds, contra Cohen, a unique status within the marketplace. Hence, it is very dangerous to allow their policies to be governed mainly by the financial aspirations of their investors and executives. Epstein responds to Relman and Angell by pointing out that all businesses are setup with the aim of maximizing profits, and the investors and creditors of the pharmaceutical industry are no different from other industry bodies in this respect. Any price regulation seeking to deny the return of profit one would ordinarily expect from setting up the pharmaceutical business will only lead to the long-term disadvantage of consumers, who need their products and services.

Epstein defends the pharmaceutical industry's practices by explaining these practices from an economic and business standpoint. He discusses seven issues here:

(1) *Drug Utilization:* Relman and Angell launch their attack on the pharmaceutical industry by pointing out the high rise in the cost of pre-

scription drugs. Epstein begins his response by noting that these price increases are not the same throughout all periods. Moreover, vital components in the overall national health care budget are attributable to matters that are entirely outside the control of the pharmaceutical industry. In fact, the overall budget is shaped mainly by a national commitment to treat health care as a right, regardless of the individual's ability to pay for it.

(2) *Price Discrimination:* Relman and Angell, who are disturbed by the pricing of patented goods, call for a weakening of the protection currently afforded to patentees of prescription drugs. However, Epstein argues that price discrimination is an indispensable feature of pharmaceutical pricing. The differences in the rates of drugs are due to the need for the patentees and the manufacturers to recover their costs quickly. Epstein defends a compromise that allows for a certain degree of price discrimination, thereby benefiting both consumers (who could then pay a uniform price throughout a drug's history) and the patentees (who need to be rewarded for their investments, if they will continue to invest in pharmaceuticals).

(3) *Price Variation for Individual Drugs:* Epstein explores the objection that the costs of particular drug prescriptions rise, in some cases, more rapidly than inflation. However, Epstein notes that the rates quoted in the statistics are average rates, which do not take into consideration the price variation to different user classes (variation which might be quite large given the institutional framework in which drugs are distributed in the United States). He also points out that it is very unclear as to exactly what inferences should be drawn from these rate increases.

(4) *The Private Public Interface:* Here Epstein considers the question of why one should use the patent system at all when government research could sponsor the development of new drugs. Epstein acknowledges that the use of government funds to sponsor basic research is a vital component in a system of drug production, but he argues that it is incorrect to conclude that such basic patents should remain in public hands, once the basic science has been established.

(5) *Me-Too Drugs:* Relman and Angell argue that the introduction of me-too drugs, created to compete with particular drugs that enjoy monopolies, does not actually lead to price reduction. Epstein exposes the short-sightedness of this argument on both economic and medical grounds. From the medical point of view, the availability of two drugs implies that the second one can be tried if there are no particular benefits from using the first one, or if the latter has some adverse side effects.

From the economic side, the presence of the second drug means that the first drug has lost its monopoly on the market.

(6) *Marketing and Advertising Practices:* From Relman and Angell's point of view, marketing is seen only as an effort to woo the medical profession into abandoning their own freedom, and to convince the public to demand or purchase new high-price drugs that are not worth their extra cost. Epstein concedes that puffery and temptations are threats associated with pharmaceutical businesses, but the question here is one of measure and proportion. And, on these accounts, he argues that his opponents overstate their case. Epstein also points to the benefits of advertising, which may in some cases justify the associated costs.

(7) *Drug Costs:* Finally, Epstein examines Relman and Angell's argument that the costs of researching and developing new drugs are not as high as they are made out to be. They suggest the drug industry has inflated its estimates of the costs of production in an effort to stave off price-control measures they deem inappropriate to this market. Epstein notes that there are various factors that add to the cost of producing a new drug—time spent on research, on experiments, on repeated failures, etc.—and that the proper mode of calculating drug costs should include the cost of capital over time.

The moral realities of the anti-market forces besetting global drug innovation are explored by Michael Rie, who proposes possible routes to recapturing a robust market morality in global drug production and distribution. He questions whether the efforts put into a drug's research and development can be divorced from considering future economic sustainability. As a case in point, he discusses the case of the drug Xigris® which has met its market resistance level, and the ethical profit making opportunities for drug companies in such an environment. Rie also calls for a resolution of drug-consumer rebellions (i.e., purchasing pharmaceuticals from Canada) before there is a drug industry implosion. He argues that there should be a moral commitment, on the part of the entire industry, to a unitary global pricing strategy modeled after those governing world commodity markets in oil, coffee, and sugar. Long term success, he argues, requires "short term discipline and corporate sacrifice of all drug companies in countries that propose to protect intellectual property rights" (p. 8). Global pricing, for Rie, promises a potential benefit to other countries as well, in that globalization of prices will be politically and morally easier to accept prior to national policy interests complicating the implementation of policy. With the globalization of prices, patients around the world will be obliged to participate more directly in the purchase of their drugs. Market efficiency will allow for new drugs to be developed, companies to be economically viable, and pharmaco-economics and marketing employees to be held accountable for upholding an unfettered market morality.

Rie then discusses the retailing value and financial valuation of Compliance Leveraging®, an all encompassing methodology of investment valuation in the biotechnology and pharmaceutical industries. Here, the quality of research activities and marketing methods will primarily determine how capital seeks out quality performers in the industry. What will remain a vital issue is the extent to which the Compliance Leveraging® reporting system will prove of benefit to internal operations of corporations and the advantage of that informational dissemination to the investment community of the world. He ties these issues to a discussion of research ethics by noting that institutions engaging in cost-containment health care have been negligent in not recognizing that their cost-containment studies are actually instances of population-based research. One way to avoid scrutiny by Institutional Review Boards (IRBs) has been to keep these activities outside the purview of research ethics, which has been practiced by researchers. Such activity, for the researchers, is an additional deadweight and resource consumptive activity, which does not add to the value of their science. He argues that a shift from regulatory culture to one of research responsibility is called for, which may find expression in the Compliance Leveraging® method for the drug industry. Rie also argues that ethical issues underlying the corporate process of care in hospitals or the health system not be conflated with the purity of research and clinical trials in the development of new pharmaceuticals. He concludes his paper by arguing that developing a policy of funding independent institutional review boards (IRBs) devoid of governmental restriction can nevertheless help to clarify the ethical confusion that exists in medical research, cost containment, and medical publication.

IV. Markets, Pharmaceuticals and Health Savings Accounts

The costs of pharmaceuticals and medical devices are set within the issue of health care costs generally. Goodman traces back some of the major anomalies of the current healthcare system in the United States to the ways in which patients pay for health care and increasingly for medical devices and pharmaceuticals. He argues that the principle payment methods are not the result of free market sources, but rather of distortions created by public policies, which reflects a failure to understand contemporary economics. Goodman goes on to suggest possible changes to public policy that might overcome these anomalies. Goodman begins by noting that it is time, and not money, which is the rationing device in American healthcare. Since demand is greater than supply, a patient spends a lot of time waiting in turn for the physician. Even if patients decide to get medical advice via telephone or e-mail, the same problem arises in light of the demand again exceeding supply. Thus, because healthcare cannot be both easily accessible and free, waiting appears to be an essential feature of healthcare. Reducing the demand through quality degeneration is not a viable option, since physicians understandably fear malpractice litigation and/or remain highly committed to their own professional ethical standards. In general, Goodman argues that it is difficult to get physicians to reduce non-price amenities (e.g., e-mail or telephone consultations, generic vs. name-brand drug counseling, etc.), since it is not in their financial self-interest. Because physicians get paid by third parties such as Medicare, they are not generally willing to implement services such as e-mail and telephone consultations or informing the patients about generic drugs which are as effective as name-brands. The result of all this is waiting. As Goodman notes, this is a poor way of delivering healthcare, as there is no way to insure that those most in need will receive service first—patients who can treat themselves can make visits to the doctor, while people who urgently need assistance may not get the required healthcare. On the other hand, while patients can reduce their own time and waiting periods by researching healthcare providers and the costs of drugs, they tend not to bother, since third parties pay for their healthcare and thereby lessen the incentive. Goodman locates the source of these problems in the third-party payment system, which is increasingly involved in pharmaceutical and medical-device markets. One solution would be to avoid the third party system all together with the aid of entrepreneurship, such as by creating patient Health Savings Accounts (HSAs), which allow for and provide incentives for patients making their own unbiased choices. However, Goodman identifies a number of problems with the current HSA system, which bears on the controversies regarding pricing and profits in the pharmaceutical industry. Until recently, HSA deposits have been subject to payroll and income taxes, whereas third party insurance premiums are often tax free. Moreover, the law requires employers to make the same deposit to every employee's account, irrespective of the fact that the actual healthcare costs may vary substantially from one employee to another. In addition, the law forces the employees to use their HSAs in a way that piggybacks onto the current payment system, rather than to challenge it. Goodman concludes his paper by suggesting possible changes to be made in public policy to overcome this situation. In particular, he critically identifies tax laws which encourage everyone to pay all medical bills through third party payers and argues that the discounted fees of doctors and discounted costs of the drugs which the insurers receive should also be provided to the patients. Employers also should be free to make different contributions to the HSAs of different employees, depending on their employees' healthcare status. Goodman argues that there also needs to be complete flexibility with respect to the setting of deductibles and copayments. Freed from the constraints of conventional health insurance, Goodman holds, the market would be free to offer products that reduce both time and money costs in patient-pleasing ways. He concludes by citing the example of South Africa, whose experience with HSAs can be used as a guide in bringing about policy changes in the United States.

The dangers of parallel trade involving prescription drugs from Canada to the US are examined in the paper by John R. Graham. Canadian entrepreneurs exploit loopholes in the system to export prescription drugs from Canada to the US, in the pretext of providing them to a significant number of individual consumers in America who could otherwise not afford them. This process continues, even though parallel trade is normally illegal both in the US and in Canada. Graham points out that parallel trade, unlike free trade, opposes the interests of the affected manufacturers. Free trade allows manufacturers to negotiate vertical restraints with distributors, such that price differences and hence competition are maintained. Parallel trade, which opposes this policy, might lead to a situation where manufactures charge only one price, which will more likely be the higher price than the lower one. In addition to making it virtually impossible for drug makers to know who actually is buying their products, parallel trade also turns out to be more expensive and less safe than free trade. Furthermore, according to Graham, the main idea behind making parallel trade illegal is that it ensures that the inventors of patented goods are free from competition from equivalent, identical products. If parallel trade is allowed, then inventors cannot prevent the parallel traders from debasing the quality of their products or from counterfeiting them. Finally, Graham also points out that there is a real danger that research-based drug makers and manufactures will totally cut-off supplies to Canada, if the law normalizes parallel trade. These manufacturers will risk continuing the supply of innovative drugs to Canada, only if the US government can completely prevent the parallel trading of generic medicines from Canada to the US. Graham ends his paper by expressing his reservations that the US government can take such a drastic step.

V. Pharmaceutical Liability: Another Source of Health Care Costs

In the closing paper, Johnson and Iltis address the issue of the costs on the development of pharmaceuticals and medical devices imposed by the less-than-optimal approaches of tort law. They offer a framework for understanding the emergence of legal judgments that do not comport with scientific evidence, resulting in imbalances which might threaten pharmaceutical and medical device innovation. They focus on the conditions that shape product liability litigation and influence outcomes, while discussing whether corporations that provide healthcare or sell health-related products (i.e., pharmaceuticals and medical devices) have special moral duties to individuals and society at large. They point out that even if it is true that corporations have special obligations to other parties, there is considerable disagreement concerning how to rank and interpret those interests. Next, they highlight the points of convergence and divergence of science and law. Attempting to demonstrate a causal connection between the product and the alleged harm is critical to determining liability in products litigation. As examples, they discuss some cases involving silicone breast implants where no strong epidemiological evidence was available to establish that silicone implants had caused any harm. Nevertheless, in many legal cases, large amounts of money were awarded to plaintiffs. Unlike science, the law does not reexamine decisions which it considers to be final. Also, the law's relatively fast-paced resolution of disputes clashes with science's slow and labored progression towards consensus. Due to these points of divergence between law and science, plaintiffs are left with a choice between not bringing a claim at all and bringing one based on insufficient scientific evidence. Johnson and Iltis point out that normally the latter option is chosen. They then analyze the principle cultural, sociological and psychological factors shaping and driving the legal decisions that result. They argue that much of the explanation for the disconnection between evidence and awards turns on the social construction of the concepts of trust, causation, proof, consent, fault, and responsibility.

This social construction of reality in courts of law depends on the ways in which a story is told (an issue of dramatization) in the context of litigation influence the judge's and jury's understanding of blame and responsibility. Johnson and Iltis point out that juries recognize something as a fact by organizing and giving significance to the facts with which they are presented by using stories that they construct themselves, emerging from their own beliefs and their own experience. They also argue that even judges understand facts through the lens of a narrative. What exacerbates this situation is that lawyers are by training, if not by personality, predisposed to accept the power of a narrative and a "social construction of reality" because these notions express the common experience in the law that different people see things differently. Next, Johnson and Ilits consider the role of trust in litigation and the extent to which a party or witness's trustworthiness or perceived trustworthiness might influence a juror's assessment of the information being presented. The history of corporate scandals and breaches of trust fuels outrage among jurors. Even when the particular corporate defendant's history is not tainted, the plaintiff's attorneys may be able to count on a general sense of outrage against corporate giants to win the jury's trust and sympathy.

All of this is compounded by the challenge of presenting scientific and statistical information to jurors. Johnson and Iltis argue that most persons have a limited understanding of basic science, statistics, statistical analysis, and the concept of risk. This allows the parties involved in the litigation to construct a reality for jurors that does not necessarily closely mirror the reality supported by the scientific evidence. Further, they highlight the fact that all drugs and devices have side-effects and carry some risk, and that patients must engage in a cost-benefit analysis to determine if the risks are "worth it" for them. This is something that neither patients nor jurors may understand. Quite different are risks of which a manufacturer knew but failed to address and/or failed adequately to warn consumers. A third scenario regarding risk and informed consent concerns a manufacturer intentionally not pursuing certain kinds of tests in order to avoid identifying problems it would be obligated to disclose. The final case involving risk is where a patient is not informed about a particular risk because it was not known. The liability issue in this case may turn on the question of whether the manufacturer could have and should have known about the risk.

The cultures of science and law differ and sometimes clash with respect to the understanding of causal connections and of how they should be established. While scientists are still gathering and evaluating data and thus are not able to make judgments, the legal system requires that suits be filed, cases be heard, and juries render verdicts. Moreover, it is very difficult, if not impossible for science to obtain absolute certainty in its inquiries. But litigation requires an end-point, a decision. In law, the assessments of causation have a finality which science lacks. The standards for the quantity of evidence required to make decisions regarding causation in litigation is not as high as it is in science. Further, the focus of questions concerning causation and the goal in assessing causation is different in the law and in science. Finally, Johnson and Iltis conclude by highlighting the exceptional role of media in products-liability. This role can hardly be overstated and takes many forms, from significantly increasing the public's faith in science and medicine, to influencing juries and inaccurately portraying a system gone wild.

VI. Toward a Richer Appreciation of the Relationship Between Profit and Innovation

The issues raised in this volume go to the heart of how in a high-technology culture one should understand the proper role of profit. It turns out that simplistic attempts to aid access to drugs and devices by limiting prices will have harms as well as short-term benefits. Attempts to control prices of pharmaceuticals and medical devices in order to advantage patients in the present will inevitably disadvantage patients in the future for whom there will not be the means to address new threats to health or to provide new ways of lowering morbidity and mortality risks. Attempts to regard advertising and profits in the pharmaceutical and medical-device industries in a light different from other areas of the economy turn out to be more difficult than one might expect. Legal judgment against pharmaceuticals and medical-device manufacturers that are excessive or scientifically unsound will advantage current litigators at the price of disadvantaging patients in the future. If innovation in the pharmaceutical and medical-device industries is as important as would appear, then Nicholas Capaldi is correct that much must be done to change the culture of suspicions against profit in general and against profit in the pharmaceutical and medical-device industries in particular. Undoubtedly, much of this distrust is rooted in broader commitments to an egalitarianism of envy, which is suspicious of any that have more, even when great equality will be to the disadvantage of most. The contributors to this volume offer a rich set of perspectives on how to meet these challenges set against the backdrop of the human condition in which persons have the aspirations of gods and goddesses, but only the limited resources and challenging circumstances of finite men and women.

This volume would never have taken shape without the insight, commitment, and generous and patient support of Beirne, Maynard & Parsons, L.L.P. In particular, the editors are deeply grateful to Martin Beirne and Peter Feldman. Reflections on the issues that led to the commissioning of these papers began in late 2002 and came to take shape in essays that were the antecedents of this volume. An earlier version of some of the papers in this volume appeared in a publication by Beirne, Maynard & Parsons in 2005 with the title "The Ethics of Entitlement". Over the last three years, other authors joined this project and earlier papers were further developed and at times radically recast. Much of the onerous editorial labor was borne by Vinod Lakshmipathy and Erica Rangel, to whom the editors owe a special debt. Although this volume was inspired and supported by Beirne, Maynard & Parsons, L.L.P., the opinions expressed herein are those of the authors and the editors and do not necessarily reflect those of the law firm or its members. We are in special debt to the authors who recast their essays over these years of work so that this volume can offer the readers an insight into a politically incorrect and often ignored but nevertheless cardinal truth, namely, that innovation in the pharmaceutical and medical-device industries necessary to maintain and improve the human condition depends on the pursuit and realization of profit.

References

Graber, M.A. & Tansey, J.F. (2005). 'Autonomy, consent, and limiting healthcare costs,' *The Journal of Medical Ethics*, 32, 424-426.

Public Citizen's Congress Watch. (2002). *America's Other Drug Problem: A Briefing Book on the Rx Drug Debate* [Online]. Available at: http://www.citizen.org/documents/drugbriefingbk.pdf.

Relman, A.S. & Angell, M. (2002). 'America's other drug problem: How the drug industry distorts medicine and politics,' *The New Republic*, 227 (25), 27-41.

The Unavoidable Goodness of Profit: The Cunning of Reason and the Realization of Human Well-Being

H. Tristram Engelhardt, Jr.
Department of Philosophy, Rice University

I. Pharmaceuticals and Medical Devices: The Importance of Profit

Many are suspicious of, or indeed jealous of, the good fortune of others. Even when profit is gained in the market without fraud and with the consent of all buying and selling goods and services, there is a sense on the part of some that something is wrong if considerable profit is secured. There is even a sense that good fortune in the market, especially if it is very good fortune, is unfair. One might think of such rhetorically disparaging terms as "wind-fall profits". There is also a suspicion of the pursuit of profit because it is often embraced not just because of the material benefits it sought, but because of the hierarchical satisfaction of being more affluent than others. The pursuit of profit in the pharmaceutical and medical-device industries is for many in particular morally dubious because it is acquired from those who have the bad fortune to be diseased or disabled. Although the suspicion of profit is not well-founded, this suspicion is a major moral and public-policy challenge.

Profit in the market for the pharmaceutical and medical-device

H.T. Engelhardt, Jr. and J. Garrett (eds), *Innovation and the Pharmaceutical Industry* (pp. 17–32).

industries is to be celebrated. This is the case, in that if one is of the view (1) that the presence of additional resources for research and development spurs innovation in the development of pharmaceuticals and medical devices (i.e., if one is of the view that the allure of profit is one of the most effective ways not only to acquire resources but productively to direct human energies in their use), (2) that given the limits of altruism and of the willingness of persons to be taxed, the possibility of profits is necessary to secure such resources, (3) that the allure of profits also tends to enhance the creative use of available resources in the pursuit of pharmaceutical and medical-device innovation, and (4) if one judges it to be the case that such innovation is both necessary to maintain the human species in an ever-changing and always dangerous environment in which new microbial and other threats may at any time emerge to threaten human well-being, if not survival (i.e., that such innovation is necessary to prevent increases in morbidity and mortality risks), as well as (5) in order generally to decrease morbidity and mortality risks in the future, it then follows (6) that one should be concerned regarding any policies that decrease the amount of resources and energies available to encourage such innovation. One should indeed be of the view that the possibilities for profit, all things being equal, should be highest in the pharmaceutical and medical-device industries. Yet, there is a suspicion regarding the pursuit of profit in medicine and especially in the pharmaceutical and medical-device industries.

This paper argues that this suspicion of profit is ill-founded because it rests on a category mistake that confuses the goodness of charitable and beneficent acts, with the view that the pharmaceutical industry should be encumbered with enforceable obligations of charity with regard to those in need of pharmaceuticals and medical devices. Another way to put the matter is that, if one grants the positive tie between the pursuit of profit and medical innovation and also affirms as a good the relief of morbidity and mortality risks this innovation promises, one must then bear the burden of proof if one disparages the pursuit of profit in the pharmaceutical and medical-device industries as opposed to the pursuit of profit in the development of new and engaging videogames. The intuition that profit is wrong if gained from the unfortunate medical circumstances of patients in need of pharmaceuticals and medical devices should be recognized as a misleading temptation. It stems from a failure to recognize that the pursuit of profit has driven many substantial scientific, industrial, and technological developments that have made contemporary life relatively financially secure, prosperous, and healthy. The energies that the market set loose at the end of the 17th and the beginning of the 18th centuries, and which radically raised the standard of living in the West, are the same energies that currently drive innovation in the pharmaceutical and medical-device industries. To appreciate the proper place and role of profit, one needs to see how self-directed pursuits often come to have remarkably beneficent societal consequences.

The importance of self-directed interests in the market is an old theme. In responding to 18th century concerns regarding the market, Bernard de Mandeville (1670-1733) in *The Fable of the Bees* captured well the fact that the pursuit of private interests can produce public goods.[1] That is, the pursuit of individual wealth set within the rule of law generally leads to the flourishing of society as a whole. As he observed,

> So Vice is beneficial found,
> When it's by Justice lopt and bound; ... (p. 37)
> Thus Vice nurs'd Ingenuity,
> Which join'd with Time and Industry,
> Had carry'd Life's Conveniences,
> It's real Pleasures, Comforts, Ease,
> To such a Height, the very Poor
> Liv'd better than the Rich before,
> And nothing could be added more. (p. 26)
> Thus every Part was full of Vice,
> Yet the whole Mass a Paradise.... (p. 24)

The point is that fallen man in a broken world often achieves more for the benefit of his fellows when he pursues his own benefit and his personal advantage, than were he simply to attempt to act altruistically. When one confuses business with charity, then business will tend not to be profitable, and charity will tend not to be sincere.

This paper examines these issues with a special focus on the pharmaceutical and medical-device industries by first showing why the market is a cardinal means for peaceable collaboration in the face of moral diversity. The very character of the human condition marked by moral pluralism sets the market in central place as a means of morally appropriate interaction. Moreover, the pursuit of profit appears intimately connected with the realization of important human goods such as a longer life with less suffering. The place of profit in the pharmaceutical and medical-device industries is then explored in light of taking seriously the finitude of the human condition and the inequalities it produces.

Special focus is given to the inclination to establish an egalitarianism of jealousy that focuses on who has more rather than altruistically focusing on cheaply aiding those who have less. The essay ends with showing the centrality of profit in the pharmaceutical and medical-device industries to the project of relieving the human condition and therefore the concerns one should have when setting policy regarding legal liability and the protection of patent rights.

II. The Market and Profit by Default and by Positive Choice

The market is not only productive of benefits, it is a default means for cooperation in the face of moral pluralism. Acknowledging the proper role of profit in the pharmaceutical and medical-device industries requires appreciating the place of the market in coming to terms with one of the defining challenges for ethics, law, and public policy: people do not affirm a common, content-full morality.[2] The market is cardinal to moral action in the face of moral disagreement. It allows moral strangers to work together with mutual consent, despite their moral differences. This is not to deny that there is an objective morality; it is to recognize that we do not agree about its character and that we require a default means for collaborating despite our moral disagreements.[3] The market presents one of the cardinal practices uniting moral strangers in peaceable, morally authoritative collaboration (i.e., collaboration bound simply by the authority of common permission).

Moral pluralism defines the human condition. It may be the case that all moralities concern similar issues such as when it is improper, licit, or obligatory to kill, to have sex, to lie, etc. Moralities nevertheless differ in the settled judgments they support about when such actions are prohibited, licit, or obligatory. These disagreements support incompatible views of the good life and of human flourishing. As a consequence, one cannot coherently compare different polities, different legal systems without in advance choosing a particular view of the good as a standard by which to make comparisons. Imagine that one wanted to determine which political system is best in terms of which best realizes the goods of liberty, equality, prosperity, and security. One cannot make a determination unless one already has determined how one should rank these cardinal concerns. If one ranks liberty as individual freedom first, prosperity second, security third, and equality last, then one will affirm the Republic of Texas as the ideal polity. If one ranks security first, prosperity second, liberty third, and equality last, then one will endorse

Singapore. To determine the best societal structure, one must first determine which background ordering of goods and values is canonical. Here, of course, is where foundational disagreements lie.

To determine the correct ordering of primary human values, one cannot appeal to intuitions to establish the standard because others can meet one's particular intuitions with their contrary intuitions. How, then, can one determine which moral intuitions are canonical and should govern? One cannot appeal to a canonical balancing of intuitions because each party will have his own intuitions about which intuitive balancing is correct, and one cannot appeal to what works, because "what works" requires a particular standard of success. One cannot appeal to a plurality of considerations unless one already knows how rightly to weigh, order, or balance such considerations. There will not be a principled agreement as to which higher-level consideration should be invoked in weighing object-level considerations until one has first established a background standard. One cannot appeal to what rational decision-makers or contractors would choose, because they must first be fitted out with a particular moral sense or thin theory of the good to guide them, and that is what is in question. The determination of which moral sense is canonical itself requires a background moral vision.

People find themselves embedded in incompatible sets of moral judgments and clusters of intuitions, in different moralities, all without the ability to resolve their differences by sound rational argument.[4] If they wish to collaborate despite these differences, they must engage a practice such as the market, which draws authority from the limited agreement of the collaborators but requires no particular view of the wishes of God, the requirements of a content-full morality, or the nature of human flourishing. That is, disputes as to which account of justice, fairness, and morality should guide public interaction by default place centrally procedural mechanisms for limited collaboration, such as the market set within the constraints of a rule of law (i.e., a rule of law established within the constraints of a limited constitutional polity that does not coercively and in a totalizing fashion impose one ideology). This default basis for human collaboration, which recognizes moral diversity, as well as the limits of plausible common agreement in common projects, accounts for the worldwide salience and success of markets.[5] Moral pluralism and the limits of secular political moral authority put contracts and market transactions in central place, because we disagree about so much. It is those who are suspicious of the market and the profit it produces who should bear the burden of proof of showing that in particular circumstances the market involves fraud so as no longer to be a mechanism of peaceable cooperation. Absent such a showing, the market and the pursuit of profit must be accepted as fundamental default mechanisms for cooperation in the face of intractable moral diversity. Given the limits of secular morality, and because the market and the pursuit of profit are integral to a cardinal means of peaceable cooperation among moral strangers, profit from the market, including profit in the pharmaceutical and medical-device industries, must be presumed innocent until proven guilty.

Insofar as one affirms the goals of affluence, human safety against new microbial threats, and decreasing human morbidity and mortality risks, one should celebrate profit in the pharmaceutical and medical-device industries as beneficent. As a result, the supporters of the market can have it both ways. On the one hand, in the face of moral disagreement, they can point out that the market is not justified by a particular ranking of values, but by an appeal to the permission underlying the peaceable collaboration of consenting participants. On the other hand, the supporters of the market and profit can also appeal to a general interest in increasing the standard of living and decreasing morbidity and mortality risks in order to support the market, especially the role of the market and profit in encouraging innovation in the pharmaceutical and medical-device industries. Those who affirm the increase of affluence and the amelioration of morbidity and mortality risks should not only accept the market as a default means of collaboration, but also affirm the market as good in being productive of significant, beneficent outcomes. In short, the market is (1) a cardinal procedure for the collaboration of moral strangers in the face of intractable moral pluralism, (2) which should in general be affirmed as good by those interested in wealth, insofar as the market produces excess wealth, and (3) in the case of the pharmaceutical and medical-device industries, by those interested in the continued adaptation and survival of humans, as well as in the lowering of morbidity and mortality risks.

III. The Agonies of Finitude: Most Want the Best of Health Care Along with Pharmaceuticals and Medical Devises, All Provided Cheaply

The pharmaceutical and medical-device industries are cardinal human responses to the human condition, a condition defined by limits, which limits are by and large unpleasant. Twelve marks of human finitude frame these limitations and the context within which the moral suspicion of profit appears plausible.

1. All humans will die; no amount of health care will postpone death forever.
2. Almost all humans will suffer sometime before death; no amount of health care will fully eliminate all human suffering, disability, injury, and pain.
3. Humans are radically biologically unequal (e.g., some will die young, others at an advanced age).
4. Humans are socially unequal because they have made different choices, have different friends, and live within families with different social resources.
5. These biological and social inequalities are often simply fortunate and/or unfortunate, but not unfair, in that they have occurred without the violation of the rule of law or of anyone's forbearance rights.
6. Even when biological and social inequalities are due to failures of the rule of law and/or the violation of forbearance rights, so that it is clear that someone or some group has been unfairly disadvantaged by others, it does not follow that it is the responsibility of the pharmaceutical and medical-device industries to make compensation, provide aid, or be specifically charitable to those treated unfairly by others.
7. Human resources, including financial resources, are limited; if one invests all one's resources in health care, one may marginally extend life and decrease suffering, but one will have no resources to enjoy the extra years secured.
8. Medical knowledge is generally probabilistic; one usually cannot with certainty know what will work and how well in a particular instance.
9. Human secular moral knowledge claims are the subject of persistent controversy (as shown in section II) so that
10. There is no agreement about how one ought to gamble with life, death, and suffering.
11. Given the different biological endowments and circumstances as well as the different social endowment and circumstances that define the basic inequality of humans, different investments will be made in medical and other life gambles that will at times blunt and at times increase the differences defining human inequalities.
12. Inequalities among persons, especially with regard to suffering and death, will often provoke jealousy, leading to the affirmation of an egalitarianism of jealousy (i.e., a concern about who has more or better) that, if established through public policy, will tend to make all worse off by diminishing the strength of the profit motive, which drives beneficial innovation.

This state of affairs defines the character of human finitude, human inequality, the jealousy the latter can provoke, and the background conditions within which the pharmaceutical and medical-device industries operate.

Choices among policies that support or hinder innovation in pharmaceuticals and medical devices are thus marked by the agonies of human finitude because all humans are forced to make decisions about how to gamble with their own lives and the lives of those whom they love, as well as the lives of anonymous strangers. This difficulty is compounded by the circumstance that there is no common understanding of the appropriate way responsibly to approach such gambles, and because different persons will have different amounts of resources to invest in such gambles, with the result that the market facilitates different approaches with consenting others and their resources. Also, and very importantly, as just observed, the outcomes will often be marked by inequalities that will provoke envy, if not jealousy. That is, those with less will not only wish they had as much as those with more, but will be inclined to want those with more not to have more, even if no one is made better off, and even if all are made worse off. Yet, in the face of moral pluralism, it is impossible to show the secular moral authority to set such inequalities aside. There are as many secular understandings of justice as there are major religions, so that none can be shown in secular terms to be the one canonical account that should be normative. In addition, given the contribution of profit to innovation, the attempt in the pursuit of equality to limit profit in the pharmaceutical and medical-device industries will tend to make most worse off by diminishing innovation. Egalitarian concerns (e.g., pricing drugs so that all can have easy access) will thus be harmful in slowing the decrease of morbidity and mortality risks.

Attempts to pursue material equality are thus fraught with moral and practical difficulties. First, attempts to realize equality among humans confront stubborn human inequalities. Humans are de facto unequal, not just in health care needs, but in their intelligence, self-control, moral understandings, and social connections, including most importantly their family circumstances. As long as, and insofar as, people are free, their free choices will lead to outcomes that will make some better off and others worse off. Persons are equal only in the limited sense of being able to give permission with the consequence that a default secular morality in the face of moral pluralism places forbearance rights, not material rights, centrally. It is because all persons are formally equal in possessing forbearance rights that the market has a clear presumptive moral standing. However, because the motive to become richer than others is productive of greater affluence for all, as well as greater relief of morbidity and morality risks, and because material equality as a moral norm depends on counter-factual accounts grounded in a normative jealousy, such egalitarian approaches are not morally compelling, since *inter alia* they would make all worse off in order to avoid having some better off than others. That is, such accounts must value equality itself higher than material affluence and the amelioration of morbidity and mortality risks. Such a moral vision, an egalitarianism of jealousy, is to be contrasted with an egalitarianism of altruism, which affirms attempts as cheaply and effectively as possible to ameliorate the status of those who are suffering without valuing equality itself.[6]

The failure to face without jealousy the intractable inequalities separating humans leads to unrealistic, and therefore unfeasible egalitarian policy positions. Among these is the attempt

1. to provide all with the best of care (i.e., providing all with any health care useful in postponing death or ameliorating significant morbidity, no matter how expensive), and thus
2. to provide equal care to all, while attempting
3. to maximize patient and physician choice, while nevertheless attempting
4. to contain health care costs.

The difficulty is that this constellation of goals is unrealizable if resources are limited. Coming to terms with the human condition in a fashion that more effectively decreases morbidity and mortality risks requires abandoning an egalitarianism of jealousy (e.g., ceasing to be concerned about who has more) in favor of at most a limited egalitarianism of altruism (e.g., seeking cheaply to provide a limited means-tested basic package of health care for those in need as a means of diminishing avoidable early death and significant morbidities).[7]

The circumstances of human finitude force health care policy to abandon an egalitarianism of jealousy and retreat to the position of

1. guaranteeing everyone a means-tested access to at least some level of health care as an insurance against significant losses at the natural lottery;
2. while not interfering with those with sufficient resources and the desire to purchase luxury care and better basic care; and also
3. not impeding those with the funds and the desire for profit to invest in the development and marketing of pharmaceutical and other innovations.

If this approach is embraced, which approach in various degrees underlies public policy in most major polities (with the exception of countries such as Canada), one has decided (as in every limited democratic polity) to recognize the unavoidability of inequality among patients at any particular time, as well as between current and future patients. Such approaches to health care policy are based on providing

1. a basic, limited, means-tested health care package, recognizing that there will be
2. unequal care, while also recognizing that
3. innovation in the market will be driven by consumer demand, investments, profit-driven forces, in addition to support from other sources such as government grants.

This last approach appreciates that the human condition sets limits to the pursuit of equality. It acknowledges as well that there are both private and public resources, and that there are disparate views as to how resources should be used. Within these constraints, there can be cost-containment and the avoidance of an egalitarianism of jealousy.

Coming to terms with human finitude requires in particular recognizing the role of profit and the market in medical innovation: humans are not moved by love alone, but also by the pursuit of self-interest. A well-structured society harnesses the pursuit of self-interest, the desire for profit, within the rule of law in a fashion that generally increases the good available to all. In the 20th century, this has been shown by the circumstance that capitalist systems by rewarding those who succeed in the market tend to increase the standard of living and the amount of resources generally available, while societies that suppress the pursuit of profit tend to be marked by scarcity. Accommodating to the human condition requires recognizing the finite ability of humans to be effectively moved by altruism or love, that is, by concerns with charity alone. Again, insofar as it is the case that medical innovation requires the investment of capital, and insofar as it is the case that the market is the most efficient means for securing and productively directing such investment, then markets and the pursuit of profit are essential for ameliorating the human condition through controlling and decreasing mortality and morbidity risks. Moreover, in a world of disparate moral views, the market, like limited democracies, is one of the prime modes of peaceable collaboration in the face of numerous, competing views regarding the nature of the human good and of human flourishing.

A general secular affirmative bioethics of money and markets can then be endorsed as integral to improving the human condition through medical technological progress. These considerations can be summarized as follows.

1. Since there are only three ways to acquire resources to support innovation in pharmaceuticals and medical devices, namely, through love (i.e., charity), coercion (e.g., taxation), and self-interest (e.g., the pursuit of profit in the market), one must always consider what patterns of approaches are most likely to produce the funds required to drive innovation.
2. In the face of moral pluralism and a diversity of goals proposed for health care, the market provides a peaceable procedural means for large-scale collaboration towards the realization of diverse goals, including diverse forms of innovation in pharmaceuticals and medical devices.
3. Insofar as the profit motive is generally the most efficient means for nurturing pharmaceutical and technological innovation, and if innovation is desired (i.e., if one wishes to lower morbidity and mortality risks), then markets and profits should be affirmed as integral to relieving the human condition and to achieving progress in health care and the biomedical sciences.
4. In summary, if resources are needed for innovations in the development of pharmaceuticals and medical devices, and if such innovation is desired, then, given the limits of charity (i.e., the limited inclination of persons to support research through charitable donations), and given the limited readiness of persons to be taxed to support such research (not to mention the greater efficiency in most areas of market responses in comparison with governmental central planning), the pursuit of profit through the market will prove indispensable and should be embraced. As a fact of the matter, the profit motive will be a cardinal source of the financial resources and the creative human energy needed to support the development of innovative pharmaceuticals and medical devices.

The very character of human finitude, including the finitude of secular moral reflection, thus places the market, money, and profit as central elements of the project of improving the human condition in the sense of increasing affluence, as well as decreasing morbidity and mortality risks.

IV. In Praise of Profit

A public policy that limits profits in the pharmaceutical and medical-device industries through imposing high litigation costs and court verdicts, as well as through limiting patient protection and controlling prices, supports goals that are in conflict with an efficient pursuit of postponing death and decreasing suffering. Such choices may result from assigning goals such as equality a priority over concerns for security from death and suffering. A further critical consideration of these issues is integral to re-assessing policy bearing on litigation, product liability, and the provision of cheaper pharmaceuticals and medical devices. Such a critical re-assessment requires taking into account the following circumstances.

1. There is no such thing as a perfectly safe drug or medical device. The choice to market a less-than-optimally-safe pharmaceutical or medical device is not in and of itself unethical, but rather reflects a recognition of human finitude: finite humans can never achieve the best. Whether any marketing choice is unethical depends on whether a manufacturer, while disclosing the known risks, followed publicly established procedures to establish safety and efficacy, which procedures are always limited and imperfect.
2. The choice easily and highly to compensate current injured patients for damages from pharmaceuticals and medical devices implicitly involves the choice to offer less innovation to patients in the future, insofar as the costs of such compensation when imposed on the makers of pharmaceuticals and medical devices will hinder the pace of innovation. There is no moral right, *ceteris paribus,* to be made whole for damages from pharmaceuticals or medical devices when users knew or should have known that their use offers not only benefits but risks from their use. The easier it is to impose liability costs on the pharmaceutical and medical-device industries, especially from the litigation costs and greater ease of adverse judgments from strict product liability, the more one tends to impose costs on all patients in the future through diverting resources from the pursuit of innovation to paying for litigation and its costs.
3. The choice between providing greater financial rewards either to plaintiff legal firms or to firms engaged in the production of pharmaceuticals and medical devices depends in part on where one wishes to reward and encourage innovation.
4. The choice to make pharmaceuticals and medical devices cheaply accessible to current patients by controlling prices and therefore controlling profits is undertaken at a cost to patients in the future, insofar as any decrease in profits hinders the pace of innovation.[8]
5. A decision to limit patent protection for expensive drugs in the developing world is tantamount to a choice (insofar as profit attracts investment, and investment supports innovation) to help current patients in the developing world at a cost to patients in the developing world in the future who will not have better drugs, since investment will tend to shift instead to addressing the ills of the developed world and thus to benefiting patients in the future in jurisdictions where patent protection is better. All else being equal, choices to limit profits through abolishing

patent protection will benefit future patients in those countries that do protect patent rights.

6. The unavailability of cheaply priced pharmaceuticals and medical devices is not to be ascribed primarily to the companies producing them, but to governments that do not tax to provide funds to purchase those pharmaceuticals and medical devices at their market price so as to distribute them at a discount (i.e., absorbing the costs of the discount), as well as to the failure of individuals out of charity to contribute funds towards such goals.
7. The choice not to interfere with higher prices for pharmaceuticals and medical devices in the United States represents a choice to advantage patients in the United States and indeed throughout the world in the future by supporting further innovation.
8. In summary, insofar as profit and financial reward through market mechanisms contribute in an important degree to innovation, and insofar as such innovation is necessary to improving the human condition, and insofar as the pursuit of such improvement is, all things being equal, a moral obligation, then limiting financial reward for the pharmaceutical and medical-device industries through (a) lowering the prices of drugs and medical devices, (b) limiting patent protection, or (c) providing large and/or ill-justified awards to injured patients is wrong.

These points display the intractable bond among profit, innovation, and a philanthropic commitment to aid humans in need. The profit motive in the market, insofar as it is positively associated with the possibility of lowering morbidity and mortality risks should be seen as integral to the project of bettering the human condition.

This state of affairs does not foreclose pursuing goals other than the development of innovative pharmaceuticals and medical devices. Some may in fact value aiding patients in the present more than aiding patients in the future. Others may value the pursuit of equality over decreasing human suffering, that is, over decreasing morbidity and mortality risks. They may support making all worse off in material wealth and in protection against morbidity and mortality risks, as long as people are made more equal. Such views are unlikely, however, to be the settled, informed view of most people, given the disinclination of most to early death and greater suffering, and given the threats posed to human well-being in the absence of continued innovation in pharmaceuticals and medical devices. That is, the inclination against the pursuit of profit generated by various forms of jealousy is likely to be counterbalanced by a fear of suffering and death.

A better appreciation of the contributions made by the pharmaceutical and medical-device industries is likely to be gained through better knowledge of the dependence of humans on pharmaceutical innovation for their very existence. In order to maintain the status quo of current morbidity and mortality risks, one needs ever new ways of controlling threatening microbial agents. This is the case because ever new risks are always emerging to threaten the survival of humans, as through microbial antibiotic resistance and the threat of new pathogens (e.g., human immunodeficiency virus and avian flu). The history of mankind until recently has been the history of recurrent devastating plagues with especially dramatic adverse impacts on urban populations. Pharmaceutical advance is necessary to protect against what have up until recently been natural, predictable occurrences. There is also a wide spectrum of sources of human morbidity and mortality, ranging from cancer to Alzheimer's, that is likely to be ameliorated over time through medical-technological developments. How long it will take to achieve those developments will depend on the resources and energies invested. The pharmaceutical and medical-device industries, supported and driven by the profit motive, are core to the project of decreasing human suffering and premature death.

There is nevertheless a suspicion of these industries and of the profit that they pursue. A better appreciation of the benefits of innovation driven by the pursuit of profit should help in controlling inclinations to an egalitarianism of jealousy that would limit and slow the ability of humans to protect themselves against new threats and to relieve the human condition. As Nicholas Capaldi in this volume argues, the pharmaceutical and medical-device industries should contribute to the common good by information campaigns directed to helping the public better appreciate that, insofar as one wishes to secure a future with a better life expectancy characterized by less disease and disability, one should critically regard policies that would limit the pursuit of profit in pharmaceuticals and medical devices. Because such information can contribute to aiding those in need, it is not only allowable but obligatory. Against temptations to an egalitarianism of jealousy, one should support a better appreciation of the benefits from the pursuit of profit in the market.

Notes

* H. Tristram Engelhardt, Jr., Ph.D., M.D., is Professor, Department of Philosophy, Rice University, and Professor Emeritus, Department of Community Medicine, Baylor College of Medicine, and Editor of the *Journal of Medicine and Philosophy.*

1. In *The Fable of the Bees,* Bernard de Mandeville argues for a powerful, positive role of the market in ameliorating the human condition.
2. At stake in appreciating the place of the market and the pursuit of profit is a contrast between content-full versus procedural moralities. A content-full morality involves normative claims that depend on particular orderings of right-making conditions and cardinal human values. A procedural morality eschews directly affirming any such ordering and instead proposes a procedure for authoritative collaboration. The first focuses on discovering a concrete, canonical pattern of appropriate behavior; the second focuses on creating a concrete pattern of appropriate collaboration. In its purest form, a procedural approach takes its form simply from the consent of the participants. The market is a pure procedure for peaceable collaboration in the exchange of goods and services. I have addressed these issues in detail elsewhere (cf. Engelhardt, 1993; 1996).
3. The author's defense of a secular moral philosophical skepticism should not be interpreted as an endorsement of a metaphysical skepticism. It is one thing to hold that secular moral philosophical reflection is insufficient to identify canonical, moral truth, and another to hold that such truth does not exist. The author is a committed and practicing Orthodox Christian. See Engelhardt (2000), and also Engelhardt (2007).
4. For a discussion of the intractable character of moral diversity and its implications for bioethics, see Engelhardt (2006).
5. Given the salience of moral pluralism, secular polities, in order to function with a generally defensible moral authority, must invoke a moral perspective that is not simply one more among the various content-full moralities competing for dominance. As a consequence, rather than appeal to a particular vision of the good or human flourishing, it must by default draw authority from the permission of those who join together in a common endeavor. It is for this reason that the United States Constitution is a formal-right constitution, not a material-right constitution. For a further account of the character of secular pluralist societies and the role of limited constitutional governments see H. T. Engelhardt (1996, Chaps. 1-4).
6. One can distinguish between an egalitarianism of jealousy and a limited egalitarianism of altruism by reference to three fictive worlds, each with ten persons. In World One, the reference world, all ten persons have 6 units of the good. In World Two, nine persons have 6 units, and one has 10. If one holds World One to be preferable to World Two, then one affirms an egalitarianism of jealousy. One is committed to making one person worse off (reducing the person with 9 units to 6), as well as decreasing the total amount of good in the world (i.e., reducing the quantity of good from 63 to 60), in order to achieve an equality that provides no benefit beyond the equality itself. World Three has nine persons each with 6 units of the good, and one person has 1 unit. If one attempts as cheaply as possible to raise that one person towards the level of the other nine and is not concerned with World Two, one is an egalitarian of altruism. One is concerned with inequalities not for the sake of inequality, but because some have less of the good than others.
7. For an account of the inferior character of health care associated with social welfare approaches to the provision of health care, see Goodman, Musgrave, Herrick, and Friedman (2004).
8. One must critically regard any health care policymakers who in public debates attack the contribution to higher health care costs made by innovative pharmaceu-

ticals and new medical devices. At best, such policymakers fail to recognize that they are lamenting necessary conditions for best lowering morbidity and mortality risks in the future, namely, the accrual of resources and the focusing of energies through the pursuit of profit in the market. At worst, they are unconcerned about these facts of the matter and are nevertheless demagogically appealing to misinformed, if not perverse (i.e., harmful) public sentiments that would support an egalitarianism of jealousy in order to garner short-range political advantage.

References

Engelhardt, H.T. (1993). *Bioethics and Secular Humanism: The Search for a Common Morality.* Philadelphia: Trinity International Press.

Engelhardt, H.T. (1996). *The Foundations of Bioethics,* 2nd Ed. New York: Oxford University Press.

Engelhardt, H.T. (2000). *The Foundations of Christian Bioethics.* Salem, MA: M&M Scrivener Press.

Engelhardt, H.T. (Ed.). (2006). *Global Bioethics: The Collapse of Consensus.* Salem, MA: M&M Scrivener Press.

Engelhardt, H.T. (2007). "Why Ecumenism Fails: Taking Theological Differences Seriously," *Christian Bioethics,* 13(1), 25-51.

Goodman, J.C., Musgrave, G.L., Herrick, D.M., & Friedman, M. (2004). *Lives at Risk: Single-Payer National Health Insurance around the World.* Lanham, MD: Rowman & Littlefield.

Mandeville, B. (1988). *The Fable of the Bees: or, Private Vices, Publick Benefits,* 2 vols. F. B. Kaye (Ed.). Indianapolis: Liberty Fund.

Corporate Social Responsibility and Business Ethics in the Pharmaceutical Industry

Nicholas Capaldi
Loyola University, New Orleans

I. The Demonization of the Pharmaceutical Industry

The pharmaceutical industry finds itself caught up in the "Perfect Storm." A variety of circumstances have conspired to place the pharmaceutical industry at the center of a maelstrom. It would be easy to dismiss or misidentify this maelstrom as the consequence of purely fortuitous and temporary economic factors, namely:

1. Falling profits
2. Patent expirations
3. Competition from generic drugs, and
4. The dearth of new blockbuster drugs.

This would be a serious misperception. The fact of the matter is that the pharmaceutical industry is being demonized. The really significant forces contributing to the storm are parts of a concerted effort on the part of various interest groups to push their own agendas at the expense of pharmaceutical corporate pocketbooks. Together they have conspired to present a portrait of the pharmaceutical industry as profiteers who (a) spend obscene sums on marketing[1] instead of research, (b) engage in dif-

H.T. Engelhardt, Jr. and J. Garrett (eds), *Innovation and the Pharmaceutical Industry* (pp. 33–45).

ferential pricing at home and abroad in an effort to gouge the American consumer, and (c) deprive developing countries of life-saving medicines. As a result, the industry is under intense pressure to make medicines less expensive.

The success of the concerted effort to demonize the pharmaceutical industry is not the product of incontrovertible facts and formidable arguments on the part of the industry's critics. No. The success of the demonization is a result of the receptivity (perhaps one should say gullibility) of the public. And why are the public so receptive? The answer is that drugs are the most visible recurring expense and the one that consumers are asked to pay, in part, directly; this, coupled with the fact that the public has not yet come to terms with the economics of contemporary healthcare has led to a crisis. *In short the real crisis is the present inability and unwillingness of the public to understand the economics of contemporary healthcare.* For reasons which will become apparent as we proceed, the burden of the social responsibility of educating the public will fall on the pharmaceutical industry.

II. How Did We Get Here?

The problems that beset the pharmaceutical industry are not *sui generis* but part of the much larger healthcare debate. To attempt to solve the problem by purely business, legal, or political means would be to see the trees but to miss the forest.

Health-care practice and policy are based on a paradigm that is no longer meaningful. Past policy reflects a "Jurassic" period when doctors could do very little and costs were comparably low. It reflects a time when the emphasis was put on bedside manner, because there wasn't anything at the bedside except some posturing. I am old enough to remember a time when going to the hospital was viewed as a prelude to death. The most important obligation of the medical profession was non-maleficence (avoiding harm), not the principle of beneficence (doing good) (Veatch & Haddad, 1999). This produced a myopia about the cost of healthcare. This myopia about the cost of healthcare was reinforced by the generosity of employers, starting in the Second World War when they were forbidden to raise wages. Employers contractually absorbed the then modest cost of healthcare. The public myopia would be further reinforced by the rapid growth in the post war period of the welfare state.

The public has been led to believe that healthcare is a right and that a right (in the current politically correct sense of the term, not the sense in which the American Founders understood it) imposes a positive obligation on government to provide such goods or benefits. How, however, does this actually work out in practice? Governments can pretend to protect your newly discovered right by controlling the supply of healthcare. They can do this, paradoxically, by cutting off access. That is, they can, among other things, restrict the number of doctors, and they can reduce the supply of medical technology. The ultimate logic of these moves will result in waiting lists or rationing. Rationing is a way of privatizing costs without monetizing them. There is one exception to this practice: prescription drugs.[2] *The only way that government can manage the quantity or supply of prescription drugs is by insisting that patients pay some of the costs directly.* That is why drugs are the most visible recurring expense and the one that consumers are asked to pay, at least in part, directly. It is also not surprising that up until recently politicians have avoided including a prescription drug plan in Medicare.

We are getting a little ahead of ourselves in our account of why the public has not come to terms with the economics of contemporary healthcare. The past, and to some extent current, paradigm in the minds of the public is that healthcare should be inexpensive. This is an outmoded paradigm. Everything has changed dramatically. In the past half-century, medical technology, as in the case of technology in general, has totally transformed the landscape. There is an enormous and ever growing amount that medical technology can provide, but the costs have risen appreciably. Neither the medical community itself nor the public nor the formulators of public policy have appreciated the need for a *paradigm shift*.[3]

Up until now, the pharmaceutical industry has tried to defend itself by rightly pointing out its preeminent role in producing, promoting and providing access to the benefits of modern medical technology along with the need for protecting intellectual property rights. This defense has fallen on deaf ears. This problem cannot be solved through a public relations defense alone; it requires a coordinated offense. That offense has to embody a new paradigm. What is the new paradigm? Preserving and improving healthcare requires full commitment to free market economy in healthcare.

This will not be an easy or swiftly accomplished task. There are a number of vested interest groups who oppose thinking of healthcare as a commodity and who would want to maintain that healthcare is a special case in which the profit motive should play no role. Let me identify the major classes of opponents:

1. There is a deeply embedded and historically rooted anti-capitalist mentality among many intellectuals, journalists, and the medical technocracy.[4]
2. There are many irresponsible politicians whose political career and reelection depend upon manufacturing ever more victimized groups whose "rights" need protecting. There are precious few politicians who aspire to a leadership role (honor) in politics as opposed to a celebrity role or a power role. There is hardly anyone out there who has either the vision or integrity to play the responsible role in the healthcare debate.
3. Many healthcare professionals are in the same position as politicians in not being able to assume a leadership role. They are too often mere technicians or self-serving or self-deceived by mission statements written in a vacuum. They too do not see the big picture.
4. There are some consumer groups who are in general in favor of capitalism except in the case of their own specific interest.
5. There are some plaintiffs lawyers who are in general against capitalism except in the case of their own profession.

III. Where Do We Want to Be?

It is time for the public and the world at large to be clear on where it wants to be, how we have got close to it, and how we can get closer. If you will allow me to condense the history of the last 500 years into one paragraph, I shall tell you what road we have been traveling. Since the Renaissance, the Western World (of which the U.S. is the preeminent example and leader) has been irrevocably committed to the Technological Project (Descartes, 1995; Bacon, 1995; 1980; Locke, 1986)[5], that is, the project to control the physical universe and make it responsive and subservient to humanity. I say irrevocably because there is now no serious possibility of giving it up. The essence of the Technological Project is constant innovation (Aoki, 2001). Since 1989, the world has come to understand that the most efficient way of pursuing the Technological Project is through a free-market economy because it is just such an economy that maximizes innovation. I won't waste time giving you the technical reasons, because you can read them in Adam Smith's *Wealth of Nations* (1990). The spread of this realization that the Technological Project requires a free market economy is what globalization is all about. A free-market economy requires a limited government, i.e., a government which recognizes that its job is to serve the market which serves the Technological Project, a government which is itself under the law—that is what we mean by the rule of law and not men, and a government which enforces, adjudicates conflicts within, and maximizes the potential for, contracts. Finally, the only way of producing and maintaining a limited government is to have a larger cultural context in which individuals are personally autonomous, that is define their own lives and take responsibility for them.

The greatest achievement of the Technological Project has been to improve the longevity and quality of human life. Medical technology has been at the forefront of that project. Let me mention just a few facts:

1. From 1900 to 2000 life-expectancy increased in the US from age 47 to age 77 (Wikipedia, Life Expectancy, p. 1).
2. Since 1986, there has been a 40% increase in life expectancy in 52 countries due to the launch of new medicines.[6]
3. The expense of new drugs often reduces the cost of hospital care expenditures (Lichtenberg, 1997).
4. Old cures often have to be replaced by new cures.
5. New diseases and medical conditions develop all the time.
6. Most of the science Nobel prize-winners, especially in medicine, are from the US and Britain—the countries most committed to a free market.
7. Our most successful research universities are privately endowed universities, endowed by the philanthropy of a culture committed to wealth production through a free market economy.

Telling this story is what the industry has tried to do so far, but unsuccessfully. We need to tell it better and to get it across more successfully (i.e., we need a marketing strategy for ideas). To do so, we need to bypass the medical technocrats and go directly to the public. It is important to connect the story to profits. The public's perception of medicine as seen on TV always focuses positively on doctors instead of researchers and entrepreneurs. The medicines appear miraculously, and, of course, the doctors get all the credit. We might want to encourage switching the focus, perhaps through selective programming and advertising. We might want, for example, to contrast the way psychological dysfunction was treated in the era of Freud and psychoanalysis with current psychiatrists who give medications. We might want to highlight the number of world leaders who come to the US for medical treatment, and stress that it is no accident that the best care is available in the country most committed to a free market.

IV. How Do We Get There?

A. Short-term

1. *Blow your horn*
   a. The pharmaceutical industry must learn to market ideas not just pills. It must do a better job of telling the story of how it has been at the forefront of medical advancement.
   b. There is one misunderstanding that should be countered. Sometimes the original research on which modern pharmaceuticals are based was funded by the government. However, what the public has not been told is that (i) that original research lies dormant until the entrepreneurial spirit of the pharmaceutical industry and its willingness to risk massive investments develops it.[7]
2. *Acknowledge and promote Pharmaceutical Industry Social Responsibility by taking the lead on the total healthcare debate:*
   a. A Nobel laureate in economics, Ronald Coase (1960; 1997) has persuasively argued that every firm or corporation faces both political and social transaction costs. The existence of political transaction costs is one reason firms, and even whole industries, employ lobbyists. Social responsibility obligations would be an example of social transaction costs. Lest I be misunderstood, it is important to note that corporate social responsibility must be compatible with the bottom line. Bad public relations hurt profits; good public relations help profits.
   b. The pharmaceutical industry, is, in some important respects, not like 'Britney Spears' or 'Coca Cola'; it is more like the defense industry. World-wide health threats are as much a matter of national defense as terrorist threats. The industry should not react to AIDS as if it were like arthritis or sexual dysfunction, and it should not simply placate special interest groups; AIDS is a serious epidemic; *but* like the defense industry, it should demand and get a profit from the government for its efforts in responding to such national threats. The defense industry is not asked to subsidize counter-terrorism; the pharmaceutical industry (which saves lives) should not be asked to subsidize dealing with epidemics.
   c. The pharmaceutical industry should and must take a leadership role in the healthcare debate. It must do so because no other institution is able or willing to lead. Let's face it: medical per-

sonnel are pampered technicians with little understanding of economics or public policy in general; non-profit organizations are run by people who spend other people's money rather than having an appreciation of how wealth is generated; most politicians have little incentive to educate the public; many of those entrusted to educate the public do so within non-profit organizations and either share the common ignorance about creating wealth or are hostile to a free market or suffer from an obsolete anti-market mentality.

To lead the way is not merely to react. The pharmaceutical industry should warn the public of the ever present possibility of newly emerging catastrophic health threats; it should rally support from groups that suffer from less chic maladies; it should remind everyone that the profit incentive is the key to innovation in medical treatment. It should, as a public service, endlessly and continually document how misguided public policy both domestically and in the UN has had an adverse effect on health and healthcare. It should name 'names'. Educating the public on healthcare is part of the cost of providing for healthcare; this cost has to be figured into any assessment of product cost and profits.

d. The pharmaceutical industry must accept reasonable limits on patents. The reason we have patents to protect intellectual property rights is to encourage innovation by rewarding it with a temporary monopoly. But long-term monopoly undermines innovation. Keep in mind that given the time frame for testing new drugs, the real life span for patents in pharmaceuticals is 12 years instead of the usual 18. Let's have a serious discussion about the reasonable economic and technological limits to patents, but let us also tailor it to differences among industries and economic reality. It is important that the pharmaceutical industry not appear as the enemy of technological progress.

3. *Promote sound public policy: What will save the most lives and improve the most lives in the long run?*

   a. **Who should pay?** Let us begin by recognizing our responsibility to take care of those who cannot take care of themselves. One group that needs protection is seniors. However, there are *only a relatively small number of seniors who lack drug coverage.* This is an access problem, not a price problem. Providing them with care is a public obligation, to be taken care of through taxes. It is absurd and counter-productive to penalize the people who make the care possible.

b. **How long should we pay?** We are caught in a time warp just as we were during the great depression, when, among other things we learned that economic and social transformations made it less and less likely that people would live among extended families and therefore did not have to worry about retirement. Our time warp is that we have only recently acknowledged that increasingly great healthcare means increasing costs. Some people were understandably unprepared. In the previous time warp *we rightly recognized the need for social security; at the same time, we wrongly made it a universal entitlement.* The result is the present social security debacle. Let us not make the same mistake. Let us (i) advocate a program only for the relatively few caught in the time warp *but* with a 'grand-person' clause; (ii) advocate privatized long-term healthcare and prescription drug insurance for the rest; (iii) advocate refundable healthcare tax credits for uninsured individuals; and (iv) warn about what will happen if we make drug coverage a universal entitlement the way we did with social security. If we do this right we have responsible public policy; if we do political business as usual we get a pyramid scheme and eventual bankruptcy.

c. **How do we help the poor?** Accept and promote the benefits of differential pricing internationally (Carey, 2001, p. 105); it's a way of helping the poor in other countries by making drugs more affordable for them.

   (i) Let us insist that richer countries like Canada contribute their fair share to the cost of the research and development costs that go into creating a new pharmaceutical product. Perhaps we can 'negotiate' with them to spend a certain percentage of GDP on basic research and then make that research part of the public domain. They get a free ride on defense; they should not get a free ride on healthcare. If we do not do this, we are consenting to a massive cost shifting to the U.S.

   (ii) We should oppose drug re-importation (Owcharenko, 2003). Differential pricing is one of the virtues of a market economy. To allow re-importation will create safety concerns, will cause the pharmaceutical industry to raise prices in poorer countries, or to cease sales in foreign countries altogether. If the latter occurs, some of those countries will violate intellectual property rights, and thereby undermine the whole relationship between markets and technological innovation. The only reason that the industry agreed to the 'shakedown' by the Canadian government was its lack of confidence in the U.S. government's willingness to protect intellectual property rights. The rest of the world is 'ripping us off', and we are allowing them to get away with it.

d. **How do we lower prices and fix distortions in the pricing scheme?**

(i) Oppose single payer systems. Where there is only one buyer you lose all of the advantages of a competitive market.

(ii) Oppose price controls. Price controls never work, they distort the market, create delays and lead to limited access.[8]

(iii) Oppose limiting profits.[9] Please pay attention to the following argument.

(a) There is no principled basis on which to base the limitation of profits. There is no consensus or economic meaning to the idea of what constitutes a 'just' profit. The idea of a 'just profit' is as meaningless as the idea of a just price or a just wage. Substituting the word 'fair' to get to a 'fair profit' doesn't help either. There is no consensus on what is 'fair'; to arrange distribution in terms of who will make the best use of resources involves a calculation that is in principle impossible to make (Hayek, 1977; Mises, 1920). To give everyone the same thing won't work because they will engage in trade and the original problem will return; to prevent the problem of the return would require a planned and despotic economy and society. This is the same general argument against all redistributive schemes.

(b) If there is no principled basis for limiting profits, then the decision to do so would have to be political. This raises the question of whether the policy to limit profits should take losses into account. If we were to limit profits but not reimburse for losses, most if not all companies would exit the pharmaceutical field.

(c) If we take losses into account, then in essence such a policy would actually reward the less efficient companies and encourages waste in Research and Development. It would lessen the incentives for innovation.

(d) Such a policy would discourage investors if other industries without profit caps were more profitable.

(e) Finally, we could eliminate investors from making investments that are inconsistent with the policy by eliminating private investments altogether, that is, by managing the entire economy. This is precisely what Hume and Hayek predicted would happen. Such a policy would undermine the technological project as we have argued above. It would undermine advances in healthcare. It would lead to a serious deterioration in healthcare, not its improvement.

(iv) The best way to lower prices is through *individual medical accounts.* Our present system of third-party payers (insurance companies, HMO's, government) discourages both doctors and patients from being responsible consumers. Patients don't investigate alternatives; doctors sometimes prescribe more expensive medication that is less effective because of fear of malpractice suits; pharmaceutical companies therefore have no incentive to compete by offering lower prices instead of "me-too" products.

(v) The PI should make a concerted effort to clarify and to defend the importance of protecting intellectual property rights.

e. **How do we confront the distribution paradox?**

(i) Even if it is granted that the technological project is best carried out within the framework of a free market economy, and even if it is granted that overall productivity is maximized, how do we know that the goods and services produced are distributed in the best manner possible? What we have is a debate about distribution. Free markets do not lead to equality of outcome.

(ii) What does it mean to have the best possible distribution? David Hume (1751) addressed this question several centuries ago. First, "best" involves a value judgment on which there is no consensus and not likely to be one. Second, to distribute goods and services on the basis of 'desert' also involves a value judgment on which there is no consensus and not likely to be one. Third, to distribute goods and services on the basis of who is most likely to make the best use of them is to invoke a principle for which there is no known algorithm (anticipation of Hayek's anti-planning argument). Fourth, to make an initial equal distribution is to solve nothing, for, in time, the workings of a market economy will lead to an unequal accumulation. Fifth, to attempt to enforce a permanent equality will lead both to the undermining of the market economy (and a consequent loss of productivity) and to the imposition of a tyrannical regime.[10]

i. Distribution and production are integrally related. By its very nature, a free market economy (i.e., one without the central allocation of resources) can no more control distribution than it can control production. Are we then better off with a market economy? The only possible answer to this question is an inductive one. The societies with free market economies are the most productive overall and the members therein have more goods and services overall than their counterparts in societies without free market economies. World-wide migration patterns confirm that this is a widely held perception. Other relevant international developments also serve as corroboration.

4. *Go on the offensive: Denounce the bad guys*
   a. Identify and denounce public officials in the U.S. and abroad who have misled the public and distorted the market (Pear, 1993).
   b. Identify and denounce health officials at the UN who have exacerbated world-wide health threats.
   c. How should we deal with plaintiffs lawyers who profit from misguided suits: these especially should be castigated as inhibitors of future research; perhaps initiate a class-action suit based on the calculation of what it will cost to clean up the healthcare mess these attorneys are creating and the delay in new products that will cost a significant number of lives.

B. Long-term

1. Educate the general public on the economic realities of healthcare; politics will eventually reflect public opinion.
2. Promote awareness, especially in college students (who are the future journalists, teachers, politicians, doctors, and researchers) about the inescapable relationship between technological advance and a free-market economy.
3. Encourage the privatization of research institutes currently housed in universities, allow them to compete directly for government sponsored research, and avoid the economic inefficiencies of universities and their demoralizing climate.

V. Conclusion

For all of the reasons given above, the pharmaceutical industry must be pro-active and take a leadership role in the public policy debate about health care. It must explain, over and over, to all and sundry why healthcare is a commodity and is best served by a free market economy.

Notes

1. Very few people who make this sort of criticism take into account that (a) without marketing there is less or no profit because potential users need to be made aware of the existence of products, and, that (b) in an age where we are constantly bombarded with information about new products, producers and marketers need to go to extraordinary lengths some times to get attention.
2. The problems associated with price regulation of drugs in Great Britain is concisely delineated in Philip Brown (1997).
3. "Although there still is a 'physician-patient relationship', it is now set within a broader healthcare nexus. In this latter context, the rights and interests of economic agents, society and other parties are both routine and proper, not exceptional or *per se* morally distasteful" (Morreim, 1991, p. 2).
4. Arnold Relman, former editor of the *New England Journal of Medicine* maintains that "healthcare [is]...a social good rather than an economic commodity" (Cohn, 1998, p. 25).
5. From its very beginnings, the Project was tied to healthcare. Consider the following statement from Descartes' *Discourse on Method,* Part VI, "...make ourselves, as it were, the masters and possessors of nature....principally for the maintenance of health, which unquestionably is the first good and the foundation of all the other goods in this life..."
6. This paper was written in late 2004. In 2005 Hurricane Katrina destroyed my entire library. I no longer have the original documents.
7. See the discussion of the importance of the Bayh-Dole Act of 1980 in *The Economist Technology Quarterly* (2002, p. 3).
8. For a discussion of this issue in the EU context see Stephen Pollard (2002). See also John R. Graham (2002) for a discussion of the Reference Drug Program in Canada.
9. For many of the economic arguments see Patricia Munch Danzon (1997).
10. In *Bad Medicine,* Milton Silverman, Mia Lydecker, and Philip R. Lee (1992) follow up their earlier critiques of the abuses of the pharmaceutical industry. They concede that in most developing nations drug-regulation agencies are corrupt, weak, underfunded, and their workers poorly trained. Bribery is a way of life throughout the Third World. Their remedy is to suggest constant surveillance, continuous consultation among consumer advocates, the drug industry, government agencies, and the medical and pharmacy professions, with the World Health Organization leading the way. This is the perfect example of the kind of tyranny that replaces markets.

References

Aoki, N. (2001, January 17). 'Brainstorm center to encourage innovation, Pfizer puts its corporate muscle behind an entrepreneurial unit in Cambridge biotechnology,' *Boston Globe.*

Bacon, F. (1995). *Essays.* Buffalo: Prometheus Books.

Bacon, F. (1980). *The Great Instauration and New Atlantis.* J. Weinberger (Ed.). Arlington Heights, IL: Harlan Davidson.

Brown, P. (Ed.). (1997). *Should Pharmaceutical Prices be Regulated? The Strengths and Weaknesses of the British Pharmaceutical Price Regulation Scheme (Choice in Welfare 40).* London: IEA.

Carey, J. (2001, April 30). 'What's a fair price for drugs?,' *Business Week.*

Coase, R.H. (1960). 'The problem of social cost,' *Journal of Law and Economics,* 3, 1-44.

Coase, R.H. (1997). 'The nature of the firm,' in L. Putterman & R. Kroszner (Eds.), *The Economic Nature of the Firm* (pp. 89-104). Cambridge: Cambridge University Press.

Cohn, J. (1998, August 17), 'Cosmetic surgery,' *The New Republic,* p. 25.

Danzon, P.M. (1997). *Pharmaceutical Price Regulation: National Policies versus Global Interests.* London: AEI Press.

Descartes, R. (1993). *Discourse on Method.* Indianapolis: Hackett.

Economist Technology Quarterly. (2002). 'Innovation's Golden Goose,' December 14, 2002.

Graham, J. R. (2002). 'The fantasy of reference pricing and the promise of choice in British Columbia's Pharmacare,' *Public Policy Sources,* 66.

Hayek, F.A. (1977). 'The Use of Knowledge in Society.' Menlo Park: Institute for Humane Studies.

Hume, D. (1751). *Enquiry Concerning the Principles of Morals.*

Lichtenberg, F.R. (1997). 'The effect of pharmaceutical utilization and innovation on hospitalization and mortality,' *National Bureau of Economic Research,* working paper 5418.

Locke, J. (1986). *Second Treatise on Civil Government.* Buffalo: Prometheus Books.

Mises, Ludwig von. (1920). 'Economic Calculation in the Socialist Commonwealth,' "Die Wirtschaftsrechnung im sozialistischen Gemeinwesen" in the *Archiv für Sozialwissenschaften,* vol. 47.

Morreim, E.H. (1991). *Balancing Act: The New Medical Ethics of Medicine's New Economic.* Dordrecht: Kluwer.

Owcharenko, N. (2003, June 26). 'Missing the point of Medicare reform,' [On-line]. WebMemo 304. [Online]. Available: www.heritage.org/Research/HealthCare/wm304.cfm

Pear, R. (1993, May 27). 'First lady sets aggressive tone for debate on health care plan,' *New York Times.*

Pollard, S. (2002). 'Saving the European pharmaceutical industry: Price regulation and recommendation VI,' *Center for the New Europe White Paper.* [Online]. Available: http://www.cne.org/ pub_pdf/ 12162002_G10_white_paper.pdf - 122k -25/Mar/2003

Silverman, M., Lydecker, M., & Lee, P.R. (1992). *Bad Medicine: The Prescription Drug Industry in the Third World.* Stanford: Stanford University Press.

Smith, A. (1990). *Wealth of Nations.* R.H. Campbell & A.S. Skinner (Eds.). Indianapolis: Liberty Press.

Veatch, R.M. & Haddad, A.M. (1999). *Case Studies in Pharmacy Ethics.* New York: Oxford University Press.

Wikipedia. [Online]. Available: en.wikipedia.org

Pharmaceutical Companies and Their Obligations to Developing Countries: Psychopaths or Scapegoats?

Pepe Lee Chang
Department of Management, University of Texas at San Antonio

I. Introduction

The 2005 documentary titled *The Corporation* advances an emotionally convincing argument that the behavior of modern day corporations resembles the behavior that we categorize typically and clinically as the behavior of psychopaths. And much like how we file individual psychopaths as unsavory members of society, the implicit message is that the same attitude should be applied toward corporate America. To ignore such abhorrent behavior is to condone it. This paper addresses how this attitude has been applied to at least one segment of the business world, that being the pharmaceutical industry.[1] I will argue that the pharmaceutical industry has been singled out unjustifiably as having a special responsibility to save lives in third world countries. Although I do not doubt the moral urgency of saving lives when able, at the end of the day, I do believe pharmaceutical companies have become the scapegoat for failing to do so.

Pharmaceutical companies have the power to save lives.[2] Because many of the drugs that are needed to save lives are already on the market and because the cost of producing them is minimal, these companies

H.T. Engelhardt, Jr. and J. Garrett (eds), *Innovation and the Pharmaceutical Industry* (pp. 46–66).

could save lives with very little effort. It would not be controversial to say that because most everyday citizens and some ethicists believe these claims to be true, they also believe that drug companies have a special obligation to save lives. Arguments for or against this obligation have usually centered around the correctness of these claims.

One side of the argument claims that the billion-dollar bottom lines are necessary to create new and innovative drugs (Van Gelder, 2005). In other words, huge profits are just part of the pharmaceutical machinery. If drug companies were required to provide drugs to people who had no money to pay for them, they would not be able to invest adequately in research and development (R&D), which would adversely affect people who need new and innovative drugs to better their lives, and who can afford to pay for them. This argument rests on the belief that it is not justified to save the lives of the poor, by providing life-saving drugs, at the expense of depriving those who can afford to pay for drugs themselves (Resnik, 2001, pp. 14-15). The other side of the argument presupposes a Good Samaritan intuition—it holds that because drug companies have the power to save lives, they ought to save lives. This intuition is frequently invoked as a defense of moral obligations.[3]

Current literature on pharmaceutical companies and their social responsibilities to the impoverished revolve around a Good Samaritan intuition, although some stipulate contingencies and limits on the requirement of helping the impoverished. For example, David Resnik, in his paper "Developing Drugs for the Developing World: An Economic, Legal, Moral, and Political Dilemma" argues that as long as the impoverished play by the rules, such as respecting intellectual property rights, pharmaceutical companies have a responsibility to provide the needed drugs to save their lives (Resnik, 2001, pp. 16-17). Norman Daniels and Dan W. Brock both claim to agree with Resnik although they seem to want more argumentation for his view (Daniels, 2001, p. 38; Brock, 2001, p. 33).

It seems that although there is much discussion about *how* the impoverished are to be aided in the current literature, the general consensus is that pharmaceutical companies *do* have a special obligation to those in developing countries who need their drugs to survive. "They have these special obligations because of the field they have freely chosen, because they are related to health care in a way others are not, because they have the expertise that others lack, and because they make their living or profit from health-related activities" (De George, 2005, p. 555). This, I believe, is a mistake.

In this paper, I will argue that there is no distinction, with respect to responsibilities, between pharmaceutical companies that produce life-saving drugs and companies that produce other products. I have two objectives: 1) I intend to show that although pharmaceutical companies manufacture the products needed to save lives, this fact should not release other types of companies from the obligation to save lives as well. I want to make it clear that my intention is not to argue that there is no moral obligation to save lives in third world countries. On the contrary, I am working under the *assumption* that there probably is such an obligation.[4] The problem is how this obligation is assigned. 2) I believe current theories of corporate obligation need to be critically reevaluated. What are these theories for and do they do what we need them to do? If not, how can they be improved? My initial goal is to examine current theories of corporate obligation to discover whether they track or fail to track our basic intuitions about corporate obligation.[5] If they do track them, then there should be no problem using them to argue for duties that represent our intuitions. If they fail to track our intuitions, then we either stand by our theories and surrender our intuitions, or we revise our theories to account for them.

First, I must mention briefly the distinction, which has already been argued for in the literature, between legal obligation and moral obligation.[6] Second, I will explain how proponents of current theories of obligation fail to justifiably assign to pharmaceutical companies a special moral obligation to save lives, even though they produce life-saving products. Third, I will argue that the inability to assign this unique responsibility stems from the inability to draw a morally relevant distinction between pharmaceutical companies that produce life-saving products and companies that produce other types of products. Finally, I will discuss briefly what this means for the intuition that there is a duty to save lives in third world countries, and how this consequence ought to affect perceptions of current theories of corporate obligation.

II. Legal Vs. Moral Obligations

It has been argued that there is a separation between law and morality (Hart, 1958, pp. 56-72). To take an obvious example, an owner who, in the same week, both throws a million dollar party for his company's CEO, and orders a layoff, on the grounds that the company is suffering from "hard times", may be acting entirely within legal boundaries.[7] But he may nonetheless be subject to moral criticism.

Proponents of standard theories of corporate obligation, such as stockholder theory, stakeholder theory, and social responsibility theories, argue from a moral point of view.[8] This means that each theory prescribes what corporations *morally ought* to do, much as standard moral theories for individuals prescribe what they *morally ought* to do. (I am assuming that a corporate theory of obligation, like a moral theory for individuals, must tell us what counts as an obligation or duty. If the theory lacks this capability, I will consider it an incomplete theory of obligation.) I will be assessing corporate theories of obligation in the same manner one standardly assesses individual moral theories: if a theory produces inconsistent views, highly counterintuitive results, or is self-refuting, etc., it is to be rejected. I will now argue that even under the broadest scope of corporate obligation, pharmaceutical companies do not have a special obligation to provide life-saving drugs to those in need—even though they could do so with very little effort.

III. Corporate Obligation

Open any business ethics textbook, and you will come across theories of corporate obligation which state either that corporate decision makers have a duty to satisfy stockholder interests, or to satisfy stakeholder[9] as well as stockholder interests, or to maximize the general good of society.

A. Stockholder Theory

Little needs to be said about the stockholder theory of obligation in regard to corporate responsibility. Under this theory of obligation, corporate decision makers have a duty to increase profits for stockholders without the use of deception or fraud (Friedman, 2002/1971, pp. 33-37). Clearly, under this theory of obligation, pharmaceutical companies have a duty to ignore the concern with saving the lives of those in need, unless acting on this concern increases profits for stockholders.

B. Stakeholder Theory

Under stakeholder theory, it is not as clear whether pharmaceutical companies have a responsibility to provide life-saving drugs to those who need them. Stakeholders include any group or individual influenced by the company's operation.[10] At first glance, it appears that because pharmaceutical companies could directly save the lives of so many, those in need of life-saving drugs count as stakeholders. If they count as stakeholders, then the drug company is obligated to consider their interests, which means that there could be an obligation to provide life-saving drugs.

But a closer look will establish the contrary. In order to count as a stakeholder, a group or individual must be influenced by or influence the company's operation.[11] The question is, however, what counts as being influenced by or influencing the company's operation? A supplier is influenced by the company's operation because it receives orders and depends on buyers to stay in business. If the company goes out of business, the supplier suffers from the loss of business. If the company grows, the supplier will experience growth in its sales. So the company's operation creates by-products that influence the supplier. That same supplier can influence the company by raising prices, discontinuing certain supplies, going out of business, merging with another supplier, etc. Using this example, we can explain "influence" as a causal concept, that is, anything that counts as "influence" must be caused by the participants. This causal connection is evident in what standardly counts as stakeholders of a company, namely suppliers, customers, stockholders, employees, etc. (Freeman, 2002, pp. 38-48).

However, if we focus on pharmaceutical companies and consider those who need life-saving drugs but cannot pay for them, we cannot identify any causal connection. A drug company's operation normally has not directly shaped the situation of faraway individuals who are unable to pay for life-saving drugs. It is not as though the drug companies have caused these people to become poor and sick. Had the drug companies never come into existence, those people would still be in need. And those who need life-saving drugs, but cannot pay for them, do not influence the drug company in any way, since they are not customers of or contributors to the company.[12]

Consequently, those who are in need of life-saving drugs but cannot pay for them typically fail to count as stakeholders. Under the stakeholder theory of obligation, as under the stockholder theory of obligation, pharmaceutical companies would not have a special duty to save lives.

The objection has been raised that drug companies perpetuate the poverty and sickness of those who cannot pay, even though they did not create them, and that this amounts to enough of a causal connection to count the impoverished as stakeholders of drug companies.[13] Although I will not be critically evaluating this point, I do want to say that if the perpetuation of poverty and sickness amounts to the right sort of causal connection, it is doubtful whether this causal connection can be traced back *uniquely* to pharmaceutical companies. If one argues that those who need life-saving drugs are stakeholders because drug companies are part of the cause of their poverty, it will turn out that too *many* parties can be considered stakeholders. (I will be discussing this particular point in more depth following this section.)

Another response is that the impoverished count as stakeholders because they cooperate with and honor laws that allow drug companies to flourish and do business. They could, as a desperate measure, revolt and create havoc for drug companies. Because companies rely on global cooperation, the impoverished turn out to be stakeholders after all. But this type of response conflates the concept of stakeholders with the more general concept of society, which is the topic of the next section.

C. Social-Responsibility Theory (SRT)

Proponents of social-responsibility theories, or what I will call SRT accounts, argue that corporate responsibility should extend to the whole of society. "Ethical responsibilities encompass the more general responsibility to do what's right and avoid harm" (Trevino & Nelson, 2004, p. 32). Their argument depends on the claim that the greatest social and economic benefit would result if corporations recognized the well being of society as a whole in their decision making process. The following are some standard accounts of social responsibility theories of corporate obligation. "Social responsibility is the obligation of decision makers to take actions which protect and improve the welfare of society as a whole along with their own interests" (Davis & Blomstrom, 1975, p. 23). "The idea of social responsibility supposes that the corporation has not only economic and legal obligations, but also certain responsibilities to society which extend beyond these obligations" (McGuire, 1963, p. 144). "[Social responsibility] implies bringing corporate behavior up to a level where it is congruent with the prevailing social norms, values, and expectations" (Carroll, 1997, p. 594). "The social responsibility of business encompasses the economic, legal, ethical and discretionary expectations that society has of organizations at a given point in time" (Carroll, 1979, p. 500). "The ethical responsibility of business includes the dictum to 'do no harm' by such activities as polluting the environment, discriminating against workers, producing dangerous products, engaging in misleading advertising, and so on" (Carroll, 1997, pp. 594).

What I take to be the most current terminology describing the social responsibilities of a corporation is "the triple bottom line." In their 2002 paper, "Responsibility: The New Business Imperative," Sandra W.

Waddock, Charles Bodwell, and Samuel B. Graves present the responsibilities of corporations as adherence to the triple bottom lines of economic, social, and environmental performance. Much like the previously mentioned conceptions of social responsibility, triple bottom line theory fails to provide explicit principles for responsible behavior. However, the implicit idea is clear—corporations ought to be concerned with, in addition to profit, their impact on society and the environment.

Given these definitions, we can see that proponents of SRT accounts demand the broadest scope of corporate responsibility.

At first glance, it seems clear that providing life-saving drugs to those in need would result in great benefits to society (Sen, 1993, pp. 52-54). Lives would be saved. And since pharmaceutical companies produce these drugs, they are in a unique position to help the impoverished in third world countries. It seems, then, that proponents of SRT accounts could hold that pharmaceutical companies have a *special* duty to save lives.

But suppose this is true: the implication is that when a company is *able* to save lives *with little effort*, there is a special duty to do so. The duty to save lives is derived from the ability to do so, and to do so with little effort.

However, drugs are not the only things that can save lives. Money can save lives as well. This could take the form of purchasing needed supplies, purchasing drugs, providing doctors, etc. Corporations that are allowed to reach and maintain a reasonable profit margin are in a position to save lives with little effort. This means that once a corporation achieves a reasonable profit margin, it should use any profit generated on top of that to save lives. If proponents of SRT accounts require pharmaceutical companies to save lives when they are able, then they must require all companies, when they are able, to save lives as well. Hence, proponents of SRT accounts who require drug companies to save lives for the good of society should also require the same of all companies that possibly could save lives. But often this is not the case—drug companies are usually singled out for special responsibility.

Companies such as McDonalds, Nike, and Coca-Cola usually are not taken to be under a moral obligation to save lives, even though their profit margins would allow them to save lives with little effort. For these corporations, being socially responsible usually is taken to consist only in not actively harming society, rather saving those in need. Consequently pharmaceutical companies should not be morally required to save lives either, just because they can. There is no moral justification for singling them out.

Standardly, we do not tolerate *special* treatment of individuals in moral theories. Utilitarianism and Kantianism have a symmetry property: moral obligations and duties apply equally to everyone. No one is free from moral requirements. For example, it is not permissible for people to neglect or harm their children (we do not single out college graduates as especially responsible to their children) and it is impermissible for anyone to plagiarize (we do not impose the prohibition only on persons with a low GPA).[14] [15] But proponents of SRT accounts usually require only pharmaceutical companies to save lives, even though many other kinds of companies have the ability to save lives as well.

The symmetry property is necessary for a coherent moral theory. It would be incoherent for utilitarians to say that some people should act to maximize happiness while others need not do so. Kantians would be regarded as unreasonable if they held that some rational beings were bound by the categorical imperative, but others were not. Currently there are no important moral theories that lack the symmetry property.[16] As with moral theories applied to individuals, the symmetry property is necessary for the coherence of corporate theories of obligation.

If the criterion for holding a corporation responsible for saving lives is the ability to do so with little effort, then all corporations that satisfy this criterion must be held responsible. The singling out of pharmaceutical companies by proponents of SRT accounts is therefore a violation of the symmetry property. As a result, because proponents of SRT accounts usually do single out pharmaceutical companies as having an obligation to save lives, their interpretation of social responsibility is incoherent.

Proponents of SRT accounts could just bite the bullet and satisfy the symmetry property by holding all successful companies morally responsible for saving lives, when they are able and when it takes little effort to do so. This currently is not the case, and it seems highly unlikely that proponents of SRT accounts will require this duty of corporations in general. I do not here propose to critically defend or criticize this option. However, I do want to say that if proponents of SRT accounts choose to bite the bullet, they will run into many theoretical and practical complications. For example, it will be quite difficult to draw a non-arbitrary line between corporations that have the power to save lives with little effort from those corporations that do not. And although it might be easy to pick out *clear* cases of corporations that are capable of saving lives, it will still be quite tricky to draw a non-arbitrary line between the *clear* and the *not quite clear* cases of capability. Arbitrary lines may be acceptable in delineating *some* moral requirements, but the competitive nature of the market is likely to encourage constant redefinition of where that line should be drawn; this would prevent such a line from having enough moral force to be taken seriously (Frank, 2002/1996, p. 256).[17]

Another option for proponents of SRT accounts is to draw a relevant and legitimate distinction between pharmaceutical companies and other types of companies.[18] If this can be established, then proponents of SRT accounts who claim that pharmaceutical companies have a special obligation to save lives may be justified.

D. Are Pharmaceutical Companies Special?

For theorists of corporate obligation to single out and hold pharmaceutical companies responsible for saving lives when they are able, they must distinguish pharmaceutical companies from other types of companies. If a morally relevant distinction cannot be established, then under no theory of obligation can pharmaceutical companies be singled out as having a unique duty to save lives.

There have been many attempts to distinguish pharmaceutical companies from other types of companies. I will now briefly review the most common attempts and why they fail.

1. Because drug companies produce life-saving products, they ought to provide these products to those who need them to stay alive, regardless of whether or not they make a profit.[19] Unlike other types of companies, pharmaceutical companies have the power to save lives. The fact that they produce life-saving products distinguishes them from other types of companies. And this distinction is enough to hold them morally responsible for saving lives (De George, 2005, p. 555). "'If it's relatively cheap to manufacture [AIDS] drugs, it makes no moral sense to let thirty-six million people die,' says James Love, director of the Consumer Project on Technology, an organization started by Ralph Nader" (Progressive, 2001).

Reply: What counts as a life-saving product? Are drugs the only products that count? Life-saving products are those products that, when provided to those who need them, prevent death under those conditions of need. Under this interpretation, when a country is suffering from famine, McDonalds produces a life-saving product. When a country is suffering from drought, Coca-Cola produces a life-saving product. When a country is at war and in need of arms and ammunition to fight their attackers, gun manufacturers produce a life-saving product. Circumstances determine what products count as life-saving products.

Since other types of companies can produce life-saving products, the fact that pharmaceutical companies produce life-saving drugs does not distinguish them from other types of companies.[20 21]

2. Marcia Angell has proposed another distinction: drug companies often benefit from public or government support, whereas other types of companies do not. The claim is that drug companies are subject to a type of *reciprocity* principle. The government support that Angell has in mind takes the form of copyright and patent protection, FDA regulation, university research, and research done at the National Institutes of Health (Angell, 2004, pp. 7-10). Her claim is that government agencies aid drug companies in their operation and success. In some cases, drug companies entirely rely on government funded organizations for their research. This, for Angell, is a relevant and legitimate distinction. Because drug companies are benefited by publicly funded organizations, they have a responsibility to the public that made their success possible.

Reply: Many industries are supported by publicly funded organizations. And many industries benefit from research done at universities, for instance, the computer industry, the textile industry, the food and cosmetics industry, and the aerospace industry. So, pharmaceutical companies are not a special case of industry benefiting from publicly funded organizations. This distinction ultimately fails. But even if Angell is right in saying that drug companies are indebted to the public because they benefit from publicly funded organizations, this does not mean that drug companies would be indebted to the people in third world countries who are in need of life saving drugs. Pharmaceutical companies, on this theory, would only be responsible to the particular society that funded them. So even if this distinction were legitimate, it would not establish the obligation in question.[22]

3. If we want to preserve the profit margins of pharmaceutical companies, we could just require them to give up their intellectual property rights, rather than the products that are sold for profit. This way, countries that need life-saving drugs to save people's lives could make the drugs themselves. "The main moral problem pits the moral principle that the inventor(s) have the right to the fruits of their labor versus the principle that priority be granted to fulfilling the basic needs or right to livelihood of those who cannot afford the innovation in question, such as a vital drug" (Steidlmeier, 1997, pp. 337-339). The distinction offered here is that, unlike other types of companies, drug companies can save

lives by sharing their intellectual property, without affecting the sales of their products to those who can pay. Other types of companies cannot do this—they would have to donate actual products or money. Since giving up products and money influences the bottom line directly, it would seem unreasonable to require them to save lives. This would not be the case for drug companies; relinquishing intellectual property to impoverished nations will not affect their bottom line, since the impoverished do not contribute to it anyway.[23] As long as enforceable procedures are in place to regulate drug distribution effectively, pharmaceutical companies could be singled out for special responsibility.[24] In short, other types of companies cannot save lives without sacrificing the bottom line, while pharmaceutical companies can.

Reply: This distinction, at first glance, is very convincing. Since drug companies are not making money from these impoverished nations anyway, allowing them to legally make their own drugs would not affect their bottom line. The claim is that drug companies are a special case where releasing only intellectual property could save lives. However, it is not true that the pharmaceutical industry is a special case. There are several industries that hold patents that, if released, could save the lives of the impoverished. Big agribusiness holds patents on genetically modified foods (Conway, 1999). Nutrient deficiencies in impoverished nations can be remedied by providing rice that is genetically engineered to contain additional vitamins and minerals (Whitman, 2000). The computer and software industry have benefited greatly from patent protection. It seems correct to say that technology has made saving lives more efficient and effective (Versweyvel, 2003). The number of energy-related patents is rising quickly. Sustainable energy for impoverished nations would no doubt save millions of lives (McAlister, 2005). These are all industries that have the potential to save lives by releasing intellectual property to impoverished nations; the pharmaceutical industry is not a special case.

4. Proponents of SRT accounts could argue that the socially responsible act is to consider the impoverished as stakeholders, not because they currently affect the drug companies' operation, but because they could affect it eventually down the line, especially since there is no obligation to give up the intellectual property that could save the lives of the impoverished. "In the intellectual property debate it is often forgotten that the property rights advocated by multinational companies are primarily based upon modern Western values and culture. In different cul-

tural settings they do not find the same legitimacy" (Steidlmeier, 1997, pp. 337-339). What reasons do the impoverished nations have for respecting property rights? The point is that regardless of whether the impoverished count as *current* stakeholders, they will inevitably count as stakeholders in the future. This is because if drug companies fail to count them as stakeholders, and if drug companies are not required to save their lives by providing the life-saving drugs or intellectual property, there would be no reason for the impoverished to abide by and respect the property rights of the pharmaceutical companies, in which case, they would have the potential to affect the company's operation negatively.[25] As a result the impoverished would *ultimately* count as stakeholders.

Reply: If this response were to be taken seriously, it would turn out that the impoverished would ultimately count as stakeholders for all successful corporations since they, too, are allowing them to suffer and die.[26] There would be no reason for the impoverished to care about any corporation's property rights. Again, it turns out, according to this argument, that what applies to pharmaceutical companies also applies to other types of companies. There is no distinction. "This point raises the question of whether (if, indeed, there is a moral obligation to aid the disadvantaged...) it is the obligation of the property owner or, rather, of society at large to do so" (Steidlmeier, 1997, pp. 337-339).

5. In 2002, according to the Fortune 500, the top seven pharmaceutical companies generated more in pure profit than the top seven auto companies, the top seven oil companies, the top seven airline companies, and the top seven media companies. Pharmaceutical companies averaged a 17.9% profit margin, which was the highest margin of any industry in the nation. Here, the distinction between pharmaceutical companies and other types of companies is based on the former's exorbitant profit margin rather than on the product that is produced (Fortune, 2002).

Reply: This seems to be the most intuitive distinction. Many people believe that people or corporations who have significantly more ought to aid and help others who have less. We can find this point in Peter Singer's "Famine, Affluence, and Morality" (1972). It is hard to get around the idea that because pharmaceutical companies make exorbitant amounts of money, they have more of an obligation to save lives. Here, the capacity to save lives is based strictly on profit margin.[27] However, although it may be true that pharmaceutical companies have the highest profit margins, this is not a distinguishing feature. Drug companies are not specially situated to make the most money.[28] It is quite possible for other types of corporations to generate the highest profit margins. "The large drug companies are now worried about revenue growth in the years ahead. Growth through mergers and acquisitions is slowing down, and consolidation has just about hit the wall as a way to produce growth" (Elliot & Schroth, 2002, p. 59). "It's hard to make the case that an industry as rich and powerful as this one...is in trouble, but it is" (Angell, 2004, p. 217). If this distinction is based purely on profits, it shouldn't matter what types of products are produced; the most profitable corporations should bear the responsibility of saving lives in third world countries. Exorbitant profit margins are not a unique feature of the pharmaceutical industry; rather, they are features of the market. My point here is similar to my reply to the first distinction—because market circumstances can lead other types of corporations to become the most successful, the fact that pharmaceutical companies currently generate the highest profit margins does not especially distinguish them from other types of corporations. (Many people believe that drug companies ought to save the lives of those dying in third world countries because they make so much money. The fact is that, currently, drug companies do make more money than other corporations. They not only make more, they make so much more that it seems immoral for them not to donate drugs to save lives. However, if a Good Samaritan duty is based on the generation of profits, it does not necessarily establish the duty to save the lives of those in need of life-saving drugs. Remember that for this distinction, the fact that drug companies produce life-saving products doesn't matter. What matters is that they make the most money. This means that Merck could fulfill their Good Samaritan duty by donating to People for the Ethical Treatment of Animals (PETA), National Organization of Women (NOW), Deseret Industries, The Foundation for Starving Artists, etc. This distinction says nothing about whom the Good Samaritan duty ought to be directed to, since it is based on profit margins. Consequently, this distinction, even if it were legitimate, would not establish the specific duty to save lives.)

I have attempted to show that common distinctions made between drug companies and other types of companies are unjustified, in which case singling out drug companies, as having the responsibility to save lives while other companies do not, is also unjustified. If we do not require other types of corporations to save lives then we should not require drug companies to do so. There is no distinction, with respect to responsibilities, between pharmaceutical companies that produce life-saving products and other companies that produce other types of products.

IV. Options

If I am right, the intuition that corporations have an obligation to save lives, when they are clearly capable, ought to extend beyond the scope of pharmaceutical companies, which would mean that there ought to be far more corporate regulation. Alternatively, since theorists of corporate obligation cannot establish this special duty, the intuition that drug companies have a moral duty to save lives, when they are clearly capable, needs to be abandoned. Since theorists of corporate obligation are left with these options, if neither of these options are acceptable, current theories of obligation turn out to be unacceptable as well, and in need of revision.

Proponents of SRT accounts are well intentioned. Concern for the greater good of society is admirable. However, if there *really* is a concern for the greater good, consistency requires extending the moral responsibility to save lives to other corporations that have this capability[29]; this obligation would reach far beyond pharmaceutical companies. Suppose a child is drowning and that there are 10 Olympic swimmers in the pool. The fact that swimmer A could save the child does not release the other swimmers from the duty to save the child (supposing that there is this duty). They all have a duty to save the child. Some have said that the swimmer closest to the child has more of a duty to save the child since he/she could get to the child sooner. However, this still does not release the other swimmers from the duty to save the child. It seems to me that the other nine swimmers have an equally forceful duty to save the child, even if it is by way of making sure the closer swimmer fulfills his/her duty to save the child.

The point is this: the fact that drug companies produce life-saving products should not release other corporations from the obligation to save lives. But it is doubtful that theorists who propose to restrict the *free* market in such an extreme manner would be taken seriously, even if they ought to be.[30]

If proponents of SRT accounts will not extend the obligation to save lives to other types of corporations, then, again for the sake of consistency, this obligation ought to be abandoned. There is no moral justification, as I have shown, for singling out pharmaceutical companies.[31] But telling people to abandon this obligation may be harder than it seems. The intuition that drug companies have a special obligation to save lives is so strong and so widely accepted that it evidently seems immoral to give the obligation up.[32] This attitude, I believe, is a mistake stemming from an assumption that obligations come only in two modalities—moral and legal. And since the belief that drug companies have a special duty to save lives is perceived as a moral one, it is too difficult to give it up. But there are other kinds of obligations that are neither moral nor legal: prudential, professional, legacy (having to do with birthrights), conventional (etiquette), patriotic, friendship, etc.[33] These kinds of obligations are easier to revise or abandon and perhaps the symmetry property does not apply to them. Since intuitions that are perceived as moral duties are too hard to shake off, and yet the intuition that drug companies have a *special* moral obligation to save the impoverished is unjustified, this intuition may need to be recast as a different type of obligation. By doing so, we can account for the intuition, without insisting on an illegitimate moral obligation.

The last alternative is to insist relentlessly that pharmaceutical companies *do* have a special moral duty to save lives. At the end of the day, this moral intuition may be too hard to abandon or recast as an alternative type of intuition. But since I have shown that current theorists of corporate obligation cannot rationally reconstruct this moral duty, that would mean that we need to look for a new theory which can. This alternative would require that we accept the inadequacy of current theories of corporate obligation, including standard interpretations of SRT accounts. Only then can we seriously move on to establish better, more rigorous and effective theories of corporate obligation.

V. Conclusion

The first objective has been to show that the responsibility to save lives in third world countries is not one that is particular to pharmaceutical companies. The fact that they produce life-saving products does not release other types of corporations from the obligation to save lives. However, if theorists of corporate obligation, such as SRT theorists, *do* release other types of corporations from this obligation, it will turn out that the obligatory force of saving lives is minimal. In other words, it would mean that proponents of SRT accounts are not really concerned with saving lives after all. This conclusion may seem unacceptable to those who believe their concern for the impoverished is genuine. For these people, current theories of corporate obligation ought to be considered insufficient for guiding business choices.

As a response to this problem, the second objective is to show that current theories of corporate obligation, including SRT accounts, need to be critically reevaluated. If we really are concerned with moral or ethical business behavior, we need theories of obligation that reflect this concern. I have used a common intuition to illustrate this point. Current theories of corporate obligation fail to be interpreted as reflecting the intuition that extremely successful corporations have a responsibility to help the impoverished, especially when doing so takes little effort.

My hope is to motivate critical reevaluation of current theories of corporate obligation. I suspect that the standard interpretations of the theories will turn out to be ineffective and irrelevant guides for business practitioners when making important decisions.[34] Recognizing and understanding how current theories of corporate obligation are deficient is, I believe, the first step to establishing and organizing an ethical and moral corporate environment.

Notes

* I am grateful to Peggy Battin, Jim Childress, Leslie Francis, Bruce Landesman, Debby Millgram, Hillel Millgram, Shaun Nichols, Anya Plutynski, and Ryan Spellecy for commenting on earlier drafts of this paper. I am also grateful to Diana Buccafurni, Daniel Scott Fischer, Elijah Millgram, Rob Sparrow, and audiences at the 2005 Academy of Management, the Centre for Applied Philosophy and Public Ethics at Australian National University (CAPPE), and the 2004 American Society for Bioethics and Humanities (ASBH) for helpful discussions.

1. I am aware that the documentary, *The Corporation,* targets all major corporations and not only pharmaceutical companies. If we take the film seriously, it would turn out that most major corporations behave as a psychopath would. My claim is that this attitude has not been intuitively applied across the board. Rather, pharmaceutical companies have been singled out as having a special responsibility. It is this intuition that is in question.
2. I will be using the words pharmaceutical and drug interchangeably.
3. Peter Singer is a well know example of someone who relies on the Good Samaritan intuition (Singer, 1972).
4. This assumption is so intuitive that the very thought of challenging it strikes many people as absurd (even though most people somehow manage to ignore the obligation). Although it would be nice if there really were this moral obligation, it is not at all clear that there is one. My task is not to establish whether or not there is this moral obligation. I am only working under the assumption that there is.

5. This paper focuses on pharmaceutical companies and our intuitions about their obligations to society. I am using our intuitions regarding pharmaceutical companies as a test case for examining our current theories of corporate obligation. But of course other intuitions could be used as test case also.
6. Whether legal obligations are based on moral obligations is another issue, which I will not discuss here.
7. There are of course instances where this act would be illegal, such as if company executives lied about their financial situation.
8. I am putting legal obligations to one side; I will not be discussing them.
9. Some business ethicists, particularly those with a background in management, talk about social responsibility as if it were a result of satisfying obligations to stakeholders. In other words, social responsibility and satisfying stakeholder obligations are synonymous. "Responsible executives have a duty to care about justice and stakeholder rights because, as part of society, it is simply the right thing to do" (Trevino & Nelson, 2004, p. 31). This way of talking about social responsibility is, I believe, a mistake. Stakeholder concerns are not always synonymous with societal concerns. If social responsibility were to be defined as the satisfaction of stakeholder interests, then there would need to be a new classification dealing directly with societal concerns, regardless of whether they correlate with stakeholder interests. Business ethics anthologies that are meant to be used in *philosophy* courses do separate theories of obligation into three distinct classifications—stockholder, stakeholder, and social responsibility theories. Because my goal is to provide an argument that is persuasive under any formulation of social responsibility theory, I distinguish social responsibility theories from stakeholder theories. This means that I have more theories to account for, hence I argue under the broadest scope of responsibility.
10. Linda Trevino and Katherine Nelson have offer a few definitions of who counts as stakeholders: "A stakeholder is any individual or group that has one or more stakes in an organization. A stakeholder is an individual or group that can affect or be affected by business decisions or undertakings" (Trevino & Nelson, 2004, p. 196). These definitions, however, are close to vacuous, since they define practically anyone and everyone as a stakeholder. This may be why Trevino and Nelson go on to distinguish between primary and secondary stakeholders. "Primary stakeholders are those groups or individuals with whom the organization has a formal, contractual relationship: In most cases this means customers, employees, shareholders or owners, suppliers and perhaps even the government. Secondary stakeholders are other individuals or groups to whom the organization has obligations, but who are not formal, contractual partners" (Trevino & Nelson, 2004, p. 196). From this definition, secondary stakeholders are not adequately identified, which is why I focus mainly on primary stakeholders.
11. See previous footnote.
12. I have been asked to consider the following scenario: suppose a group of impoverished people buy stock in a drug company which produces the needed life-saving drugs—they would then be stakeholders. My immediate response to this is as follows: These stockholders, which are what these impoverished people would be, would benefit the same way as other stockholders. They receive the same as any other stakeholder. I don't believe that being *impoverished* stockholders warrants additional benefits. If it did, stockholders could claim benefits according to their

own needs rather than according to company performance. This would be a startling departure from standard practice.

13. I am grateful to Jim Childress for this point.
14. One might object that while parents have the obligation to care for their children, other people don't have this obligation, which means that the symmetry property is not enforced. That, I believe, is a mistake. If one is not a parent, the duty is not applicable. This, however, doesn't mean that one is free from this duty. People are required to tell the truth, but this doesn't mean people who are never in a position to lie are free from this duty.
15. This point should not be obscured by the imperfect duties (O'Neil, 1980). Kant's distinction has to do with determining how much one is required to do in order to discharge one's duties, whereas I am talking about determining who counts as having the duties. Imperfect duties leave it up to the agent to decide when and how to perform them; nevertheless, the duty pertains to everyone similarly situated. The issue of who is subject to the duties is taken care of, for Kant, by the symmetry property.
16. There are individual moral theories like Ross's (1930) account of *prima facie* duties and Jonathan Dancy's (1993) particularism that may not satisfy the symmetry property. What is characteristic of these theories is that they very quickly arrive at a point where they cannot adequately explain their prescriptions or principles. This failure to provide an adequate explanation influences the legitimacy and importance of the theory. Moral principles need to be explicable if they are to be taken seriously. This is why I am not using theories like Ross's and Dancy's as models for theories of corporate obligation.
17. This means that proponents of SRT accounts, if they were to draw an arbitrary line in order to bite this bullet, would have established a somewhat trivial duty to save lives in third world countries. This is not their goal.
18. It is not enough to say that the former produces drugs and the latter does not; just a slightly closer look will disclose the moral irrelevance of this distinction.
19. This, of course, is under the assumption that they will still be making a reasonable profit from those who can pay.
20. Klaus M. Leisinger argues that private enterprises such as pharmaceutical companies can only be as socially responsible as they are capable of being (Leisinger, 2005, pp. 582-583). This implies that different enterprises have different capabilities. My argument focuses on what I think are mistaken conceptions of "capability." To think that pharmaceutical companies have a *special* capacity to save lives is misguided.
21. It has been brought to my attention that in some cases, a pharmaceutical company may be the only producer of what is needed to save lives. This would then establish a distinction between that drug company and other companies like Coca-Cola, since Coca-Cola is not the only company producing water. However, I contend that even if a company is the only producer of what is needed to save lives, that company should not be the only party held responsible for saving lives. It is not as though the life-saving product could not be acquired and distributed through other means, such as government subsidies. My point is that a pharmaceutical company's ability to save lives does not release other parties from the duty to save lives. (I am grateful to Thomas Pogge for helping me realize this point by adamantly disagreeing with me.) Richard T. De George has also made this point.

"Clearly, pharmaceutical companies are not the only health care providers and the entire obligation to fulfill the rights in question does not fall on them. And clearly if they have special obligations, that does not mean that government, individuals, families, NGOs, and so on do not also have obligations" (De George, 2005, p. 559). However, what De George has missed, as I have been arguing, is that pharmaceutical companies do not have a special obligation and so should not be assigned a specific and separate placement within the chain of responsibility.

22. This would also be true of David Resnik's reciprocity principle: "[I]f a companies sponsors a study using a specific population, then members of the population that participate in the study should derive some benefits from their participation. In particular, the drug should be made available to members of the population at a reasonable price" (Resnik, 2001, p. 19).
23. Pharmaceutical companies have been severely criticized for lack of leniency with regard to patent restrictions. Marcia Angell explains the influence that drug companies have on the government, which not only has resulted in weak and ineffective attempts to aid the impoverished; this influence has motivated the government to prevent the impoverished from being helped (Angell, 2004, pp. 206-208).
24. The worry is that "secondary markets would develop, whereby people in Africa would buy the drugs cheaply and resell them at a mark-up in the West" (Progressive, 2001).
25. I am grateful to Rob Sparrow for this point.
26. Recall that drugs are not the only things that can save lives. Money can save lives as well. Money can buy the needed drugs. Money can establish private research geared specifically toward the impoverished. Money can send doctors to care for the suffering.
27. I am treating this intuition seriously since it is difficult to shake. I am ignoring the is/ought problem here, that is, just because it is the case that drug companies can save lives doesn't mean that they ought to. Pointing out this logical fallacy doesn't seem to effectively negate the intuition and so I will not be using it to undercut the distinction.
28. Although it is true that pharmaceutical companies are allowed monopoly privileges as a result of patent laws, the intent is to allow them to make back the money that they put into R&D. The intent of this privilege is not for drug companies to generate the highest profit margins.
29. I referred to this earlier as a symmetry property.
30. Moral restrictions work in the same way that moral permissibility works. They influence how actions are judged—they produce judgments that are either praiseworthy or blameworthy. One way to avoid blameworthiness is to play down the seriousness of the restriction.
31. As a reminder, theories of corporate obligation are *moral* theories. If theorists can't produce the special obligation to save lives, this means that they cannot morally justify this special obligation.
32. This intuition does not extend to other types of corporations, which I believe is the reason that theorists of corporate obligation do not extend the responsibility to save lives to other corporations. The inconsistency in intuitions is what initially motivated this project.
33. Explicit examples include: the obligation to prepare for retirement, the obligation to take and give messages to co-workers, the obligation to have a will, the obligation

to turn off mobile phones during a movie, the obligation to stand during the national anthem, and the obligation not to betray friends.

34. It has already been suggested that standard individual moral theories such as utilitarianism, Kantianism, and virtue ethics fail to provide guidance for business decision making (Soule, 2002, p. 115). I am suggesting that this is also true of *corporate* theories of obligation such as stockholder theory, stakeholder theory and social responsibility theories of obligation.

References

Angell, M. (2004). *The Truth About the Drug Companies: How They Deceive Us and What to Do About It.* New York: Random House.

Brock, D.W. (2001). 'Some questions about the moral responsibilities of drug companies in developing countries,' *Developing World Bioethics,* 1, 33–37.

Carroll, A.B. (1979). 'A three-dimensional conceptual model for corporate social performance,' *Academy of Management Review,* 4, 497-505.

Carroll, A.B. (1997). 'Social responsibility (entry),' in E.R. Freeman & P. Werhane (Eds.), *Encyclopedic Dictionary of Business Ethics* (pp. 594). Oxford: Blackwell Publishing.

Conway, G. (1999). *GM foods can save lives–if we use them sensibly* [Online]. Available: http://www.biotech-info.net/saving_lives.html.

Dancy, J. (1993). *Moral Reasons.* Oxford: Blackwell Publishing.

Daniels, N. (2001). 'Social responsibility and global pharmaceutical companies,' *Developing World Bioethics,* 1, 38–41.

Davis, K. & Blomstrom, R. (1975). *Business and Society: Environment and Responsibility.* New York: McGraw-Hill.

De George, R.T. (2005). 'Intellectual property and pharmaceutical drugs: An ethical analysis,' *Business Ethics Quarterly,* 15, 549–575.

Elliot, L.A. & Schroth, R.J. (2002). *How Companies Lie.* New York: Crown Publishing.

Feinberg & H. Gross (Eds.). (1977) *Philosophy of Law,* 5th edition (pp. 56-72). Belmont: Wadsworth Publishing Company.

Fortune Magazine. (2002). *2002 Fortune 500.* [Online]. Available: http://money.cnn.com/magazines/fortune/fortune_archive/2002/04/15/321417/index.htm.

Frank, R.H. (2002). 'Can socially responsible firms survive in a competitive environment?,' in T. Donaldson, P. Werhane, & M. Cording (Eds.), *Ethical Issues in Business: A Philosophical Approach* (pp. 252–262). Upper Saddle River: Prentice Hall.

Freeman, R.E. (2002). 'Stakeholder theory of the modern corporation,' in T. Donaldson, P. Werhane, & M. Cording (Eds.), *Ethical Issues in Business: A Philosophical Approach* (pp. 38–48). Upper Saddle River: Prentice Hall.

Friedman, M. (2002). 'The social responsibility of business is to increase its profits,' in T. Donaldson, P. Werhane, & M. Cording (Eds.), *Ethical Issues in Business: A Philosophical Approach* (pp. 33–37). Upper Saddle River: Prentice Hall.

Hart, H.L.A. (1995/1958). 'Positivism and the separation of law and morals,' in J. Feinberg & H. Gross (Eds.), *Philosophy of Law, 5th edition* (pp. 56-72). Belmont: Wadsworth Publishing Company.

Kant, I. (1996/1797). *The Metaphysics of Morals.* Mary Gregor (Ed.). Cambridge: Cambridge University Press.

Leisinger, K.M. (2005). 'The corporate social responsibility of the pharmaceutical industry: Idealism without illusion and realism without resignation,' *Business Ethics Quarterly*, 15, 577–594.

McAlister, R.E. (2005) *Energy-related inventions* [Online]. Available: http://www.lightparty.com/Energy/AmericanHydrogenAsso.html.

McGuire, J.W. (1963). *Business and Society*. New York: McGraw-Hill.

O'Neill, O. (1980). 'Kantian approaches to some famine problems,' in T. Regan (Ed.), *Matters of Life and Death* (pp. 285–294). New York: McGraw-Hill.

Progressive, The. (2001). *Aids culprits—multinational drug companies overpricing in Africa.* [Online]. Available: http://www.thirdworldtraveler.com/Health/AIDS_Culprits.html.

Resnik, D.B. (2001). 'Developing drugs for the developing world: An economic, legal, moral, and political dilemma,' *Developing World Bioethics*, 1, 11–32.

Ross, W.D. (1930). *The Right and the Good*. Oxford: Oxford University Press.

Sen, A. (1993). 'Does business ethics make economic sense?,' *Business Ethics Quarterly*, 3, 45–54.

Singer, P. (1972). 'Famine, affluence, and morality,' *Philosophy and Public Affairs*, 1, 229–243.

Soule, E. (2002). 'Managerial moral strategies–in search of a few good principles,' *Academy of Management Review*, 27, 114–124.

Steidlmeier, P. (1997). 'Intellectual property (entry),' in E.R. Freeman & P. Werhane (Eds.), *Encyclopedic Dictionary of Business Ethics* (pp. 337–339). Oxford: Blackwell Publishing.

Trevino, L.K. & Nelson, K.A. (2004). *Managing Business Ethics: Straight Talk about How to Do it Right*. Hoboken: Wiley Publishing.

Van Gelder, A. (2005) *NGO's on drugs*. [Online]. Available: http://www.aegis.org/news/wsj/2005/WJ051001.html.

Versweyvel, L. (2003). *Cedara and Alion join forces to develop life-saving technology for military medical emergencies.* [Online]. Available: http://www.hoise.com/vmw/04/articles/vmw/LV-VM-01-04-12.html.

Waddock, S.A., Bodwell, C., & Graves, S.B. (2002). "Responsibility: The new business imperative", *Academy of Management Executive*, 16(2), 132–147.

Whitman, D.B. (2000) *Genetically modified foods: Harmful or helpful?* [Online]. Available: http://www.csa.com/discoveryguides/gmfood/overview.php.

Autonomy, Constraining Options, and Pharmaceutical Costs

James Stacy Taylor
Department of Philosophy, The College of New Jersey

I. Introduction

There is growing concern within the United States and elsewhere about the continued rise in pharmaceutical spending. In particular, there is growing concern that patients are purchasing expensive name-brand medications rather than equally effective generic brands, and that this purchasing trend is causing spending on pharmaceuticals to increase without patients receiving any additional healthcare benefits. There is also concern that this increase in spending on pharmaceuticals is causing insurance rates to rise. This, in turn, will lead to people who purchase their own insurance being less able to afford it, and people whose insurance is provided by their employer having their level of coverage diminished, or else having their coverage eliminated altogether.

M.A. Graber and J.F. Tansey (2005, pp. 424-426) have recently argued that such worries about the effects of rising spending on pharmaceuticals would be best addressed through practices that exhibit a greater respect for patient autonomy and a greater concern with social justice. They argue that insofar as healthcare consumers are misinformed about the side effects, risks, and relative efficacy of different pharmaceuticals they cannot give their informed consent to the prescription of such prod-

H.T. Engelhardt, Jr. and J. Garrett (eds), *Innovation and the Pharmaceutical Industry* (pp. 67–79).

ucts. Furthermore, Graber and Tansey argue, patients cannot give their informed consent to the prescription of pharmaceuticals insofar as they are unaware of the social and economic effects that result from their being prescribed name-brand products rather than generic products. Given this, they hold, both respect for personal autonomy and concern for social justice require that patients be informed both of the relative efficacy of name-brand and generic pharmaceutical products, as well as of the social and economic effects that result from the prescribing of the former. They thus conclude that patients should be required to sign a formal document stating that have been informed of, and understand, both the relative efficacy of name-brand and generic pharmaceutical products and the social and economic effects that result from the prescribing of the former.

In this paper I will argue that although Graber and Tansey have correctly identified a problem that is generated by the patient preference for name-brand pharmaceuticals they are mistaken to argue that respect for autonomy should lead to the solution that they propose, for they misunderstand the relationship that holds between autonomy and informed consent. Moreover, I will argue, the solution that Graber and Tansey propose for the problem that they identify will not work. With these arguments in place I will offer an alternative solution to the problem that Graber and Tansey identify—one that is considerably more radical than theirs.

II. The Problem, and Graber and Tansey's Proposed Solution

Graber and Tansey (2005, p. 424) note that the cost of pharmaceuticals is continuing to rise. As a result of this, they claim, the cost of healthcare insurance is rising also. This rise in the cost of healthcare insurance means that persons who pay for their own insurance either have less disposable income, or else they might choose to forgo healthcare insurance altogether. This also results in fewer businesses providing such insurance for their employees, while those businesses that continue to provide their employees with coverage will reduce the quality of the coverage that they provide. According to Graber and Tansey the cost of pharmaceuticals is continuing to rise in part "because of patient demands for medication 'as seen on TV' or in other media." (2005, p. 424). Such consumer demand for name-brand medication is further compounded by the unrealistic views that both patients and physicians have concerning the safety of such medication. For example, nearly half of all patients believe that advertised drugs are "completely safe", which healthcare professionals "often prescribe new drugs based on faulty information and persuasion provided by the pharmaceutical industry" (2005, p. 424; see also Wood, 1999, p. 1753). This consumer demand for name-brand pharmaceuticals, together with "a climate in which doctors are judged on patient satisfaction," leads to a situation in which "doctors may feel pressure to allow the consumer to drive the decision making process to maintain what is perceived as good patient-doctor relationships" (2005, p. 424). This, Graber and Tansey claim, results in a situation in which physicians will prescribe a name-brand pharmaceutical product for their patients even if they believe that the product in question is suboptimal, either medically, or because it is more expensive than an equally efficacious product. This, Graber and Tansey claim, "impedes the informed consent process [of patients] since inadequate information is available with which to make a fully autonomous choice" (2005, p. 425). Furthermore, note Graber and Tansey, the consumer preference for name-brand pharmaceuticals and the belief that doctors are primarily judged by how satisfied their patients are with their performance occur within a healthcare system where the costs of the pharmaceuticals prescribed are not transparent, for there is often "no out-of-pocket costs or a limited co-pay at the time of visit" (2005, p. 425). These factors contribute to the rising cost of healthcare, and so contribute to a morally problematic situation in which some persons' medical health is compromised as a result of their no longer being able to afford adequate medical coverage.

To remedy this situation Graber and Tansey propose two solutions. First, they propose that physicians "educate themselves about the costs and adverse side effects of medication," and that both physicians and healthcare professionals limit their interactions with pharmaceutical companies (2005, p. 425). This first solution is aimed at removing the impediments to securing patients' informed consent to their treatments. Second, and more importantly, they suggest that patients become fully informed about both the risks and costs associated with the pharmaceuticals that they are considering taking, or requesting that their physicians prescribe. Here, Graber and Tansey are clear that patients should not only be educated about the costs that they themselves will incur when they are prescribed certain pharmaceutical products, but that they should also be educated about the economic impact of such prescriptions. In particular, argue Graber and Tansey, patients should be made aware that if name-brand pharmaceuticals are prescribed over equally efficacious but less expensive products this will contribute to the rise in healthcare costs, and, as such, will affect the ability of others to secure healthcare coverage. To achieve this, Graber and Tansey advocate the use of formal documents, such as this (2005, p. 425):

> I, the patient, am requesting that my provider prescribe drug ________ for me. I understand that there are less expensive medications that are also effective. I understand that by requesting this more expensive medication I am increasing healthcare costs to others, increasing the cost of insurance, using resources that could be used elsewhere in the healthcare system and may be taking an additional risk to my health as all the side effects of new drugs may not be known. The reason that I am asking for this medication is ________. I believe that the benefit to me outweighs the potential risks and resultant harms to others .

III. Clarifying the Relationship Between Automomy and Informed Consent

Graber and Tansey are concerned that the marketing of drugs, both directly to patients and also to healthcare professionals, is undermining patients' ability to give their informed consent to their pharmaceutical treatments. They are also concerned that patients' failure to recognize what they term the "social costs" of requesting name brand pharmaceuticals further undermines their ability to give their informed consent to their pharmaceutical treatments. With these claims in hand, Graber and Tansey hold that unless healthcare professionals take steps to remedy these ways in which patients' ability to give their informed consent to their pharmaceutical treatments is undermined they will be exhibiting "a disrespect of patient autonomy" (2005, p. 425). Thus, Graber and Tansey conclude, documentation such as that outlined above must be provided to patients to ensure that their autonomy is respected.

There are, however, three significant problems with this argument. The first two arise as a result of Graber and Tansey misunderstanding the relationship between autonomy and informed consent; the third arises as a result of their misunderstanding what it is for one person to respect the autonomy of another. In arguing that documentation such as that outlined above must be provided to patients to ensure that they can make autonomous choices concerning their treatments, and hence to ensure that their autonomy is respected, Graber and Tansey write that "A patient, influenced by marketing and with limited expertise in interpreting the evidence based nature (or lack thereof) of advertising claims, requires doctors to provide information about the true costs, both financial and social, of the medication being considered..." They continue: "Failure to disclose such information as morally relevant to the choice of medical options constitutes an impediment to patient decision-making capacity—a disrespect of patient autonomy" (2005, p. 425). Prior to making these claims Graber and Tansey had asserted that "Failing to consider the principle of justice within the therapeutic relationship...impedes the informed consent process since inadequate information is available with which to make a fully autonomous choice" (2005, p. 425). For Graber and Tansey, then, it is clear that for a person to make an autonomous choice concerning her treatment options she must be provided with all of the information that could be relevant to her decision, including that which pertains to its implications concerning the distribution of resources. But this is mistaken, for two reasons. First, a person is autonomous with respect to her choices and decisions if it is she, and not some other person, who is directing her making of them. (Indeed, this is precisely what is meant by "autonomy", which stems from two Greek words, *autos,* "self", and *nomos,* "law". The autonomous person is thus one who gives the law to herself; that is, who directs her own choices, decisions, and actions.) As such, a person can be fully autonomous with respect to her choices and her decisions *even if* she lacks information that she would have otherwise drawn upon in making them.[1] For example, the physicians who, prior to 1961, prescribed thalidomide to their pregnant patients may have done so fully autonomously, even though they would not have done had they been aware of the birth defects associated with this drug. Such physicians were making their own choices and decisions; they were not under the direction of another. To be sure, these physicians were not exercising their autonomy in making the choice to prescribe thalidomide in the manner that is most likely to result in their achieving the ends that they were pursuing (e.g., the well-being of their patients). However, to claim that they were thus not fully autonomous with respect to their choices is to confuse a person's being autonomous with respect to her choices with her choice of an action being, in Gibbard's terms, "advisable", where an action is advisable if it is "[w]hat it makes sense to do objectively, in light of all the facts" (1990, p. 89). Since this is so, then, Graber and Tansey are mistaken to believe that for a person to make an autonomous choice concerning her treatment options she must possess all of the information that could be relevant to her decision. Instead, all that is required for a person's autonomy to remain intact in such a situation is that she makes her own decision in the light of her own value system, free from interference by another.

This first objection to Graber and Tansey's account of why respect for autonomy should lead to certain measures (such as requiring that patients sign documents such as that above) being taken to combat the rising cost of pharmaceuticals leads to the second. Graber and Tansey claim that a failure to consider the "principle of justice" will adversely affect a person's ability to give her informed consent to a drug prescription, since this failure would leave her with inadequate information "with which to make a fully autonomous choice." As well as mistakenly conflating a person being autonomous with respect to her choice with that choice being advisable (in Gibbard's sense) Graber and Tansey here impose an objective criterion on what values a person must consider when making her decision for her to be considered autonomous with respect to it. But there is nothing in the concept of autonomy that requires a person to consider the "principle of justice" in making her decisions. A person who is completely indifferent to the demands of justice can choose to ignore them if she so wishes, and yet still be autonomous, still be self-directed, with respect to her consequent choices and decisions—just as can a person who is so completely blind to the demands of justice that she does not even choose to ignore them.

Finally, Graber and Tansey are mistaken to claim that a healthcare professional must "provide information about the true costs, both financial and social, of the medication being considered…." if she is not to disrespect patient autonomy. Note that a person will disrespect the autonomy of another if she deliberately takes action to thwart it, or to usurp it. Hence, a physician who deliberately withheld information about thalidomide in order to thwart her patient's autonomous choice to have a healthy baby would disrespect her patient's autonomy, as would a physician who manipulated her patients into taking drugs that she was being paid to prescribe by an unscrupulous pharmaceutical company.[2] A physician who simply failed to provide her patients with information about the "true costs" of the medication being considered, then, would thus not necessarily disrespect her patient's autonomy. She would only do so were she deliberately to withhold this information to usurp control from her patient over her treatment decisions.

Two points of clarification should be made here before progressing to the next section of this paper. First, the above objections to Graber and Tansey's argument are intended to show that they are mistaken to hold that respect for autonomy should lead one to provide such documentation to patients as they outline above. In particular, these objections to Graber and Tansey's argument are intended to show that respect for patient autonomy need not lead one to acquaint patients with the social and economic implications of their choosing name-brand pharmaceuticals over their generic counterparts. Second, it might seem at first sight that the arguments offered here support the counterintuitive conclusion that physicians need not take care to educate themselves about the risks involved with the drugs they prescribe. This is because if these arguments are correct, a failure to do so would neither adversely affect their patient's autonomy nor serve to disrespect their autonomy, provided that it did not occur as a result of the physicians in question trying to usurp control over their patients' decisions or thwart their ends. Yet although it is true that a patient's ignorance will not in itself adversely affect her ability to exercise her autonomy, a physician's moral duty to be concerned for the well being of her patients should lead her to educate herself about the drugs she prescribes. As such, provided that one is not solely concerned with patient autonomy (which would itself be a highly counterintuitive position to adopt) the above argument does not support the counterintuitive conclusion outlined above.

IV. Why Graber and Tansey's Solution Fails

Graber and Tansey's argument that respect for the autonomy of patients requires that their healthcare professionals make them aware of the economic and social consequences of satisfying their preferences for name-brand drugs thus fails, both because they misunderstand the ways in which a person's autonomy can be compromised, and because they misunderstand what it is to disrespect a person's autonomy. Moreover, Graber and Tansey's approach to making patients aware of these factors in an attempt to curtail the rise in the cost of pharmaceuticals would fail, too.

In suggesting that patients be required to sign informed consent documents such as that outlined above Graber and Tansey assume that patients will altruistically be motivated to forgo the name-brand pharmaceuticals that they prefer once they realize that choosing them will have deleterious effects on persons' access to healthcare. However, patients reading such documents will realize that their individual forgoing of the name-brand pharmaceuticals that they prefer will have a negligible effect on the amount of money that is spent on pharmaceuticals. They will also realize that for the spending on name-brand pharmaceuticals to be reduced to a degree that would slow or reverse the current trend of such spending being so great as to limit persons' access to healthcare a significant number of patients would have to forgo their preferred pharmaceuticals. Given this, the rational patient would reason that if enough persons chose to forego their preferred pharmaceuticals his choice to do so to would have little effect on the spending on pharmaceuticals, and, as such, his forgoing of his preferred pharmaceuticals would have little effect on persons' access to healthcare. Since choosing to forgo one's preferred pharmaceuticals would be costly to the person who chose to do so (insofar as he would then receive a product that he valued less than the one he chose to forgo), and since the rational patient would recognize that his own individual choice would have only a negligible effect on the spending on pharmaceuticals, the rational patient would not chose to forgo the name-brand pharmaceuticals that he preferred. Reinforcing the rational patient's reasoning will be her recognition that other rational patients are reasoning in the same way. The rational patient will thus recognize that other patients will not forgo their preferred name-brand pharmaceuticals. As such, the benefits that will accrue to the set of patients by persons choosing generic pharmaceuticals will not transpire, and so she will, again, come to believe that it would not be rational for her to forgo the name-brand pharmaceuticals that she prefers. Thus, when confronted by an informed consent document of the sort proposed by Graber and Tansey, and outlined above, the rational patient would not, as they wish, choose to forgo her preferred name-brand pharmaceuticals. Instead, she would rationally decide to continue to exercise her autonomy in satisfying her preference for them just as she had before. Such documents, then, would not serve the purpose that Graber and Tansey wish them to serve, and so their proposed solution to the problem that they identify would fail.

V. Autonomy, Constraining Options, and the Rising Costs of Pharmaceuticals

Yet even though Graber and Tansey's argument as to why respect for patients' autonomy requires their healthcare professionals to provide them with documentation such as that outlined above fails, and even though such documentation will not achieve its purpose, Graber and Tansey are not wrong to claim that a concern for patient autonomy should lead one to attempt to limit the rise in the cost of pharmaceuticals that stems from patients exercising their preference for name-brand drugs. This is because in the context of the current healthcare system the option to choose name-brand pharmaceuticals is an autonomy-compromising constraining option.

A constraining option is an option which, if chosen, is likely to limit the ability of person(s) to exercise their autonomy in the future. The classic example of a constraining option is the option to sell oneself into slavery. Although a person might autonomously choose to do this, once he has done so his ability to exercise his autonomy is likely to be severely curtailed.[3] The option to sell oneself into slavery is thus an "individual constraining option"—an option which, if chosen, is likely to compromise the autonomy of the person who chooses it. Another type of constraining option is a "group constraining option". Such an option is an option which, if a person chooses it, is likely to compromise the ability of the other individuals in the set of individuals to which the chooser belongs to exercise their autonomy. T. L. Zutlevics argues that the option to sell a kidney in an international current market for human transplant organs is a constraining option of this kind (2001, pp. 207-302). Zutlevics argues that if such a market exists it will be likely to be persons in poor countries who would participate in it as vendors, while persons in rich countries would participate as buyers. This situation, she claims, would provide an incentive to the rich countries to reduce or eliminate aid to the poor countries so that they do not improve their economic situation, and so continue to have an incentive to sell their organs. With these claims in hand, Zutlevics accepts that the persons who sell an organ in such a market are likely to be made better off by so doing. Thus, for Zutlevics, an international market for human organs would provide a group constraining option to the poor of the developing world. Even though the option to sell a kidney would enable the seller to exercise his autonomy more fully, his choosing this option is likely to adversely affect the ability of other poor individuals from the developing world to exercise theirs, as the seller's choosing to sell would adversely affect the amount of aid that they would receive.[4] Finally, in addition to both individual and group constraining options there are also "ultimate constraining options".[5] Such constraining options are options that, if chosen, are likely adversely to affect the ability of *both* the person who chooses them *and* that of the other members of the set of individuals of which he is a part to exercise their autonomy as they see fit. As such, such constraining options are, from the point of view of a person who values personal autonomy, either instrumentally or intrinsically, the worst type of constraining option. And, in the context of the current system of providing healthcare, the option to choose name-brand pharmaceuticals over their cheaper generic counterparts is a constraining option of this sort.

The reasons why the option to have name-brand pharmaceuticals prescribed rather than their generic counterparts is an autonomy-compromising ultimate constraining option can be drawn both from Graber and Tansey's outline of the background as to why increasing spending on pharmaceuticals is problematic, and also from the objection to their solution to this problem that was outlined above. As Graber and Tansey note, under the current system for the provision of healthcare the increased spending on pharmaceuticals leads to a situation in which some persons' access to healthcare is curtailed or eliminated. If a person's access to healthcare is curtailed or eliminated then he will have an increased risk that he will be unable adequately to treat any injuries or illnesses that befall him. As a result, he will run the risk of being less likely to exercise his autonomy in the ways that he wishes owing to such inadequate treatment of his injuries or illnesses. Given that under the current system of healthcare provision increasing pharmaceutical costs will result in persons' access to healthcare being curtailed or eliminated, options that are available to persons that will, if chosen, lead to such cost increases will be ultimate constraining options. If such options are chosen then persons whose access to healthcare could be adversely affected by this would have their ability to exercise their autonomy compromised. Moreover, since the persons choosing such options would be members of the set of persons whose access to healthcare could be adversely affected by the rising costs of pharmaceuticals, their choosing such options would be likely to adversely affect their own ability to exercise their autonomy.[6] As such, then, given the current system for paying for the provision of healthcare the option to choose name-brand pharmaceuticals is one that if chosen, is likely to result in a diminution in the ability of the chooser to exercise his autonomy. Moreover, if this option is chosen it is likely that the ability of other persons (i.e., those who are also faced with this option) to exercise their autonomy would also be adversely affected. Given the current system of healthcare provision, then, the option to choose name-brand pharmaceuticals is an autonomy-compromising ultimate constraining option.

If one is concerned with protecting personal autonomy, then, one has three options to draw from in addressing the problem that the option to choose name-brand pharmaceuticals is an autonomy-compromising constraining option of this sort. First, one could advocate eliminating this option of from persons' choice-sets. Since this solution is, however, likely to involve a significant degree of coercion of healthcare professionals, the pharmaceutical industry, and patients, and since successfully subjecting persons to coercion compromises their autonomy, this solution is not likely not to be one that is amenable to persons concerned with the protection of personal autonomy. Second, one could, with Graber and Tansey, advocate measures to make the option of choosing name-brand pharmaceuticals less attractive than it currently is. Unfortunately, the solution proposed by Graber and Tansey is likely to fail, for the reasons outlined above. Finally, one could shift one's focus from the existence or the appeal of the option to choose name-brand pharmaceuticals to the underlying cause of this option being an ultimate constraining option: the current system of how healthcare is paid for.

VI. The Solution: Individual Medical Accounts

The fact of rising pharmaceutical costs and the problematic implications that Graber and Tansey note that this has for persons' healthcare coverage is generated by a combination of two factors: patients' preference for name-brand pharmaceuticals, and a system of healthcare delivery in which physicians are unwilling to demur from patients' requests, where most healthcare payments are made by third parties, such as insurance companies, HMOs or the Government. Given this, rather than focusing on altering patients' pharmaceutical preferences one could address the problematic implications of rising pharmaceutical costs by reforming the system of healthcare payment. As Capaldi (this volume) notes, "The best way to lower prices is through *individual medical accounts.*" Such an approach to healthcare payment would encourage patients to be more responsible consumers, in part by encouraging them to compare both the relative cost and efficacy of name-brand pharmaceuticals with their generic counterparts. Moreover, the replacement of third-party payers by such accounts would serve to individuate persons' healthcare costs. As such, those who continued to exercise their preference for name-brand pharmaceuticals would not affect the healthcare costs of others. Thus, even if some persons did continue to exercise their preferences for name-brand pharmaceuticals (and the individuation of their medical accounts would encourage them not to) the satisfaction of such preferences would not result in others' access to healthcare being curtailed or eliminated. Rather than focusing on the existence or the appeal of the option to choose name-brand pharmaceuticals, then, one should instead adopt a more radical approach to the problem at hand and advocate the reform of the underlying payment system that leads to the problem.

VII. Conclusion

Two lessons should be learned from this discussion of Graber and Tansey's solution to the problematic implications of the continuing rise in pharmaceutical spending. First, and most obviously, Graber and Tansey's own solution to this problem is mistaken, and should be replaced with a more radical one: the replacement of the current system of third-party payment by a new system of individualized medical accounts. Second, the above discussion highlights the importance of philosophical theory for medical ethics. Graber and Tansey's autonomy-based argument for their solution failed because they failed to recognize the relationship that holds between autonomy and informed consent, with this latter failure being a direct result of their lack of understanding of the nature of personal autonomy. Similarly, their solution to the problem that they identified was flawed owing to their failure to engage with elementary game theory. To paraphrase Harry Frankfurt (1999, p. xi), then, contemporary medical ethicists should not just be familiar with the medical, technological, economic, or political issues that generate the ethical problems and dilemmas that they address: they should also make sure to keep their eyes on the philosophical ball.

Notes

1. This is so provided that the persons in question did not lack the information that they would have otherwise acted upon as a result of its being withheld from them by another, who was doing so in an attempt to exert control over them by directing their actions in a particular way.
2. To "disrespect" a person's autonomy is not the same as failing to respect a person's autonomy. A person can fail to respect another's autonomy without actively disrespecting it. She might, for example, simply negligently ignore his wishes in making her decisions concerning their joint future.
3. Note that this does not mean that respect for autonomy should lead to the prohibition of persons having this option. A person might respect autonomy for its instrumental value in securing the well-being of those who exercise this capacity, and, if so, might allow persons autonomously to sell themselves into slavery if their well-being will best be secured this way.
4. Zutlevics' argument was criticized in Taylor (2002).
5. This account of what an ultimate constraining option is was first outlined in Taylor (2004).
6. This claim is, of course, a generalization, for there will be some wealthy persons

whose access to healthcare will be unaffected by either their own choices or those of others. But even though this is so, if such persons' choices affect the healthcare costs of others their option to choose name-brand drugs will still be a group constraining option, and, as such, of moral concern to the defenders of autonomy.

References

Capaldi, N. (Forthcoming.) 'Corporate social responsibility and business ethics in the pharmaceutical industry,' in H. T. Engelhardt & J.R. Garrett (Eds.), *Innovation and the Pharmaceutical Industry: Critical Reflections on the Virtues of Profits.* M&M Scrivener Press.

Frankfurt, H. (1999). *Necessity, Volition, and Love.* Cambridge. Cambridge University Press.

Gibbard, A. (1990). *Wise Choices, Apt Feelings: A Theory of Normative Judgment.* Cambridge, MA: Harvard University Press.

Graber, M.A. & Tansey, J.F. (2005). 'Autonomy, consent, and limiting healthcare costs,' *The Journal of Medical Ethics,* 32, 424-426.

Taylor, J. S. (2002). 'Autonomy, constraining options, and organ sales,' *Journal of Applied Philosophy*, 19, 273 – 285.

Taylor, J.S. (2004). 'Plea bargains, constraining options, and respect for autonomy,' *Public Affairs Quarterly,* 18, 249-264.

Wood, A.J.J. (1999). 'The safety of new medicines: the importance of asking the right questions,' *Journal of the American Medical Association,* 28, 1753.

Zutlevics, T.L. (2001). 'Markets and the needy: Organ sales or aid?' *Journal of Applied Philosophy,* 18, 297-302.

Pharmaceutical Advertising and Patient Autonomy

Andrew I. Cohen
Jean Beer Blumenfeld Center for Ethics, Georgia State University

I. Introduction

The pharmaceutical industry is a business. There are products that must be created, distributed, and sold. Competing manufacturers often vie for a similar customer base. Management is accountable to shareholders for company performance. Each company markets its products to build brand recognition, to cultivate and maintain customer allegiance, and to persuade people that its products are beneficial. The norms governing pharmaceutical advertising then need not differ in any substantial way from those governing the promotion of any other consumer product.

Writers often point out, though, that medications are not SUVs, dish soap, running shoes, or any other standard consumer product.[1] The differences between drugs and other products might seem to warrant more stringent government oversight of pharmaceutical ads. Perhaps advertisers ought to be required by law to go beyond standard prohibitions against fraud, libel, misrepresentation, and deception. In what follows I would like to begin to argue against this view. My approach is indirect; I discuss how key arguments in favor of greater regulatory oversight are importantly inconclusive.

Even though public health economics certainly play a crucial role in arguments about the merits of regulations, this essay usually passes

H.T. Engelhardt, Jr. and J. Garrett (eds), *Innovation and the Pharmaceutical Industry* (pp. 80–99).

over such considerations and focuses on how and whether pharmaceutical advertising is consistent with a concern for patient autonomy. Section II considers why pharmaceuticals might seem to be in a special category of consumer product. There I consider whether the differences between the pharmaceutical market and other markets are sufficient warrant for any special regulatory oversight. Section III highlights how pharmaceuticals are a consumer product like any other.

I should note that this essay focuses on "direct-to-consumer" (DTC) pharmaceutical advertising, often with special attention to conditions in the United States. The ads can be for prescription or over-the-counter (OTC) medications. I note any relevant differences for the two cases as I proceed. A few words are in order about what this essay does not do. The essay does not consider the various forms of marketing and promotions that target physicians and other providers.[2] This essay focuses neither on arguments about the merits of advertising as such nor on arguments regarding the justice of the market system, though it may have implications for such discussions. The essay also does not address the complicated legal issues involved in pharmaceutical regulation. Insofar as it has any legal implications, this essay only discusses what sorts of considerations ought to guide the law. The essay focuses only on the role for and ethics of pharmaceutical advertising targeting consumers.

II. Pharmaceuticals Are Not Dish Soap

Pharmaceuticals are importantly unlike dish soap and decisions to buy them are made in a context that differs significantly from that for standard consumer products. The history of the pharmaceutical industry is marked by extensive government regulation, professional gatekeeping, significant public-private entanglements, and recently and most notably, a third-party payment system. The target market of many pharmaceuticals may also typically be unable to evaluate the science underwriting the industry. It may then seem that regulating pharmaceutical advertising to protect patient autonomy is a modest response to the distinctive features of this market.[3] But I would like to raise some doubts about this line of argument.

A. A Quick History of Pharmaceutical Regulation

Quacks and bogus patent remedies were common in the nineteenth century (Pinkus, 2002, pp. 143-150). The social context had prized self-reliance (which translated into a reason for being one's own doctor).

Medical knowledge and practice were so primitive that people regarded seemingly properly trained physicians with understandable caution. Physicians of the day were also reluctant to commodify their skills, so medicines were generally the province of hucksters and hustlers. Exposés of the dangers of patent remedies in the popular press along with the increasing professionalization of medicine combined to elevate the influence and status of trained physicians and their scientific approach for assessing the effectiveness of drugs. With the 1906 Pure Food and Drug Act and the later 1938 Federal Food, Drug and Cosmetic Act, physicians had the power to dispense drugs available only by prescription, and the government regulated drug labeling (Pinkus, 2002, pp. 150-151; Pure Food and Drug Act of 1906). Of special note is that manufacturers are legally required to prove their products safe and effective before selling them.

Currently the Federal Trade Commission regulates advertising of OTC drugs, while the FDA supervises advertising of prescription drugs (Pinkus, 2002, p. 151). My remarks hereafter focus on the case of prescription drugs. If we can raise doubts about arguments that advertising for such drugs is consistent with patient autonomy only with regulation stricter than what governs other consumer products, then arguments regarding OTC drug advertising would likely follow a similar course toward a similar conclusion.

In the 1980s, pharmaceutical companies acquired the legal power to engage in DTC advertising. The regulations were modified in 1997. Drug companies are still expected to solicit preliminary FDA feedback about their ads' content (Pinkus, 2002, pp. 151-152).[4] The most recent regulations from 1997 liberalized the requirements for ads. Manufacturers are no longer required to dedicate significant advertising space or time to extensive descriptions of likely or possible side effects and contraindications (Manning, 2005). The result has been an explosion of ads and ad spending since the late 1990s (Stevens, 1998; Pinkus, 2002, p. 153).

B. Pharmaceutical Promotions in the Current Regulatory Regime

Ads now tend to fall into roughly three categories. One sort of ad is mainly educational by encouraging consumers to pursue a medical intervention (e.g., "women over the age of 40 should regularly get mammograms"). Ads of a second sort encourage people to speak with physicians about a particular medical condition, but do not mention any specific drug by name. Ads of a third sort encounter the strictest government scrutiny. They name a drug as a treatment for a specific condition.

Advertisers must list leading possible side effects and contraindications, and they must provide consumers with routes for gathering further information (such as a website or a toll free number) (Pinkus, 2002, p. 152; Stevens, 1998).

Pharmaceutical advertising certainly has one beneficial effect: it promotes consumer awareness of medical problems and a willingness to seek medical intervention (Goetzl, 1999, p. 22; Manning, 2005; Pinkus, 2002, p. 152; Stevens, 1998; Holmer, 1999). The blessings are admittedly mixed. Some patients consult doctors and request (or demand) advertised drugs, which may be costlier than roughly equivalent generics (Wilkes, Bell and Kravitz, 2000, p. 152). On the other hand, the conditions thereby treated (even with newer, costlier drugs) might lead to an overall improvement in public health. Medical conditions might be more effectively treated in the long run (over other costlier options, such as surgery), or the quality of life in an increasingly aged society might improve. Of course much here depends on complicated empirical issues; the data are still coming in on this front.[5]

This is not the place for a full discussion of autonomy, but let us suppose that autonomy is generally (at least in part) a sensitivity and responsiveness to reasons. Protecting patient autonomy would seem to involve a concern with patients' abilities to understand and respond to their medical interests. Are pharmaceutical promotions in the current regulatory climate consistent with patient autonomy?

DTC ads do seem to promote a shift in medical care toward regarding the patient as a consumer. The shift may be animated by an increasing emphasis in health care on patient autonomy over the beneficence of health care providers (Pellegrino, 1994). Some physicians complain that patients in the new health care milieu are more demanding (and sometimes more of a hassle) (Wilkes, Bell & Kravitz, 2000). All these trends tend to undermine the traditional doctor/patient relationship in which a physician was the gatekeeper of medical care and medical information.

While a full treatment of this shift in health care norms is beyond the scope of this essay,[6] a few remarks are in order. Access to medical information would seem to help patients better to tend to their health and to seek out medical interventions as appropriate. This is not to dispute the need for expert guidance. Consumers can and do seek out such guidance in this and other fields driven by science and technology.[7] The key issue concerns how patients may access and act on such information.

Insofar as promoting patient medical knowledge is part of an argument for pharmaceutical ads, then a defense of stricter regulatory norms must either establish that pharmaceutical advertising threatens patient autonomy or that it would not do so only under strict regulation.[8] Were DTC pharmaceutical advertising restricted or forbidden, physicians would resume their role as the main conduits of medical information. Are physicians and regulators uniquely suited to fulfill this role? An argument for this point must confront an important challenge: some incentives and institutions might distort their commitment to advancing patients' interests, including patients' autonomy interests.

The 1938 Federal Food, Drug and Cosmetic Act required labeling of drugs, but there was an important exception for prescription drugs. Any labeling containing medical information about such drugs was to be inaccessible to the standard lay reader.[9] Legally establishing such a gatekeeping role for physicians entrenches their control over medication and medical information. But it also privileges them with a form of what economists call *rent*, here a form of income guaranteed to them by restricting patient access to the prescription drug market (Tullock, 1967; Krueger, 1974).[10]

There may be sound public policy reasons for allowing such rent-seeking. On the other hand, leaving pharmaceutical advertising on a par with promotions for other products may provide patients with an alternative information source and thereby increase the chances that their interests can be satisfied. The challenge for proponents of restricting or forbidding pharmaceutical advertising is then to show that the rent guaranteed to doctors (and pharmacists) does not impair their ability to promote patients' significant interests. Clearly much of this is an empirical issue for social scientists to investigate.[11]

Pending such data, the proponent of unrestricted pharmaceutical advertising must realize that rent-seeking is not confined to doctors and pharmacists. The pharmaceutical companies are among the biggest rent-seekers in the land. As with creators of other products, they benefit from patents. The 1984 Hatch-Waxman act also nearly doubled the typical patent life of pharmaceutical products.[12] The FDA confers another monopoly on pharmaceutical companies in the form of exclusive marketing rights.[13] Furthermore, the 1980 Bayh-Dole act allows private companies to profit from publicly funded research (via grants through the National Institutes of Health). Pharmaceutical companies and other private entities can own (or share) the patents for discoveries emerging from such research and they can profit from the royalties from government guaranteed exclusive marketing rights (Angell, 2004; Gross & Allen, 2003).

Just as proponents of unregulated pharmaceutical advertising may worry about rent-seeking physicians and bureaucrats, critics can point to public/private entanglements and industry rent-seeking to raise doubts about the merits to patients of any pharmaceutical advertising.[14] Perhaps worries about the autonomy impeding spillover effects of rent-seeking are not so much a reason for regulating or forbidding DTC pharmaceutical ads as they are a reason for eliminating or containing the relevant institutions of rent-seeking. Since this is significantly an empirical issue, let us defer here to public health economists and set this aside in favor of exploring whether pharmaceutical promotion as such is compatible with patient autonomy.

C. Pharmaceutical Promotion and Patient Autonomy

Pharmaceutical promotions might be morally suspect because persons in target markets may seem to be of diminished autonomy at the start. For this to be a problem distinct to *pharmaceutical* marketing, this cannot be a species of the familiar objection to advertising that marketing restricts autonomy by creating needs in consumers.[15] So, for instance, the issue is not whether pharmaceutical promotions bring otherwise healthy persons to believe wrongly that they need some drug. That might be true, but then the argument would revolve around the merits of advertising as such and leave pharmaceutical promotions on the same footing as dish soap advertising. What matters is whether *pharmaceutical* advertising is uniquely or distinctly a threat to consumer autonomy.

There are at least four sorts of arguments that pharmaceutical advertising uniquely or distinctly clashes with patient autonomy. What I call the *no-magic-bullet argument* maintains that drug marketing impedes autonomy by promoting misguided instrumental beliefs about the likely personal health consequences of taking some drug. A second sort of argument, which I call the *bad bullet argument,* holds that drug marketing hinders autonomy by enabling consumers to achieve the wrong goals. A third sort of argument, which I call the *crowding-out argument,* claims that persons in pharmaceutical target markets are inherently less responsive to reason in virtue of their desire or need for medical intervention. The last sort of argument, which I call the *confounding science argument,* holds that since pharmaceutical science is beyond the understanding of typical consumers, unregulated pharmaceutical marketing is inconsistent with reasoned consumer choice. I next consider the first three sorts of argument; I postpone consideration of the fourth until Section III.

1. The No-Magic-Bullet Argument

According to the *no-magic-bullet argument* (hereafter NMBA), drug marketing encourages misguided views about the likely health impact of some drug. It may seem, for example, that promotions for some cholesterol-reducing drug may tend to encourage consumers to believe that taking the pill substitutes for healthy lifestyle and diet.[16] Now, one version of this argument builds from a worry that marketing contributes to false instrumental beliefs. Were that the only worry, pharmaceutical promotions would be allowed to stand or fall with those for dish soap. In the same way that marketing may encourage consumers falsely to believe that a dish soap will improve their love lives, so too may consumers wrongly infer from some commercial that taking some drug will be better than dedicating themselves to regular exercise. But then *pharmaceutical* advertising would not uniquely jeopardize autonomy, and the discussion would reduce to a familiar one about the merits of advertising as such.

For NMBA to be a distinct issue for pharmaceutical marketing, there would need to be something unique about pharmaceutical decisions that has typical consumers less sensitive and responsive to reason. Suppose this were true. Proponents of restricting or forbidding pharmaceutical ads would then need to show that doing so promotes (or does not hinder) patient autonomy—especially in light of the potentially worrisome rent-seeking considerations discussed earlier. In any case, if consumer autonomy is more fragile with respect to health matters, this worry transforms into the crowding-out argument. Before considering that argument, consider first the bad bullet argument.

2. The Bad Bullet Argument

The bad bullet argument (BBA) does not have the instrumentalist cast of NMBA. BBA says, in effect: patients would not be mistaken to believe that some drug is likely to have a certain effect on their health. Achieving that health effect, however, would be incompatible with autonomy properly construed.

BBA presupposes a notion of autonomy informed by some substantive value(s). Autonomy would not be a function of mere desire satisfaction but more a function of some sort of properly informed desire.[17] Which is the proper conception of autonomy is fortunately something we need not resolve here; for now note that BBA, just like NMBA, has pharmaceutical promotions on par with those for dish soap, and we would return again to arguments about the merits of advertising as such but this time from a somewhat different angle.

Suppose instead that BBA were a unique complaint about pharmaceuticals. Were it to be the start of an argument for restricting pharmaceutical ads, then just as NMBA it would need to show that such restrictions are better suited to promoting autonomy (here construed as informed desire) than leaving consumers to assess the claims of comparatively unregulated pharmaceutical promotions. BBA would also need to overcome the rent-seeking worries about any regulatory regime.

It seems that both NMBA and BBA rest heavily on the idea that decisions about health care are inherently susceptible to nonrational considerations. This brings us to consider the crowding out argument.

3. The Crowding-Out Argument

According to the *crowding-out* argument (COA), typical consumers are less responsive to reason when reflecting on health matters. While we can be autonomous in many other domains of choice, COA seems to say that attending to health considerations crowds out our abilities to be sensitive and responsive to reason. But what is it about attention to health that is distinctly autonomy undermining? Whatever our specific conception of autonomy, there is at once a danger that an account of the autonomy-undermining properties of attention to health considerations may prove too much by eroding the possibility of meaningful human autonomy. But this would not be just a problem for pharmaceutical advertising. We will have then come up against a limit of human autonomy. Perhaps, for instance, a person's autonomy is impeded whenever she reflects on her cholesterol level, her degree of skin moisture, her hay fever, or her occasional constipation. But given the reach of health considerations, it would seem people could never be fully (if at all) autonomous agents. Woe unto us?

That may indeed be an important discovery. But we would then have worries more important than the impact of pharmaceutical promotion on autonomy. We would need to rethink many moral and political commitments.

Before resigning ourselves to such a task, perhaps COA can localize the autonomy-undermining effects of attention to health considerations. Though I cannot imagine how the argument would do so, suppose it was possible. COA would then need to explain how restricting or forbidding pharmaceutical advertisements would curtail such effects on autonomy. Much would hinge on difficult empirical questions, and we would still need to overcome the earlier rent-seeking worries about a regulatory regime.

One important remaining objection to pharmaceutical advertising focuses on the specialized nature of pharmaceutical knowledge. I take this issue up in the next section.

III. Pharmaceuticals Are Just Like Dish Soap

Deciding to acquire and consume a medication is importantly similar to deciding to purchase one brand of dish soap over another. People acquire pharmaceuticals because they believe doing so will enhance their welfare given their perceived needs and wants. Human beings have variable personal goals, life experiences, risk tolerances, and levels of understanding, all of which contribute to different interests in any product, pharmaceutical or otherwise. Their interests in any given product compete with other demands on their resources. Their decisions to pursue any product also arise in a context of limited personal knowledge and are subject to many common cognitive biases.

The impact of advertising on consumer preference formation and purchasing patterns has been widely studied, so here I highlight two key market considerations to illustrate the comparability of medication to dish soap: (1) advertising is a mix of information and puffery and (2) all consumer decisions are made in conditions of bounded rationality. In each case pharmaceutical products and DTC promotions are little different than what we find in other markets.

A. Advertising: Information Hyped

Pharmaceutical companies promote their products using advertising that skillfully blends information and puffery. If advertising puffery is morally objectionable, then it is not uniquely so for pharmaceutical promotions. Puffery may be traced in part to the space and time constraints facing promoters of any product. Marketers must also compete for consumers' attentions in a crowded field. Some critics claim advertising is "not a source of factual consumer information" (Chandra & Holt, 1999, p. 364). This is surely an exaggeration. Ads often provide valuable information about a product's observable characteristics. The ads may also cite reliably gathered verifiable statistics about a product's use and performance. Puffery itself sometimes provides valuable information about market trends and leaders.[18] Puffery does not necessarily crowd out facts; at worst (if at all) it undermines consumers' abilities to distinguish facts from hype.[19]

Were such a complaint valid, it would be about advertising as such, not about pharmaceutical advertising. We would then need to revisit the earlier discussion about the merits to consumer autonomy of restricting or forbidding pharmaceutical promotions. But we will then not have discovered something distinct about pharmaceutical promotions.

B. Advertising and Bounded Rationality

Cognitive biases are inevitable, nearly ubiquitous, and perhaps incorrigible.[20] All such biases impede autonomy by restricting a person's ability to respond appropriately to reasons relevant to her case. The relevant agency-restricting considerations are not unique to pharmaceutical marketing.

Consider just a few examples. Much empirical psychology shows the intractability and prevalence of the hyperbolic discounting bias (individuals tend to discount larger payoffs later for smaller payoffs sooner), the availability bias (we tend to prefer options easily visualized over other alternatives), the recency effect (individuals disproportionately prefer options of recent acquaintance over others), and the overconfidence bias (we overestimate our ability correctly to evaluate and draw inferences from data).[21] These biases do not uniquely affect pharmaceutical buying decisions. They impair decisions to buy dish soap, chewing gum, and motor oil as well. The merits to personal autonomy of regulating pharmaceutical advertising (and any advertising, for that matter) might then turn significantly on empirical issues concerning whether a regulatory regime curtails the effects of such biases.

Perhaps pharmaceutical decisions, though, are distinctly vulnerable to cognitive bias (and the attendant autonomy distorting influences) because sensitivity to reasons in this context requires a grasp of science that is beyond the reach of typical human beings. This brings us to the *confounding science* argument.

C. The *Confounding Science* Argument

According to the confounding science argument (CSA), the complexities of chemistry, statistics, and many other sciences are beyond the grasp of the layperson. Without a grasp of these fields, consumers are insufficiently sensitive to reasons relevant to pharmaceutical decisions. And so, CSA continues, unless consumers receive information distilled by experts, they are more likely to make pharmaceutical decisions based on irrelevant considerations (such as glitzy marketing).

On the one hand, CSA is quite compelling. Our bounded rationality has us making many decisions without a complete understanding of the relevant science. Without the help of available expertise, consumers might fail to respond to the reasons relevant to their cases with respect to some product.

Of course technical complexity as such does not impede our autonomy in a domain of choice. We often have epistemic shortcuts that help us to respond to the reasons relevant to our cases. Some of these shortcuts depend on the signals of epistemic authorities. Sometimes individuals have a reason not to have a full (or fuller) grasp of the reasons relevant to their cases. In this way decisions about pharmaceuticals are not importantly different from decisions about dish soap or any other consumer product.

Consider the complexities involved in being sensitive and responsive to reasons relevant to automobile purchases. The engineering, aerodynamics, physics, and electronics involved in making a car are beyond the understanding of typical consumers. Even the best-trained scientists and engineers rarely have a complete grasp of the technical details outside their fields and subfields. But consumers can make responsible decisions by following the advice or recommendations of authorities that have a better grasp of the relevant science and engineering. Some examples are the reviews by independent evaluators (*Consumer Reports, Motor Trend, Motor Week*) or word of mouth from friends or family (your Uncle Lou the car mechanic, your friend Chris the car fanatic, your neighbor Bob who recently did a lot of research on the subject, and so forth). Gathering such reports can provide consumers with important information relevant to their interests, and the very process of accumulating and assessing the information can put them in a relationship with the reasons that bind them conducive to promoting their autonomy (however construed).

The availability of epistemic shortcuts is neutral with regard to autonomy. Much depends on the reliability of the shortcuts and the reasons for abiding their recommendations. Much also depends on a consumer's other interests. It is possible, for instance, that a consumer is rationally ignorant of the details underlying the reports on the merits of cars. He may prefer to buy a car model he often sees on the road and devote his scarce resources elsewhere.

None of this is to deny that epistemic shortcuts can lead one astray, fail to promote autonomy, or give a poor excuse for failing to be sensitive and responsive to reasons. Sometimes consumers have poor reasons for abiding by another's advice. Alternatively, they may have good reason to listen to the advice of some authority even though, unbeknownst to them, that authority has become corrupt or insane. They may even unwittingly become sensitive and responsive to reasons but for irrelevant or wrong reasons. (Terry might follow Pat's advice on car purchases, for example, but not because Pat is a car expert, but because Terry is romantically interested in Pat.) Perhaps their choices comply with reason but only by accident. The availability of publicly acknowledged authorities can also provide an excuse for intellectual laziness. Ultimately, epistemic shortcuts—and the reasons for abiding their advice—are corrigible.

A fuller discussion of epistemic authorities would need to consider such and related issues and their connection to personal autonomy, but this is beyond the scope of the discussion.[22] The point here is that having access to such shortcuts can (and often does) help agents to be sensitive and responsive to the reasons relevant to their own cases. Much now turns on how consumers have such access and the form(s) it takes.

The task here is not so much to defend pharmaceutical advertising but to explore whether DTC drug promotions deserve stricter regulatory oversight than what governs other consumer goods—especially in light of a concern with consumer autonomy. Consumers routinely make autonomous decisions in circumstances of limited knowledge and bounded rationality when facing other complex matters. If they can do it with cars in light of all the extensive puffery, then it may seem they could do so with pharmaceuticals, at least provided sufficient shortcuts.

D. The Risks of Ordinary Pharmaceutical Use

One important objection to allowing regulatory oversight for pharmaceutical promotions to be on par with other consumer products is this: pharmaceuticals are significantly different from other consumer products precisely because of the high stakes involved. A pair of bad pantyhose will not kill a consumer, but a defective pharmaceutical very well might.[23] There are two versions of this objection, a restricted version and an expansive version. Neither one conclusively shows that pharmaceutical advertising merits stricter regulatory oversight than other consumer products.

The *restricted* version of the objection holds that drugs and drugs alone merit greater advertising regulations because pharmaceuticals as a class of consumer product are inherently riskier than any other class of consumer product. Combined with other features about drugs (such as what the confounding science argument might suggest), it may seem that greater regulatory scrutiny is appropriate. This version of the argument seems untenable, however, because other consumer products—including technically complex ones—regularly expose consumers to risk of death from defects or misuse. Food and automobiles are the obvious examples. Just like promotions for pantyhose, those for food and automobiles are free to boast their virtues as long as they steer clear of libel, fraudulent representations, and the like.

The *expansive* account is the more plausible version of the objection. This objection is willing to regulate promotions strictly if they are for consumer products whose use entails risks on a par with those for pharmaceuticals. The expansive account holds that regulatory oversight for promotions should track the danger of mishaps from using the product in question, other things being equal. The expansive account might then advocate *increasing* the oversight of promotions for food, soap, and automobiles to bring them up to the level of scrutiny devoted to pharmaceuticals.

The expansive version of the objection can defend greater oversight for pharmaceuticals only by making controversial claims about risk. No doubt defects or misuse with regard to drugs can kill a consumer, but the same is true for what people take to be innocuous consumer products such as pantyhose or bottled water. Promotions for bottled water are not required to warn consumers of the dangers of misuse, yet there clearly are such dangers. Excess consumption of bottled water can deprive a person of the fluoride she might have otherwise received by drinking tap water. This might contribute to tooth decay. More worrisome is the danger that a person can suffer a life-threatening condition called inhyponatremia, which is a dangerous imbalance of water and sodium in the body. In some cases, brain swelling, coma, and death may result. This is a particular threat for the physically active, who are routinely told to stay hydrated. Ads for Dasani or Deer Park are not required to state "use only as directed" or to warn of such dangers. It is then tempting to deflate any supposition of great risk: if consumers can figure out how to use water correctly without special oversight for the relevant promotions, then they should be able to do so with drugs.

Critics might reply that the ordinary and intended use of bottled water does not expose consumers to risk of death, but using a drug for the purpose for which it is intended very well might. This seems plausible. But consider the risks from the use of pharmaceuticals. Either a person does not use it for the purpose for which it was intended, or a person suffers a rare complication, or the product is defective. But none of these cases give conclusive reason to provide stricter regulation of pharmaceutical ads—especially when we are mainly animated by a concern with patient autonomy. Any of these cases can be handled with a reasonable regime of liability. Specifying what that would be is of course beyond the scope of this paper, but the point is that strict government oversight for pharmaceutical promotions is not necessary as a vehicle for promoting consumer autonomy. If a pharmaceutical manufacturer fraudulently misrepresents what its product does or its product is defective, it can and should be held liable.

Pharmaceutical manufacturers use promotions to inform consumers of a product's intended use, and consumers can then determine what to do with that information in light of their other knowledge and their interests. And once again, consumers seem entirely capable of making informed decisions about pharmaceuticals, just as they can with their food, their cars, and their pantyhose. They can, if they wish, evaluate the merits of pharmaceutical promotions in light of expert advice and other information.

Besides being able to consult doctors and pharmacists, patients now have the advantage of drug reports from the nonprofit Consumers Union. Such reports help consumers and physicians to compare the effects and costs of competing drugs (Voelker, 2005). Critics still worried about the pernicious or misleading effects of pharmaceutical advertising puffery might also consider various private options available that could elevate the caliber of advertising content. One idea is that non-profit non-governmental bodies might vet DTC ads for ethical considerations. The EthicAd Council, for instance, offers drug ads the "EthicAd Seal of Approval" if they comply with various standards for communicating pharmaceutical information (Wechsler, 2000).[24]

This is not the place for an exploration of alternative private information sources regarding pharmaceuticals. Just as the Confounding Science Argument did not clearly point us to having regulations stricter than what governs automobile promotions, so too the appeal to the high stakes of pharmaceutical use is an insufficient argument. Since gathering expert advice is often a key ingredient in being sensitive and responsive to reasons, the government need not be regulating pharmaceutical ads to make sure that consumers have such information.

Allowing that the pharmaceutical industry might do well to police itself through independent, nongovernmental regulatory bodies might seem to be conceding much to critics of pharmaceutical ads. Perhaps a concern with consumer autonomy would justify stricter regulations for other consumer products (especially those flagged by the CSA) along with pharmaceuticals. It may simply be that other moral and political considerations (such as free speech concerns and an entrenched history of a comparative lack of regulation) take precedence over this concern with autonomy. DTC pharmaceutical promotions, on the other hand, might present a unique opportunity to help persons be more sensitive and responsive to reasons. Consumers are historically willing to accept some greater regulation in this area, so some stricter oversight might seem politically possible and morally warranted.

Much hangs again on empirical matters concerning how best to promote consumer responsiveness to reasons. This is not an issue of what is best for the consumer overall nor is it mainly an issue of how to curtail health care costs (though both have great moral significance). The issue here is autonomy. Some market environments might do better at promoting autonomy than others. Would consumer autonomy be promoted more by letting patients wade through myriad pharmaceutical information (sometimes laced with puffery), or does a concern with autonomy allow or require some stricter regulatory oversight of DTC promotions?

Sometimes puffery may help consumers to realize what their desires are. Sometimes sorting through puffery is an important part of the process of realizing what one's interests are. Of course, puffery can distort preferences. But then the argument seems again to return to a traditional discussion about the merits of puffery with respect to consumer autonomy. We might set all this aside and simply argue that having consumers in the right relationship with the reasons that bind them requires leaving them to use whatever epistemic shortcuts they deem appropriate to assess the competing claims from all available sources of the merits of any product. This seems just as plausible for pharmaceuticals as it does for dish soap.

IV. Conclusion

Pharmaceutical advertising blends information and puffery for consumers who seldom understand the science underlying the industry's claims regarding safety and effectiveness. It may be that pharmaceutical advertising merits some stricter regulation than what currently governs other consumer products, but it would seem that the reasons for such a view would apply to many or all other consumer markets. Much hangs on empirical issues: strict regulation might enhance autonomy, but there are potential dangers given any regulatory context. Of course, advertising puffery may be morally objectionable, and perhaps especially so for pharmaceuticals. The puffery can dangerously exacerbate disturbing externalities in a context where rent-seeking players compete in a pharmaceutical market featuring a morally hazardous third-party payment system. But this is not clearly an autonomy-based argument for stricter regulation. It may instead be a reason for reassessing the current institutional context and its regrettable spillovers and impact on personal autonomy.

This essay has focused purely on whether pharmaceutical advertising merits regulation stricter than what governs promotions for other consumer products. There has been no discussion of the law, nor has there been any extensive appeal to other significant moral and political considerations, which might root a compelling argument to leave DTC ads unregulated. The essay has also passed over a discussion of the merits of restricting access to some drugs by prescription. Pharmaceutical advertising seems to stand or fall with other promotions, so we must return again to arguments about the merits of advertising as such.[25]

Notes

1. "It's not like buying a car or tennis shoes or peanut butter," Senator Debbie Stabenow says of prescription drugs (Angell, 2004, p. 53). See also Lars Reuter (2003), and Jerry Avorn (2004).
2. These are a source of much concern among medical ethicists. The marketing and promotion comes in many forms, including gifts of trinkets such as pens, pads, and coffee mugs, free samples, generous consulting fees to speak at professional conferences, outright cash grants, marketing that some complain masquerades as education (e.g., sponsored research, research with massaged data, suppressing research that conflicts with company aims, brochures promoting new drugs, showcase clinical trials, abundant perks courtesy a well-paid and well-trained drug company sales force), and most notably, sponsored conferences in pleasant locations. Whether these practices are consistent with medical providers' roles is an issue I do not address here.
3. Minimally, advertising content must not be fraudulent or libelous and is subject to ordinary standards of tort liability. This essay explores whether any further regulation is warranted, such as content or form requirements, or needing the approval of some regulatory body before an ad can appear.
4. But apparently this is infrequently observed; it is not a binding requirement. Some politicians have proposed requiring FDA approval of ad content. See, for instance, Julie Schmit (2005).
5. See Wilkes, Bell and Kravitz (2000) for a helpful discussion of this point. Even if the data do eventually show that DTC ads contribute to increased health care costs,

much then hangs on how and for whom those costs are incurred.

6. But for a glimpse of the rich, extensive discussions on this issue, see, for instance, Gerald Dworkin (1988, pp. 100-120), Lainie Friedman Ross (2002, pp. 57-62), Tom Sorrell and Heather Draper (2002, pp. 335-352), H. Tristram Engelhardt, Jr. (1996), Benjamin H. Levi (1999), Donald C. Ainslie (2002, pp. 1-28), and R. S. Downie (1994).
7. I develop this point later.
8. Again, here I pass over the relevant public health economics. Note, though, that even if the numbers suggested drug ads ultimately cost more public health dollars than they saved, there would still need to be a moral argument to show that those costs are sufficient reason to discount the importance of any putative gains to patient autonomy. Furthermore, even if there were a moral argument that discounted the precedence of patient autonomy in favor of some other principle (such as beneficence), strict regulation of pharmaceutical ads may be inappropriate given other significant moral or political considerations.
9. As the act reads: "All representations or suggestions contained in the labeling [must] appear only in such medical terms as are unlikely to be understood by the ordinary individual." (Emphasis added.) As quoted in Kerry Howley (2005, p. 41).
10. The health care market exhibits many forms of successful "rent-seeking," such as physician and pharmacist licensing laws, which restrict entry and access to a market.
11. Given the third-party payment system dominant in the US health care market, consumer choice is significantly (and often entirely) divorced from pricing signals. Private insurance absorbs the costs of much medical care, and the government is a significant and growing source of funds for the remainder. Publicly funded health care may then invite medical decisions to be guided less by medical necessity and a concern with patients' morally significant interests than by political considerations and the upshot of industry lobbying. See Reuter (2003) and Angell (2004) for illuminating discussions of this point. Of course all this would be beside the point if health care should not be a commodity. Establishing such an alternative view (or doing so just for the case of pharmaceuticals) would indeed be a decisive objection to pharmaceutical advertising with any marketing purpose.
12. Though intended to promote the then-nascent generic drug market, the upshot was to increase the patent life for all drugs, hence delaying the market entry of less expensive generic copies of drugs. For a discussion, see Angell (2004). The economics on this issue are certainly beyond the scope of this essay. Note, though, that delaying the entry of generics to the market may increase health care costs for at least three reasons: (1) patients would be required to visit doctors before getting prescriptions for drugs, (2) without the market pressures of less expensive generic rivals, price points for most prescription drugs are set higher, and (3) patients operating at the margin of medical care will often delay or shun seeking medical intervention until their conditions escalate to the point of requiring more costly treatment. See Ryan H. Sager (2000).
13. See Angell (2004) for a discussion.
14. They might also worry that pharmaceutical advertising will often promote patent-protected newer (and thus, more expensive) drugs over older or generic drugs that would be less expensive but might medicate just as well. Often, though, newer drugs compare favorably with older generics by medicating patients better and by saving more money than the added expense they entail by reducing or shortening

hospital stays or by improving patient health. See Marie Bussing-Burks (2001) and Frank Lichtenberg (2001). Indeed, pharmaceutical companies frequently use legal tactics to stall the entry of generics on the market, such as by disputing their equivalence to brand name medications (Burton, 1998).

15. For examples of this line of argument, see, for instance, Richard Lippke (1989 & 1999), Roger Crisp (1987), and John Kenneth Galbraith (2001, pp. 387-391).
16. See, for instance, Ashish Chandra and Gary A. Holt (1999, p. 363) for worries that vitamin advertising is guilty of this charge.
17. For a helpful discussion of a related distinction, see Richard J. Arneson (2005).
18. See, e.g., Phillip Nelson (1987). For a discussion of the signaling functions of advertising, see Philip Nelson (1974).
19. This is a common criticism of advertising. See Richard Lippke (1989 & 1999), Roger Crisp (1987), John Kenneth Galbraith (2001, pp. 387-391).
20. See, for instance, J.D. Trout (2005).
21. For an account of these and other biases, see, for instance G.W. Ainslie (1975 & 2001) and the helpful overview in Trout (2005, pp. 399-408).
22. See, for instance, Robert Pierson (1994), John Hardwig (1985), Joseph Raz (1986 & 1989), and Richard T. DeGeorge (1970).
23. I am grateful to Peter Lindsay and anonymous reviewers for stressing the importance of this point.
24. Another possible example: the Pharmaceutical Research and Manufacturers of America (PhRMA) adopted a code of advertising conduct in January of 2006, which requires members to uphold certain standards in their advertising content and to submit their ads to the FDA for advice. See http://www.phrma.org/files/2005-11-29.1194.pdf. Of special note among the list of fifteen "Guiding Principles" for advertising is number 12, "All DTC advertising should respect the seriousness of the health conditions and the medicine being advertised." Interestingly, PhRMA elaborates in the "Question and Answers" section: "While humor and entertainment may not be appropriate in conveying all messages, they may be effective tools for attracting public attention to a particular disease or treatment" and having other significant public health benefits.
25. An earlier version of this paper was presented at the 2006 meetings of the Association of Practical and Professional Ethics. I am grateful for the feedback I received there. I also thank Peter Lindsay and anonymous reviewers for their detailed comments.

References

Ainslie, D.C. (2002). 'Bioethics and the problem of pluralism,' *Social Philosophy and Policy*, 19, 1-28.

Ainslie, G.W. (1975). 'Specious reward: A behavioral theory of impulsiveness and impulsive control,' *Psychological Bulletin*, 82, 463-496.

Ainslie, G.W. (2001). *Breakdown of Will*. Cambridge: Cambridge University Press.

Angell, M. (2004, July 15). 'The truth about drug companies,' *The New York Review*, 52-58.

Arneson, R.J. (2005). 'Joel Feinberg and the justification of hard paternalism,' *Legal Theory*, 11, 259-84.

Avorn, J. (2004). *Powerful Medicines*. New York: Alfred A. Knopf.

Burton, T.M. (1998, November 18). 'Why generic drugs often can't compete against brand names,' *Wall Street Journal,* xx-xx.

Bussing-Burkes, M. (2005). 'Benefits of newer prescription drugs exceed their costs,' *National Bureau of Economic Research Digest.* [Online]. Available: http://www.nber.org/digest/oct01/w8147.html.

Chandra, A. & Holt, G.A. (1999). 'Pharmaceutical advertisements: How they deceive patients,' *Journal of Business Ethics,* 18, 356-66.

Crisp, R. (1987). 'Persuasive advertising, autonomy, and the creation of desire,' *Journal of Business Ethics,* 6, 413-418.

DeGeorge, R.T. (1970). 'The function and limits of epistemic authority,' *Southern Journal of Philosophy,* 8, 199-204.

Downie, R.S. (1994). 'The doctor-patient relationship,' in R. Gillon (Ed.), *Principles of Health Care Ethics* (pp. 343-347). New York: Wiley and Sons.

Dworkin, G. (1988). *The Theory and Practice of Autonomy.* Cambridge: Cambridge University Press.

Engelhardt, H.T. Jr. (1996). *The Foundations of Bioethics,* 2nd ed. New York: Oxford University Press.

Friedman-Ross, L. (2002). 'Patient autonomy: Imperfect, insufficient, but still quite necessary,' *Journal of Clinical Ethics,* 13, 57-62.

Galbraith, J.K. (2001). 'The dependence effect,' in W.M. Hoffman, R.E. Frederick, & M. Schwartz (Eds.), *Business Ethics: Readings and Cases in Corporate Morality* (pp. 387-391). New York: McGraw Hill.

Goetzl, D. (1999). 'Second magazine study touts value of DTC drug ads,' *Advertising Age,* 70, xx-xx.

Hardwig, J. (1985). 'Epistemic dependence,' *Journal of Philosophy,* 82, 335-49.

Howley, K. (2005). 'Locking up life-saving drugs: Prescription laws make us sicker and poorer,' *Reason,* Aug-Sept, 41.

Krueger, A. (1974). 'The political economy of the rent-seeking society,' *American Economic Review,* 64, 291-303.

Levi, B.H. (1999). *Respecting Patient Autonomy.* Champaign-Urbana: University of Illinois Press.

Lichtenberg, F. (2001). 'The benefits and costs of newer drugs: Evidence from the 1996 Medical Expenditure Panel Survey,' *National Bureau of Economic Research* Working Paper No. 8147, March.

Lippke, R. (1999). 'The "necessary evil" defense of manipulative advertising,' *Business and Professional Ethics Journal,* 18, 3-20.

Manning, A. (2005, February 15). 'Plugged into prescription drugs: Companies spend billions marketing directly to patients,' *USA Today,* D1.

Nelson, P. (1974). 'Advertising as information,' *Journal of Political Economy,* 82, 729-754.

Nelson, P. (1978). 'Advertising and ethics,' in R.T. DeGeorge & J.A. Pichler (Eds.), *Ethics, Free Enterprise, and Public Policy* (pp. 187-198). New York: Oxford University Press.

Pellegrino, E.D. (1994). 'Patient and physician autonomy: Conflicting rights and obligations in the physician-patient relationship,' *Journal of Contemporary Health Law Policy,* 10, 47-68.

Pierson, R. (1994). 'The epistemic authority of expertise,' *Proceedings of the Biennial Meetings of the Philosophy of Science Association,* 1, 398-405.

Pinkus, R.L. (2002). 'From Lydia Pinkham to Bob Dole: What the changing face of direct-to-consumer drug advertising reveals about the professionalism of medicine,' *Kennedy Institute of Ethics Journal,* 12, 141-158.

Raz, J. (1986). *The Morality of Freedom.* New York: Oxford University Press.
Raz, J. (1989). 'Facing up: A reply,' *Southern California Law Review,* 62, 1153.
Reuter, L. (2003). 'The ethics of advertising strategies in the pharmaceutical industry,' *Ethics and Medicine,* 19, 171-175.
Sager, R.H. (2000, August 8). 'Over-the-counter is the right prescription,' *Wall Street Journal,* xx-xx.
Schmidt, J. (2005). 'Where drug advertisements often cross the lines,' *USA Today.* [Online]. Available: http://www.usatoday.com/money/industries/health/drugs/2005-05-31-drugs-ads-side_x.htm.
Sorrell, T. & Draper, H. (2002). 'Patients' responsibilities in medical ethics,' *Bioethics,* 16, 335-352.
Stevens, T. (1998). 'To your health,' *Industry Week,* 247, 56-58.
Trout, J.D. (2005). 'Paternalism and cognitive bias,' *Law and Philosophy,* 24, 393-434.
Tullock, G. (1967). 'The welfare costs of tariffs, monopolies and theft,' *Western Economic Journal,* 5, 224-232.
Voelker, R. (2005). 'Easy-to-use drug reports help patients and physicians weigh costs, benefits,' *Journal of the American Medical Association,* 294 (2), 156-166.
Wechsler, J. (2000). 'Health plans and payers attack DTC advertising, seek objective information on medication value,' *Formulary,* 35, 616-17.
Wilkes, M.S., Bell, R.A., & Kravitz, R.L. (2000). 'Drug research and development,' *Health Affairs,* 19, 110-115.

Why America Does Not Have a Second Drug Problem[1]

Richard A. Epstein
University of Chicago Law School
Hoover Institution, Stanford University

I. Open Season

There have been in recent years a number of books and articles that are sharply critical of the pharmaceutical industry, root and branch.[2] In this paper, I shall not address these works directly, but comment only that they are part of a continuing drumbeat on that subject, which goes back for several years. Two earlier scorched-earth critiques of the pharmaceutical industry were published under the title "America's Other Drug Problem." One study was prepared by Public Citizen (Public Citizen's Congress Watch) and the other by two eminent physicians, Arnold Relman and Marcia Angell (2002). Their purpose was (and remains) to bring into disrepute the traditional methods that have been used to develop and market new pharmaceutical drugs. The short term sources of discontent from which they drew strength were both simple and powerful when they wrote their initial attacks, and the overall situation on the ground has changed little since that time. Prescription drug prices are high, and getting higher, but they are subject to wide variation within the United States and across different countries. These price dif-

H.T. Engelhardt, Jr. and J. Garrett (eds), *Innovation and the Pharmaceutical Industry* (pp. 100–127).

ferentials create a general perception of unfairness, and they spur multiple efforts to arbitrage the markets, by shipping drugs from locations in which they can be bought relatively cheaply to those in which they are more expensive. Trent Lott, the Republican Senator from Mississippi, announced his support for legislation that would allow importation of foreign drugs by saying, "I can't explain to my mother why she pays twice as much for her drugs" (Rovner, 2004) in the United States than elsewhere. Any single dramatic price increase, such as the four-fold increase for Norvir, provokes widespread cries of indignation and calls for patent invalidation or new forms of state regulation.[3] The talk of price controls for patented pharmaceuticals is, moreover, commonly bandied about, even by individuals who are uneasy about the prospect of their arrival (Editorial, Chicago Tribune, 2004).

These current debates bring back in microcosm the longstanding debate over the proper organization of the means of production and distribution of goods and services in the United States. Although the participants of today's debate tend to view it as an exercise in current events, the larger issues that it raises hearken back to the long simmering dispute over the respective merits of capitalism and socialism that occupied central stage in the first half of the twentieth century. At bottom, that debate was directed toward two issues that constantly recur today. The first of these asks who should own the means of production, the state or private individuals. The second asks what is the ideal distribution of wealth derived from that production. In tackling these issues it is easy to identify two extreme positions that surround an array of intermediate possibilities. At the one end of the spectrum lies the socialist dream that insists that it is possible to have the best of both worlds: to use a system of government-run centralized planning to insure that all resources are put to their highest value uses, and then, independently, to adopt an equal income policy on the ground that a dollar of wealth is worth more to a poorer person than a richer one.[4] On the other side of the debate lies the strong version of capitalism that insists that only a decentralized system of prices can supply the information that allows independent traders and entrepreneurs to decide which investments to undertake and which ones not (Hayek, 1945; 1940). On this view, inequalities of wealth are needed in order to generate the economic vitality which in the end will redound to the benefit of individuals all across the income spectrum. This market-oriented view of the world leaves, of course, an important role for government insofar as it provides social order and the physical and legal infrastructure which is needed for the operation of markets. The laissez-faire model, as it were, is treated as tantamount to anarchy, only by its opponents, never its supporters.[5]

As a matter of general economic history, notwithstanding its distinct echoes in the current debate over pharmaceutical policy, today socialism in its extreme form has few if any friends as a general political philosophy. The problems of political incompetence and corruption are so endemic to any system of state-run enterprises that nations throughout the world have systematically sought to privatize their major industries in a slow but inexorable move toward market liberalization. Even the once-ardent socialists have abandoned any claims for the superiority of government-owned businesses, and have instead put their faith in systems of state regulation that exert some control over the types of goods produced, and the prices for which they can be sold, in the marketplace. The key questions today, therefore, do not concern the stark choices between capitalism and socialism that dominated the intellectual landscape more than half-a century ago. Today's pale shadow of socialism finds its most powerful expression in New Deal-like efforts to regulate those markets that are thought to be subject to inequalities of bargaining power. For example, the labor markets are subject to minimum wage requirements, collective bargaining statutes, and antidiscrimination laws, which are opposed by those, like me, who work in the free market tradition (Epstein, 1995).

Outside of labor markets, the struggle between market institutions and regulation more often than not takes place on an industry-specific basis. In this context, the strongest case for regulation involves those goods and services that are most efficiently provided by a natural monopoly, that is, an industry in which the cost of supplying an additional unit of service is declining over the relevant domain, so that a single supplier can furnish goods at lowest cost to all comers (Posner, 1969). Public utilities, transportation and telecommunications have been the traditional industries that have fallen into this class, but the history of regulation in this area has been spotty at best,[6] and continues to give rise to major litigation to this very day.[7]

II. The Extra-Ordinary Pharmaceutical Industry

This debate over regulation has spilled over into all aspects of the health care industry, including the long-standing debate over whether some form of universal health care is preferable to a system of unregulated markets for medical care, or the ungainly mixed system that combines some form of regulation with extensive levels of subsidy through Medicare and Medicaid. I shall sidestep that huge debate in this essay[8] and confine my analysis to the pharmaceutical industry, which has become the lightning-rod in the debate over the nature and function of regulation. In particular, I shall focus on a 2002 Relman and Angell broadside, backed up as it is by the work of Public Citizen. In speaking about the pharmaceutical industry as this nation's second drug problem, neither source pauses to speak about the benefits to life and health that have come from pharmaceutical innovation (Public Citizen's Congress Watch). Instead, they concentrate all their considerable efforts to explain why this nation should redouble its effort to rein in the industry. At its broadest level, the Relman/Angell critique updates vintage socialist arguments by insisting that while in "ordinary markets," for-profit firms may perform a useful social function, they should not be allowed to dominate in areas as sensitive as health care. They argue that "the market for drugs is not like other markets," so that it is dangerous to allow their policies to be "impelled primarily by the financial aspirations of their investors and executives" (Relman & Angell, 2002, p. 27). It is evident that this world-view extends the legitimate scope of state regulation of private firms beyond the control of harmful externalities (e.g., pollution) or monopoly, things at the core of the standard market-based account of a legitimate sphere for government action. Given its broad sweep, this argument sets the stage for all that follows and embodies at least two common misconceptions that need to be exposed before considering the more particular charges.

The first of these is the undefended assertion that the pharmaceutical industry is not like ordinary markets.[9] That common but dangerous ploy is used in virtually every modern instance to expand the scope of regulation over the goods and services that firms supply to markets. The extensive forms of price regulation for farm goods is justified on the ground that food, which is necessary for survival, cannot be left to the operation of the market, especially if the competitive forces that bring lower prices might also result in the bankruptcy of some farmers, which they always will. Rent control is justified on the grounds that housing is also a unique good. The above mentioned extensive regulation of labor markets starts from this same residue of socialist belief on the pervasive nature of market failure. But in each and every case, the network of regulations in question has produced more harm than good, by adding frictions to the operation of a whole range of economic systems, and distorting the behavior of individuals and firms as they maneuver either to avoid the regulatory sweep or to gain its protections. Broad claims of this sort do not have any form of uniqueness associated with them. What should always be required is some showing of a specific evil that regulation is able to combat, without introducing greater evils of its own. It is on that ground that regulation for safety and efficacy under the Food and Drug Administration has been justified, and it is on precisely that means-ends correction that regulation is subject to attack, which may call for a streamlining instead of an elimination of the entire regulatory apparatus in an effort to speed new drugs to the market. Thus, the insistence that pharmaceuticals are not "ordinary goods" rises to the level of theology, which makes little sense to dispute at all.

The rhetorical anti-market trope is subject to yet a second objection. There is of course *no* business that does not wish to maximize the income of investors and employees of the firm. But it hardly follows from that commonplace observation that firms will succeed only by a single-minded devotion to this parochial end. The great intellectual achievement of Adam Smith in the *Wealth of Nations* was that he showed how within the framework of a competitive industry the firm that sought to maximize its profits would also maximize overall social welfare. Under competition all goods that are worth producing are produced, while those whose costs exceed their benefits are not. The ability of consumers to enter and exit the market is the only constraint that is needed to make sure that the for-profit firm is attentive to the interests of its customers and will not go elsewhere. Indeed, the constant effort of Relman and Angell to set up the welfare of the firm in mortal opposition to consumers does an enormous disservice to the consumer interests that they assiduously seek to protect. A firm is not some disembodied entity that has utility or wealth of its own. It is a collection of individuals, both investors and creditors, who put money up in certain ventures in the expectation of a return that will compensate them for the risk of the business that they enter into.[10] A system of price regulation that denies that return will lead them to exit the business in question, which will only work to the long-term disadvantage of the consumers who so desperately need their products and services. It is an easy economic demonstration that any imposition of price controls results in an excess of demand over supply at the stipulated price, creating shortages in the short run and investment dislocations in the long run. On this question at least, there is nothing special about the pharmaceutical industry relative to any other. Starting from the global assumption that profit-making firms should not be entrusted with important components of health care forcibly brings back the specter of the socialist case for centralized planning. What are needed are more specific charges to explain why and how "the drug industry distorts medicine and products" (Relman & Angell, 2002, p. 27).

Given their general framework, Relman and Angell mount a three-front attack on the practices of the pharmaceutical industry. The component that I shall emphasize here looks at the various practices in the development, pricing and marketing of patented prescriptions. Since space does not permit, I shall not address in any detail the many issues that concern the role of the Food and Drug Administration (FDA) in the regulation of prescription drugs. Nor shall I address the distinctive patent questions that arise in the pharmaceutical area, many of which concern the interaction between the patent system and health and safety regulation under the FDA.[11]

In dealing with these various development and marketing issues, it would be foolish to advance any claim of perfection for the pharmaceutical industry, which has surely made its fair share of errors. Yet by the same token, overall popular sentiment has shifted very much against the industry so that there are few issues today on which it could hope to get treatment more favorable than that which is supplied to firms that populate those other "ordinary" industries. The proposals for legislative reform, such as various price control and importation systems, all tend to find ways to reduce the ability of firms to run their own affairs, to subject them to greater scrutiny under the FDA and to limit the duration and strength of their patents. In most instances these reforms, many of which are championed by Relman and Angell, are off the mark. But the issue demands individuated examination of the charges leveled against the industry and the proposals for reform. In this paper, I cannot consider all these issues, but will examine several. These include rates of drug utilization, the role of price discrimination in the market for patented pharmaceuticals; the price movements of individual drugs; the respective spheres of public and private support for drug innovation; the place of "me-too" drugs; the role of advertisement in drug pricing; and the cost of research for new wonder drugs. All of these themes meld together, because once the standard principles of business and economic analysis are understood, the practices of the pharmaceutical industry look much less out of whack than their critics suppose.

III. Drug Utilization

Relman and Angell launch their initial salvo on the pharmaceutical industry with the common perception of the high cost of prescription drugs, which they, in line with general estimates, place at about $170 billion per year, as a rapidly growing fraction of the national health budget of $1.4 trillion. Indeed, as of this writing, the estimates for annual prescription drug sales are at $275 billion a year (Saul, 2007). Relman and Angell write: "Greater overall use of drugs, higher prices for new drugs, and steady increases in the prices of existing drugs all contribute to an annual inflation rate in drug expenditures of 14 percent (down from a high of 18 percent in 1999)" (Relman & Angell, 2002, p. 27). This general criticism, which lumps together some many disparate elements, offers an accurate thumbnail description of the current state of affairs. But it does not in and of itself supply the needed indictment of industry practices.

The first point in response is that these price increases are not uniform over all periods. In contrast with the account offered by Public Citizen is that which the Pharmaceutical Research and Manufacturers of American (PhRMA) has offered in its own defense. It notes that the increase in retail prescription drug prices was about 1.5 percent in the period between November 2003 and March 2004.[12] Moreover, it is likely that these price increases will slow down, or perhaps reverse themselves for drugs that currently generate $60 billion of the $275 billion annual market for patented products will go off patent, and thus face generic competition sometime in the next five years. (Saul, 2007). The larger point, however, does not turn on which statistic is quoted at any given point in time. Rather, the key insight is that huge components of the overall national health care budget are attributable to matters that are wholly outside the scope and control of the pharmaceutical industry. In large measure, this budget is shaped by an extensive national commitment to treat health care as a right, regardless of the individual ability to pay. That general commitment rests in part on the basic ethical conviction, which I do not wish to dispute, that wealth is a poor proxy for utility in contexts that involve life or death issues.[13] The inability to pay for treatment does not mean that a person whose life is at risk has no intrinsic social worth. Indeed, the entire system of charitable care in the United States and elsewhere grew up with the explicit recognition that a standard of willingness to pay suffers major defects in this area.

There is, alas, no easy fix to this serious problem, for the effort to supply all health care without regard to market constraints creates a second and larger problem of its own. Quite simply, no one has ever found an effective means to ration the amount of health care provided, so that individuals who are spared the need to pay for the health care services will consume excessive quantities—more in fact than they would purchase if they had sufficient funds of their own to spend as they please. In the end, it may well be the case (empirical evidence is hard to find) that the huge tax burden of the current health care system contributes to a *shortening* of life, by reducing the disposable income that ordinary people would otherwise have available to stay outside of that system, especially in the final years of life when costs are so high. The dollars spent on taxation are not available for new tires, airplane trips, food or, even a good time, all of which could keep injury or illness away from one's doorstep. For the same dollars, it is better to add a year to life before one enters an ICU than a week to life after that occurs.

Within this overheated framework, it is hard to know exactly how to credit or attack the pharmaceutical industry, which of course benefits indirectly from the large national subsidy to health care. But the exact level of its benefit is hard to determine because the elaborate set of government regulations is designed in part to set price limitations on the amount that pharmaceutical firms can charge to Medicaid patients, for example, so that the subsidies to the poor are not captured in full by the firms that supply them.[14] In some sense, therefore, the critique of the pharmaceutical industry, especially by champions of a system of universal health care, cannot rest on the charge that too many national resources are devoted to this sector. Rather, the more precise charge must lie in how that money is spent. On this point it is a clear mistake to attack the pharmaceutical industry for grabbing an increasing fraction of the health care dollar. To see why, recall that before any pharmaceuticals were on the market, the industry fraction of expenditures was zero. Clearly the initial set of increases was most welcome because it provided avenues of relief that could not be as easily met by other means. The same dynamic continues to this current day. An increasing fraction of expenditures on health care could be doubly welcome. In the first place, it represents the substitution away from other treatments (e.g., surgery) that pose greater risk and promise smaller benefits than the new drug treatments that could be used in their place. Second, the new treatments could shorten time for recuperation and lower overall expenditures on medical care. The former produces gains that are not recorded in the health care sector, but are instead buried either in general increases in productivity (for those who work), or personal happiness (for those who don't), or, in many cases, a felicitous combination of the two.

The real question, in a word, is whether the new expenditures mark a social improvement of the expenditures that they replace. Neither Relman and Angell's nor Public Citizen's critique of the higher costs address the social consequences of this substitution toward drugs. Nor are there any independent reasons to believe that the greater expenditure on drugs represents some systematic decline in social welfare. Indeed, in many cases the most common critique is that treatments are not made available to individuals who are in a position to benefit from them, which suggests that the level of drug expenditures is as likely to be too low as it is too high. It also makes it all the more inexplicable that Relman and Angell are strongly opposed to direct-to-consumer advertisement (2002, pp. 36, 40), which offers some hope of reaching patient populations in need who are unable to make regular trips to the doctor.

IV. Price Discrimination

A more pointed way to make the criticism is to examine the variation in pricing for particular drugs. That calculation is difficult to make because of the multiple ways in which drugs are sold. In the United States there is no single price at which any patented or off-patent drug is sold. Rather, the basic pattern is that drugs are sold in many different segments at the same time, often at different prices, and often with rebates that are not publicly announced. The source of the complexity for patented goods arises from the exclusive right to sell that is conferred on the successful drug inventor as a reward for creating the drug in the first place. The recognition of this exclusive right often results in the creation of a short-term *economic* monopoly, but only if there are no close substitutes for the patented product. Relman and Angell do not call for the abolition of the patent system, but they are obviously distressed with the peculiar forms of pricing of patented goods, and urge for a weakening of the protection now afforded patentees of prescription drugs (2002, p. 36). In order to see how this works, it is useful to first understand the issue from the point of view of the patent holder, and then to ask how its self-interested strategies map out against social welfare.

On this basic issue, pharmaceutical patents take a different profile than those in other industries. With computers, for example, many patents are of small scope, and their useful life is short given the rapid rate of technical advance. There is an extended debate within the industry on whether patent protection works in this segment of the larger market, given the fragmentation risks that are associated with the so-called anticommons (Heller & Eisenberg, 1998; Epstein & Kuhlik, 2004). But there is no debate about that in the pharmaceutical industry where a few key patents acting alone or in combination with one or two others, hold their economic value throughout their entire patent life.

These patents give their holder some real economic might, such that the basic problem faced by the holder of the patent is how much to charge for each unit that it sells. One possible method is to charge each person the cost for the marginal production of each additional unit that comes to market. Here it is generally the case that the initial pill will have very high costs—how much is an issue to which I shall return in a moment—while the subsequent pills could be produced for a tiny fraction of the original cost. The root of the difficulty is that pharmaceutical drugs go through extensive research and development costs, with clinical trials and regulatory approval, all of which have to be incurred before a *single* pill is offered to the market. Everyone, therefore, is keen to pay for the *second* pill, but no one wants to pay for the *first* one. But if that strategy is followed uniformly, the first pill will never be produced, and hence all others will not be produced either. Yet it is clear that no potential user of the patent drug is better off in a world in which the drug is simply not available relative to one in which it is available, albeit to some at a very high cost.

This problem of high fixed versus low variable costs has long been recognized as a fundamental objection to the competitive market ideals of a laissez-faire system (Robinson, 1935). The harder question is what to do about it. On this point, the only feasible, if imperfect, solution is one that shifts some of the cost from the initial user and places it on subsequent users. In order for this system to work, however, it is necessary that all subsequent users pay enough above the marginal cost for their own pills in order to cover the cost of initial production over the drug's limited lifetime. That solution creates an inefficiency of its own, because now the higher price for the subsequent pills means that some people will be forced to do without the new treatment even if they can afford to pay the marginal cost of production. The point here is not new, but represents in the area of pharmaceutical patents an issue that has come up in other contexts with other sorts of monopolies (Coase, 1946). It may cost $1,000,000 to build a bridge that is *costless* to maintain. To charge nothing for its use means that tax revenues (which create distortions in other markets) have to be used to fund the construction of this bridge, raising the risk that pork barrel politics will lead to the construction of many bridges that should never be built at all.

This same set of insights applies to the patent area (Duffy, 2004). Since no one wants to pay for the first pill, that cost has to be spread out over other users. But there is no unique way in which that allocation can be made because each potential buyer will seek to pay as little of it as possible. One possibility is to constrain the holder of a patent so that it can charge a uniform price to all users. That price can be set above marginal cost and might well allow the patentee to recover its front end costs. But that system has the unfortunate side effect that any individual who can afford to pay something above the competitive price but below the monopoly price is shut out of the market, while people with very high demands (often individuals with great wealth) are allowed to reap a substantial consumer surplus (i.e., a large difference between their willingness to pay and the price they are charged). In practice, therefore, some measure of price discrimination may well both increase the profits of the patentee and improve social welfare simultaneously by seeking to charge everybody a uniform price that is just below the maximum prices that they are prepared to pay.

From this brief account, it is clear that price discrimination, notwithstanding Trent Lott, is an essential feature of pharmaceutical pricing because different prices are charged to consumers even if the marginal cost of provision to them is the same. But just how does that discrimination manifest itself in the market? In practice, it turns out that large health benefit plans (which often have members of limited means) have a systematic advantage over ordinary consumers (whose prices appear to be the concern of Relman and Angell, who are not, however, explicit about the consequences of market segmentation). The health plans with their own dispensaries are able to go to the supplier of a given drug for which there is a viable competitor and say that unless it gets rock-bottom prices it will shift its entire purchase order to the rival. Often both parties will keep the rebate secret, for the buyer knows that if the information becomes public, its size will perforce be reduced, as the manufacturer may be forced to offer a like deal to other firms. In contrast, however, the ordinary pharmacy has to stock a full line of products for its full-range of individual customers and thus does not have that flexibility. But any system of state-imposed price controls that required all firms to give most-favored-nation status to all individual users would not increase overall efficiency. The lowest prices would start to rise, which would cut some individuals out of the market, while the high demanders would receive the benefit of lower prices. It follows, therefore, that some form of price discrimination is necessary to keep the pharmaceutical markets operative, and will emerge without any form of collusion among manufacturers in violation of the antitrust laws.[15]

In light of this helter-skelter system of industrial organizations, there is no single "price" at which any drug is sold. Further, the problem becomes more acute when foreign markets are thrown into the mix, for as Relman and Angell rightly note, prices in the United States are higher than they are elsewhere in both developed and undeveloped nations, by amounts that vary between 50 and 64 percent (Public Citizen, p. 24). But all this reflects not only the inveterate need of patent holders to engage in price discrimination to recover their fixed costs, but also the stated policies of foreign governments to set the prices at which drugs are sold in their country. This is easily implemented in nations like Canada where there is only a single national health care service, which can now act as a monopsonist that will get its way: so long as the foreign nation is willing to bite off some portion of the fixed cost, no supplier is willing to abandon that market, at least if it is confident that goods which are sold in that country will not be resold elsewhere (Epstein & Kuhlik, 2004, pp. 54-58).

But for many reasons it is pointless to protest these developments as well. There is nothing that can be done by pharmaceutical companies to stop foreign nations from acting in their own self-interest, even when to do so hurts American consumers.[16] The most that could be expected, with little prospects of a positive return, is that the United States, which is often regarded as a bully in international trade in any event, will take up the cause. Yet that is most unlikely because one of the most common criticisms of the pharmaceutical industry is that it does not offer cut rate prices on drugs to destitute third-world countries especially for treatment of AIDS. More generally, the higher prices in the United States also reflect a more robust demand for drugs in this country related to the higher overall levels of income.[17] The issue of pricing is so complex that it becomes quite impossible to draw any negative inference from the change in overall price levels or the distribution in prices within or across countries, at least as long as we use the patent system.

V. Price Variations for Individual Drugs

A more telling objection, perhaps, is that some evidence suggests that the cost of particular drug prescriptions is rising in some instances more rapidly than inflation. Public Citizen, for example, notes that the price of particular drugs have risen by more than inflation—Acutane (22.7%), Oxycontin (15.4%), Glucophage (14.4%) and Allegra (10.9%) (Public Citizen, p. 16). But the presentation of isolated bits of information is not the same as a systematic examination of the available data. Here are some of the problems that have to be faced in dealing with the problem.

First, the rates that are quoted are average rates, and thus do not take into account the price variation to different user classes, which are likely to be large given the institutional framework on which drugs are distributed in the United States. In addition, the retail prices also reflect downstream price increments that are attributed to wholesalers, pharmacists and the prescription drug managers of various health plans over which the pharmaceutical houses exert little or no control. This problem, moreover, is not confined to patented drugs, but also gives rise to risks in the generic sector, where once again hefty-markups are always possible.

Second, it is unclear what inferences should be drawn from these increases in any event. Some portions of the market basket will always increase more rapidly than the rate of inflation. It is important, therefore, to know the source of the increase. In these cases, there is no hint of collusion or other illegal activities that explains the price increases. The possible explanations are multiple. A drug could have been perceived as risky at the time of launch, only to prove itself more successful over time. The higher level of safety commands a greater premium. Alternatively, the product in question could have proved its value in lower dosages or in combination with other drugs, which again increases its demand. Finally, the price increases could reflect changes in one portion of the overall market to the exclusion of changes in other portions of the market.

I list these possibilities not just as theoretical abstractions. Each of them has played its part in the recent furor over Abbott Laboratories' four-fold price increase with respect to its popular AIDS drug Norvir, from $1.75 per day to $8.57 per day.[18] That increase provoked a strong outcry, which led to demands that Abbott be stripped of its exclusive rights to market Norvir under the so-called "march-in" rights under the Bayh-Dole Act, which are triggered whenever a patentee fails to exploit his patent in a "reasonable" fashion.[19]

Looking solely at one number is sufficient to raise eyebrows, but these should be lowered in light of the full case. Here are some of the particulars from the newspaper reports. First, the additional revenues generated were to be plowed back into further AIDS research. What fraction and for what projects is hard to say, but the larger point remains true. An increase in patent revenues during the life of a drug is an additional spur to the initial creation. It would be senseless as a matter of basic policy to insist that price increases from initial prices should be prohibited or limited to the level of inflation. The net effect of that rule would be to induce drug companies to charge higher prices at the outset of drug treatment, thereby limiting early uses. As with any "ordinary" product, users are willing to pay higher prices when doubts about the drug's safety or efficacy have been removed or eased through actual usage. The same process works in reverse, those drugs that have limited effectiveness or substantial side effects will see a reduction in market share and price. Price movements offer powerful signals of the worth of various goods and services that are every bit as useful for patented commodities as with any other goods.

Second, the price increase for Norvir did not cover all shipped units. At the same time that Abbott raised its prices in the commercial sector, it guaranteed that free supplies would be provided for uninsured individuals, regardless of income. In addition, Abbott agreed to a permanent price-freeze for sales to the two major programs available to AIDS patients. Both these decisions may have been made in a self-interested mode to forestall a government response under Bayh-Dole, but, if so, that is an argument against the aggressive reading of the statute that leads to choices that would not be made in an unregulated market. In any event, it certainly requires a downward recalibration of the stated price increases.

Third, the new uses of the drug give some explanation as to its repricing. When originally sold in 1996, Norvir was used in high dosages as a stand-alone drug, and was priced accordingly. Subsequently, research established that Norvir, when taken in conjunction with other AIDS drugs in small quantities improves their effectiveness. In effect, the new use has made the drug more valuable in smaller dosages. A per unit price system ignores the positive synergetic effects from lower dosages, which should be reflected in market prices.

In light of these variations, it is no surprise that ex-Senator Birch Bayh testified that he did not think that the march-in rights under the basic statute were meant to usher in a de facto system of price controls, but should be reserved for (the thus far nonexistent) cases in which market forces were wholly ignored in the use and dissemination of government-funded drugs. The point is of special relevance because it turned out that the United States had contributed about $3 million, or roughly one percent of the cost for the commercialization of the product, chiefly to sponsor some early clinical trials. The obvious point is that the entire public/private partnership under Bayh-Dole could not survive if that small hook is construed to authorize government control over pricing. Who would take a $3 million carrot which comes with a $1 billion stick? James Love, the President of Essential Inventions, who led the futile charge for this novel exercise of march-in rights insisted that it is wrong to ask consumers to "pay twice" for Norvir given that they had funded "the research" on the drug. How easy it is to inflate contributions: some research is not 'the' research, and the novel invocation of Bayh-Dole would wreak havoc on the long-established patterns of funding research.

VI. The Private Public Interface

This last observation leads to the next question: why use the patent system at all when government research could sponsor the development of new drugs? This point, which Relman and Angell suggest but do not fully endorse, is of course subject to objections that bring us right back to the socialist calculation debate in the first half of the last century (Relman & Angell, 2002, pp. 30-32). As noted in dealing with the case of the bridge, a decision for government construction has at least two perils. The cost of construction could be higher owing to the inefficiency of government contracting, and the need for the bridge cannot be independently established by an appeal to private demand (which for these purposes is measured by the *maximum* amounts that all users are prepared to pay). The same problems arise in the pharmaceutical industry. There is no doubt that the use of government funds to support basic research is an important component of any sensible system of drug production. But it is wrong to think that it follows that the process of commercialization of these basic patents should also be left in public hands once the basic science has been established by research that falls in the public domain.

There is within the patent literature endless debate over the question whether a single firm with a monopoly position will do more to innovate on the patented invention than will a competitive industry in which no one enjoys a position of patent protection.[20] The issue is again hopelessly clouded at the theoretical level, because there are advantages each way. The exclusive right means that the holder of the patent will spend lots of money for successful commercialization because it knows that it does not face competition. But that exclusive protection keeps out all sorts of other innovators unless they can negotiate deals with the patent holder, which can sometimes be done by licensing.[21] This ambiguity is not new, for in the nineteenth century there was much uncertainty as to whether any franchise given to build a bridge over public waters should be exclusive or nonexclusive, given the arguments that could be made both ways.[22] Even today there is strong disagreement as to whether brokerage commissions should be exclusive or shared. And it is beyond doubt that Congress itself is somewhat leery of the public domain insofar as the Bayh-Dole Act takes affirmative steps to require government grantees to make good faith examinations of potential innovations to see if they are worthy of patents.[23]

Yet however close that debate turns out to be in principle, the one solution that is bound to fail is that which seeks to place the full responsibility of commercialization in public hands. Without some consideration of which projects will generate a market demand, the state will in this regard be as much at sea as it is in any other area where it purports to make social calculations without the benefit of prices. The current system in contrast offers a more intelligent division of labor. There is a strong prohibition against the patenting of any natural substance on the ground that these are most efficiently utilized when left in the public domain.[24] (Note that this rule is in contradistinction to a rule that allows for the patenting of a *process* to isolate and purify a natural substance.) Once that basic work has been done, any private firm can seek to develop a worthwhile marketable product based on it. That will still lead to patent races, but those races will take place over a shorter course, which means that the drugs in question can be developed in greater number at lower costs. In addition, the same basic research could lead to the development of two or more patented drugs that work in competition with each other, which allows for greater choice in responding to treatments.

VII. Me-Too Drugs

Relman and Angell are skeptical about this last point as well, by arguing that these "me-too" drugs add nothing to the pharmacopeias, and do little to reduce the prices in question (2002, p. 32). But this position seems to be exceptionally short-sighted from any of multiple perspectives. On the first, any me-too drug has to be sufficiently different from the original in order to be able to meet the standards for patent protection. Obvious extensions and imitations are denied patent protection under the law as it is, notwithstanding protestations from Relman and Angell to the contrary (2002, p. 36). And those small differences in chemical composition could really make a difference in the grand scheme of things. No one could analogize these patents to some mechanical device that moves one lever to the front or the back of a machine. From the regulatory side, we know that chemical differences really matter because no one would argue that the me-too drug is sufficiently similar that it could be let on the market without going through testing and other standard regulatory procedures. From the medical side, the availability of two drugs means that a second one could be tried if the first provides no additional benefit or has some adverse side effects. From the economic side, the creation of a second drug means that the holder of the exclusive rights to market the first drug has lost its economic monopoly by the presence of a new competitor. Relman and Angell pooh-pooh this last possibility, claiming that they observe little or no price competition with the advent of me-too drugs. But, as noted above, while this may be true in the independent druggist segment of the market, it is not true in the managed care sector where professional buyers are able to trade off the one drug against the other.

Dr. Thomas H. Lee supplies one useful illustration of the impact that a second product has on the first. He notes that the first-in-class of a new kind of cardiac stent produced a land office business until a second form of cardiac stent came along to provide it with some competition (Lee, 2004). It is, therefore, difficult to disagree with Lee's assessment that "[m]e-too products reflect and create competition among drug and device manufacturers, and that competition is also a powerful driver of better quality and lower cost" (2004, p. 211). The point here has, if anything, deeper implications for industrial policy. In expressing their desire that drug companies go for new chemical entities that open up new vistas for treatment, Relman and Angell are promoting a frame of mind that hearkens back to the old socialist command and control economy. Sitting back in their armchairs, they think that we are all better off with high-risk/high return investments than with low-risk/low return investment. They also are critical of the FDA for using a standard that compares a new treatment to a placebo and not to established drugs. All this is quite mistaken for there is no reason why they, or anyone else who sits on the sidelines, should have better information as to what strategy is better for what firm. If it turns out that some company is prepared to market the fifth statin to lower cholesterol it must believe that it can do something to persuade physicians and patients to leave their current product in exchange for a new one. In cases of "ordinary" markets, we welcome new entry as a way to expand consumer choice. There is no reason not to do the same here. The FDA should not be turned into an arbiter of marketability.

All this is not to say, however, that sound business acumen points inexorably to a strategy that favors "me-too" drugs. In principle, there is absolutely no reason to think that any uniform strategy will work for all market players, or even for all large pharmaceutical houses. In practice, it is possible to adopt any one of a countless number of research strategies, based on the knowledge of the strengths of one's own business and the apparent strategies of various competitors.

In making this general declaration, nothing assures us that for-profit firms will adopt a winning strategy. Indeed, the recent and thorough Bain study on the entire industry castigates the large pharmaceutical houses for choosing the wrong strategies.[25] In the view of the Bain study, Big Pharma is too transfixed with mergers and too preoccupied with doing research across the board in the vain hopes of discovering the next Lipitor that will carry its profitability over the next generation. As jacks-of-all-trades, and masters of none, they constantly lose out to smaller, more focused operations that have defined targets to which they can bring genuine expertise. The Bain study notes further that the rate of innovation in the small firms has been on average higher than those for larger firms (Gilbert, Henske, & Singh, 2003).

One clear implication from this study is that Big Pharma should probably make deals with smaller producers who are proving themselves to be the more successful innovators. Perhaps this diagnosis better fits some firms than others. If so, we should expect some large firms to hire Bain as others spurn their advice. But for our purposes, the question is not whether this diagnosis is on the money (which I suspect that it is) but whether we think firms, commentators, or legislators have the incentives to get to the bottom of the problem. The key point is that there's no reason to think that outsiders will do better on this question than insiders. Since we don't have problems of monopoly or collusion, it is best not to prescribe firm strategy.

Yet rather than following the market test on this critical question, Relman and Angell march off in the wrong direction. In their view, the way to measure the success of a large firm is to look at the percentage of its budget that is devoted to drug research as opposed to marketing and other activities. To be sure, this figure is far higher for pharmaceutical corporations than it is for most industries—about 18 percent versus 4 percent. But these numbers should be understood as descriptions of how business is, or has been done. In and of themselves they have no normative pop. To be sure, Relman and Angell, as good commissariats, would like to see that percentage increased, especially at the expense of advertisement and marketing. But perhaps the opposite strategy would work better both for the firm and their customers. If large firms are not focused in their research, perhaps they should *reduce* the percentage of expenditures on research and specialize instead in "in-licensing," that is licensing from smaller firms promising treatments that they have not developed. That strategy, which seems to be on the rise, may well be a market response to the Bain criticism in that firms that have had mixed internal research results have decided to concentrate their efforts on other portions of the process of getting products from conception to the market. If so, we have seen a form of market specialization that at least holds out the possibility of some gains from trade. It is hardly the retreat from social responsibility that Relman and Angell make it all out to be.

VIII. Marketing and Advertisement Practices

Relman and Angell's conviction that large pharmaceutical companies should have a commitment to do (as oppose to contract for) basic research leads them to condemn their advertisement and marketing practices. The marketing issues are seen as efforts to woo the medical profession into abandoning their own independence and to persuading the public at large to either demand or purchase new high-price drugs that are not worth their extra cost. In responding to this point, it is important not to give a blanket endorsement to each and every pharmaceutical marketing practice that has ever been deployed. Puffery and temptation are risks in "ordinary" business, and they are risks in the pharmaceutical business as well. But once again the key question is one of measure and proportion, and on that score Relman and Angell overstate their case.

The first point to note is that advertisements are not just a set of costs; they also provide a set of benefits that in some cases at least justify the associated costs. Here the relevant argument is not distinctive to the pharmaceutical industry but applies across the board to any industry with high-fixed and low variable costs. The key effort is to find ways to spread the cost of that first pill across as many users as is feasible, for otherwise the product will not reach the market at all. Thus, assume that we have a drug whose first pill costs $1 million to make, and each additional pill costs $2. The simple increase of one to two buyers cuts the cost per customer by almost half. That simple insight means that it makes eminently good sense from a social point of view to expend resources on advertisement to make public the benefits of new treatments. If one thousand individuals now use the pill, then the fixed costs are reduced to $1000 per person. If a million pills are sold, then those costs are at $1 per person, well within the ordinary ability to buy. But those other 999,999 individuals will not just find out about the drug unless it is advertised. If, for example, it took $1,500,000 to spread the word, the cost per customer drops sharply, for now the total expenditures of $3,500,000 mean that the pill can cover its costs at roughly $3.50 per pill. The additional expenditures on advertisement serve to lower the cost per unit, to increase the overall profit of the firm, and to offer benefits to individuals who would otherwise not know to make the drug expenditure in question. What the advertisements do is to allow the fixed costs of development to be amortized over a larger class of users. Once the additional advertisement costs add more to the cost of medicine than they save through this amortization process, the ads will cease. This is not a situation in which there is a conflict of interest between the welfare of the firm and that of the public at large. Only if we ignore the gains from broader dissemination could we treat all advertisement expenditures as a waste.

In dealing with advertisements, Relman and Angell spend little time on the basic economics and more time on the endless efforts of "detail" men and women to move new drugs at lavish conventions staged for physicians. I think that it is wrong to dismiss these events as wholly useless even though there is much that looks unseemly in this effort. But the important judgment is not mine, but of those within the medical profession, who are capable of resisting these blandishments if they choose. Indeed, there is evidence that greater resistance to traditional modes of promotion has already taken place. The Bain study notes: "Physician details have become almost twice as expensive, evidenced by the drop in sales representatives' productivity of nearly 50% over the past seven to eight years" (Gilbert, Henske, & Singh, 2003, p. xx). Yet even this news is not an unalloyed good, because some advertisement channel is necessary for needed therapeutics to reach their largest audience.

IX. Drug Costs

The analysis thus far has concentrated on how drugs are sold and the revenue that they produce. Of equal importance is the cost of new production of these drugs. It is here that Relman and Angell take the strong position that the drug industry has inflated its estimates of the cost of production in a disingenuous effort to stave off the price-control measures that they think appropriate to this market. In their view the costs of research and development of new drugs are not all that high, and represent a smaller fraction of the overall bill than the costs of advertising, to which they attach little benefit. Indeed, they take issue with the standard estimation of the cost of a new chemical entity of DiMasi, Hansen and Grabowski (2003), which places that figure at around $800 million, preferring instead to adopt the estimate of $100 million taken by Public Citizen. They would surely be apoplectic at the figure announced in the Bain Report, which, based on more recent data, ups that number to about $1.7 billion (Gilbert, Hensky, & Singh, 2003).

The root of the difficulty starts with a very simple question: what counts as the cost of a new drug launch. Here everyone agrees that it covers the various efforts directed toward the discovery and synthesis of the new molecules, work which often takes years. In addition, there is the daunting array of pre-clinical and clinical trials, which are designed to deal with both the safety and efficacy of the drugs in question. It is also clear that the costs of new drug development must cover the cost of failed innovations. As in the oil industry, the successful wells must produce enough revenues to cover the dry holes in order for any firm to remain in business. Looking just at the DiMasi study, it is easy to isolate the two sources of the sharp bump in cost estimates. The Bain report explains that the costs of clinical trials, particularly at Phase II and Phase III,[26] have gone up sharply, while the percentage of drugs that make it through trials to successful launch has dropped from about 14% to 8% from the 1995-2000 to the 2000-2002 period.

The Bain data is by necessity somewhat limited, and the extrapolations from the DiMasi study may well be overstated, but those differences in estimation are not what accounts for the huge gulf between their work and the conclusions of Relman and Angell. That difference kicks in at a much more fundamental level, stemming from the conviction that the proper mode for calculating drug costs should *not*, repeat **NOT,** include the cost of capital over time. Here it is critical to quote Relman and Angell's key passage which critiques DiMasi for assigning a cost of capital of nine percent per annum for each year between expenditure and realization:

> [T]he final estimate of the cost per drug is not the actual out-of-pocket cost, but what the authors [DiMasi, et al] call the "capitalized" cost—that is, it includes the estimated revenue that might have been generated over the long development period if the money spent on R&D had instead been invested in the equity market. This theoretically lost revenue is known as the "opportunity cost," and it is added to the industry's out-of-pocket costs of R&D. The authors seem to justify this interesting accounting maneuver on the grounds that from the perspective of investors, a pharmaceutical company is really just one kind of investment, which they chose among other possible investment options. But while this may be true for investors, surely it is not true for the pharmaceutical companies themselves. The latter have no choice but to spend money on R&D if they wish to be in the pharmaceutical business, so they have no "opportunity costs. (DeMasi, Hansen, & Grabowski, 2003, p. 29)

This passage only confirms the enormous gulf between economics and medicine, which remind us today about the laments of the gap between "two cultures."[27] There is of course nothing unique about the pharmaceutical industry in this respect. One could say as well that no corporation faces opportunity costs because they could all go out of business, so that we should always ignore the first maxim of finance theory that all future cash flows should be discounted to present value. But rather than recognize the manifest economic absurdity in denying the conventional wisdom, Relman and Angell cast digs at DiMasi and his colleagues, whose standard procedures are treated as some kind of parlor trick that eagle-eyed physicians are duty bound to unmask. After all, they tell us, no one can be confident of what takes place on Wall Street in light of recent events. In this quixotic revisionist history of finance theory, they follow the lead of Public Citizen, which also believes that the only expenditures that matter are out-of-pocket expenses, and not the carrying costs of the deal.[28] The upshot is that half the costs of financing new drugs, which often take eight to 12 years to reach market, are treated as though they were not incurred at all. From that point it is easy to argue that other deductions from the ostensible cost figures should take place because, for example, expenditures in research and development (R&D) are deductible. But the corresponding adjustment for after-tax income is not made as well.

All this is not to say that anyone can speak with confidence that DiMasi has gotten the right numbers, or whether the higher Bain estimate will be confirmed when the recent data become more ample or are reviewed dispassionately by others. Nor is it to deny that the use of a single number to cover the widely disparate paths of new drug development may conceal as much as it reveals. But with that said there is at least one simple test that says something about the overall state of health of the pharmaceutical industry today. Which way does the investment flow? If Relman and Angell are correct in their assertions, there is no reason why capital should not flow into pharmaceuticals, with stock prices trending sharply upward. After all, the costs are low, the marketing expenses are largely redundant, and the prices are astronomical. But that pattern of robust growth is not what we saw in 2004, and it is not what we see as of 2007. New firms could avoid some of the problems that derive from the all-purpose research programs of the mega-firm simply by building a better business model. Established firms can mend their ways or reinvent themselves, and may be doing that as we speak. But there are other problems that simply won't disappear that easily. The constant threat of price controls is pooh-poohed by Relman and Angell on the ground that so long as the profits of the industry exceed the costs of their R&D there is nothing to worry about. "Prices," they assure us, "could be lowered substantially without coming close to threatening the R&D budgets of drug companies, much less their economic survival" (Relman & Angell, 2002, p. 28). But once again this statement bears no recognizable connection to any standard form of financial analysis. The simplest test of market value relies on some capitalized value of the entire income stream. A firm that just covers its costs and no more will be worth zero. If a firm finds that the profits over its entire base of expenditures falls by one-half across the board, as a first approximation its capital value will fall by a like amount. And in this environment when the rate of return on new investments may be as low as five percent, if the Bain survey is to be believed, it is idle to assume that the position of firms will be improved by placing additional restrictions on how they conduct all aspects of their business.

X. Conclusion

There is, I think, little reason to belabor the deep differences between myself, on the one side, and Angell and Relman, and Public Citizen on the other. Our substantive differences on the behavior of the pharmaceutical industry depends as much on world view as it does on the particulars of the case. In this regard, their mindset sees government as a source of strength, not as a source of mischief, when it goes beyond the usual functions of the laissez-faire state. I see it as a strength. There was a time when their critique of markets cut across all sectors of the economy. Today it represents a holdout against a shift in general opinion that has moved sharply away from the planned economy. Our forensic positions are quite different. I need only explain why the general logic of strong property rights and voluntary exchange can carry over to the pharmaceutical industry. They have to explain why that translation does not work. But if they concede, as they seem to do, that markets work well enough for ordinary products, then they face this challenge. Just why in their view do markets work well in other sectors? I do not think that they could give an answer that is so specific to insurance, or banking, or real estate that did not rely on the logic of the mutual gains through specialization and trade. Any neutral observer who looks at this situation will be hard pressed to find some structural element about this industry that lends any comfort to critics of the pharmaceutical industry whose initial premise is the desirability of the command and control economy.[29]

Notes

1. The original version of this article was prepared some years ago for a conference on pharmaceuticals that never took place. A version of it has been published in somewhat different form by the Institute for Policy Innovation. Since that time I have published my 2006 book on the Pharmaceutical Industry, *Overdose: How Excessive Government Regulation Stifles Pharmaceutical Innovation.* I have not been able to make extensive revision in this paper, but I have tried to rewrite in a way that reflects the more recent developments in the field.
2. Goozner (2005); Kassirer (2004); and Angell (2004). For my review of the Kassirer and Angell books, see Epstein (2005b).
3. For discussion, see Public Citizen's Congress Watch (p. 16).
4. For an early statement of this view, see generally Lange and Taylor (1938).
5. *See, e.g.,* Viner (1960). ("I will carefully avoid using the term laissez faire to mean what only unscrupulous or ignorant opponents of it and never its exponents mean, namely, philosophical anarchism, or opposition to any governmental power or activity whatsoever.")
6. For the most recent Supreme Court foray into this area, see *Duquesne Light Co. v. Barasch* (1989), noting the different methods that have been tried to achieve the two goals of effective regulation: the elimination of monopoly profits without confiscating the major investments made by the regulated industries.
7. One major example is in telecommunications, in which there was much effort to introduce competition to displace the statutory monopoly given to various local exchange carriers, or LECs. See, e.g., *Verizon Communications v. Federal Communications Commission,* (2002); *AT&T Corp. v. Iowa Utilities Board,* (1999). For discussion, see Douglas Lichtman & Randal C. Picker (2002).

8. I address it in *Mortal Peril: Our Inalienable Right to Health Care* (Epstein, 1997).
9. For a recent elaboration of this theme, see Richard A. Epstein (2004).
10. For a defense of this proposition, see Easterbrook and Fischel (1991).
11. Bruce Kuhlik, formerly General Counsel of PhRMA and currently General Counsel of Merck & Co.,, and I have addressed some of these (2004).
12. *See* PhRMA, Prescription Drug Price Trends are in Line with Medical Inflation, (Spring 2004), at www.phrma.org/publications/twopager//2004-04-29.986.pdf. The figures offered were designed to counter the charge that pharmaceutical companies had systematically raised their prices in anticipation of the discounts that will be available under the Medicare Modernization Act, as of June 1, 2004. Enrollment in that program has in fact proved spotty in the early going.
13. For my development of this theme, see Epstein (1997, p. 31–37).
14. *See, e.g., Pharmaceutical Research & Mfrs. of Am. v. Walsh,* (2003) upholding a Maine plan to extend the Medicaid benefit to other needy individuals against a challenge that the entire matter was controlled under federal law.
15. For a clear discussion of these issues, see *Brand Name Prescription Drug Litigation,* (1999).
16. It is important to be clear as to the source of the harm. It does *not* arise because an increase in prices in foreign markets will lead firms to reduce their price in the American market. No profit making firm would give up profits at home because it makes additional profits overseas. Rather the social loss arises because investors that see limited returns from overseas will cut back on the number of drugs that they produce or delay their introduction to reflect the lower rate of return.
17. See Patricia M. Danzon and Michael F. Furukawa (2003) concluding that the differential in drug prices across countries are roughly in line with income and smaller than the differences in the supply of other services.
18. For some relevant sources, see Bruce Japsen (2004a; b); *Abbott Laboratories Comments at NIH Public Meeting Regarding Norvir and Bayh-Dole March-in Provisions* (2004).
19. See Bruce Japsen (2004a). The statutory text on which the argument is based is 35. U.S.C. § 203, which reads in relevant portion as follows:

    § 203. *March-in rights*

    (a) With respect to any subject invention in which a small business firm or nonprofit organization has acquired title under this chapter [*35 USCS ßß 200* et seq.], the Federal agency under whose funding agreement the subject invention was made shall have the right, in accordance with such procedures as are provided in regulations promulgated hereunder to require the contractor, an assignee or exclusive licensee of a subject invention to grant a nonexclusive, partially exclusive, or exclusive license in any field of use to a responsible applicant or applicants, upon terms that are reasonable under the circumstances, and if the contractor, assignee, or exclusive licensee refuses such request, to grant such a license itself, if the Federal agency determines that such--

    (1) action is necessary because the contractor or assignee has not taken, or is not expected to take within a reasonable time, effective steps to achieve practical application of the subject invention in such field of use;

    (2) action is necessary to alleviate health or safety needs which are not reasonably satisfied by the contractor, assignee, or their licensees;

    (3) action is necessary to meet requirements for public use specified by Federal reg-

ulations and such requirements are not reasonably satisfied by the contractor, assignee, or licensees; or

(4) action is necessary because the agreement required by section 204 has not been obtained or waived or because a licensee of the exclusive right to use or sell any subject invention in the United States is in breach of its agreement obtained pursuant to section 204.

Standing alone, the text could be read as to make the possibility of government intervention a routine business, but in fact the interpretation of the statute has consistently gone the other way. See, e.g. Evelyn H. McConathy & Lisa Burgin Conte (2002, p. 23) noting that the objective of the Act is commercialization, so that the United States "government is not anxious to exercise its march in rights."

20. For the seminal paper on the question, see Edmund Kitch (1977). For a modern reiteration of the problem, see John F. Duffy (2004a). For a more skeptical view, see Mark A. Lemley (2004).
21. For a discussion of these issues, see Epstein (2003).
22. For the judicial decision that construed grants as nonexclusive when they were silent on the question, see *Charles River Bridge v. Warren Bridge* (1837). The decision was by a 4 to 3 vote, with Story, J., in dissent. For a general history see Kutler (1971).
23. 35 U.S.C. §§ 200–211 (2000). Note that the commercialization rationale for the statute was explicitly endorsed by Joseph Allen, a former Bayh staff member: "What the public gets back is that these drugs will be commercialized." Japsen (2004a).
24. See *Funk Brothers Seed Co. v. Kale Inoculant* (1948). For the limits, as applied to human-made bacteria, see *Diamond v. Chakrabarty* (1980).
25. See Jim Gilbert, Preston Henske & Ashish Singh (2003).
26. The usual protocol runs as follows. Phase I clinical trials are given to small numbers of individuals to determine the maximum levels of exposures that can be tolerated, taking into account adverse side effects. Phase II trials work off larger groups and experiment with different dosage levels to determine effectiveness. If a drug passes at this level, Phase III Clinical trials are enormous undertakings, often on thousands of patients, which are intended to make more definitive judgments about safety and effectiveness. The logistical elements here are formidable because if a new therapy promises a small improvement it may have to be tested on huge populations. Ideally, these studies should be conducted in academic institutions where the controls are best, but the sheer size of the work requires that many different types of facilities be brought into the picture, creating higher costs and serious questions of quality control. For a brief account, see Relman and Angell (2002, p. 28).
27. See Snow (1959). Snow referred to the gap between literature and physics from the standpoint of one who was extraordinarily proficient at both. He did not allude to the gap between medicine and finance which years later looks every bit as large.
28. "50% percent of the $802 million figure [of DiMasi] is theoretical: Companies don't actually spend $802 million to discover and develop new drugs. That's because one-half of the $802 million figure represents the 'opportunity cost of capital" (Public Citizen's Congress Watch, p. 46).
29. I should like to thank Uzair Kayani, University of Chicago Law School, Class of 2009, for his valuable research assistance in rounding this article into final shape.

References

35 U.S.C. §§ 200–211. (2000).

Abbott Laboratories Comments at NIH Public Meeting Regarding Norvir and Bayh-Dole March-in Provisions. (2004, May 25). PR Newswire Association. [Online]. Available at: http://www.aegis.com/news/pr/2004/PR040534.html.

Angell, M. (2004). *The Truth About Drug Companies: How They Deceive Us and What We Can Do About It.* New York: Random House.

AT&T Corp. v. Iowa Utilities Board. (1999). 525 U.S. 366.

Brand Name Prescription Drug Litigation. (1999). 186 F.3d 781, 786-789. 7th Cir.

Charles River Bridge v. Warren Bridge. (1837). 36 U.S. 420.

Coase, R.H. (1946). 'The marginal cost controversy', *Economica,* 13, 169-182.

Danzon, P.M. & Furukawa, M.F. (2003). 'Price and availability of pharmaceuticals: Evidence from nine countries', *Health Affairs,* 22(6), W521-W536

Dickenson, H.D. (1939). *The Economics of Socialism.* New York: Oxford University Press.

Diamond v. Chakrabarty. (1980). 447 U.S. 303.

DiMasi, J.A., Hansen, R.W., & Grabowski, H.G. (2003). 'The price of innovation: New estimates of drug development costs', *Journal of Health Economics,* 22, 141-185.

Duffy, J.F. (2004a). 'The marginal cost controversy in intellectual property', *University of Chicago Law Review,* 71, 37.

Duffy, J.F. (2004b). 'Rethinking the prospect theory of patents', *University of Chicago Law Review,* 71, 439.

Duquesne Light Co. vs. Barasch. (1989). 488 U.S. 299.

Easterbrook, F.H. & Fischel, D.R. (1991). *The Economic Structure of Corporate Law.* Cambridge, MA: Harvard University Press.

Editorial, (2004, June 3). 'Attacking high drug prices', *Chicago Tribune,* 22.

Epstein, R. (1995). *Simple Rules for a Complex World.* Cambridge, MA: Harvard University Press.

Epstein, R. (1997). *Mortal Peril: Our Inalienable Right to Health Care?* Reading, MA: Addison-Wesley.

Epstein, R. (2003). 'Steady the course: Property rights in genetic material', In F. Scott Kieff (Ed.), *Perspectives on Properties of the Human Genome Project* (pp. 153-194). London: Elsevier Academic Press.

Epstein, R. (2005a). *Free Markets Under Siege: Cartels, Politics, and Social Welfare.* Stanford: Hoover Institution Press.

Epstein, R. (2005b). 'Pharma furor', *Legal Affairs,* January/February, 60.

Epstein, R. (2006). *Overdose: How Excessive Government Regulation Stifles Pharmaceutical Innovation.* New Haven, CT: Yale University Press.

Epstein, R. & Kuhlik, B.N. (2004). 'Is there a biomedical anticommons', *Regulation,* 27 (2), 54-58.

Funk Brothers Seed Co. v. Kale Inoculant Co. (1948). 333 U.S. 127.

Gilbert, J., Henske, P., & Singh, A. (2003). 'Rebuilding big pharma's business model', *In Vivo: The Business and Medicine Report,* 21, 73.

Goozner, M. (2005). *The $800 Million Pill: The Truth Behind the Cost of New Drugs.* Berkeley, CA: University of California Press.

Hayek, F. (1940). 'Socialist calculation: The competitive 'solution'', *Economica,* 7, 125-149.

Hayek, F. (1945). 'The use of knowledge in society', *American Economic Review,* 35(4), 519-530.

Heller, M.A. & Eisenberg, R.S. (1998). 'Can Patents Deter Innovation? The Anticommons in Biomedical Research', *Science,* 280 (5364), 698-701.

Japsen, B. (2004a, May 21). 'Abbott AIDS drug pricing leads to Review of Patent', *Chicago Tribune,* C1.

Japsen, B. (2004b, May 26). 'Abbott defends price boost on AIDS dug at U.S. Hearing', *Chicago Tribune,* C1.

Kassirer, J. (2004). *On the Take: How Medicine's Complicity with Big Business can Endanger Your Health.* New York: Oxford University Press.

Kitch, E. (1977). 'The nature and function of the patent system', *Journal of Law and Economics,* 20, 265-290.

Kutler, S. (1971). *Privilege and Creative Destruction: The Charles River Bridge Case.* Philadelphia: Lippincott.

Lange, O. & Taylor, F.M. (1938). *On the Economic Theory of Socialism.* Minneapolis: Lippincott.

Lee, T.H. (2004). "Me-too" products—friend or foe?', *New England Journal of Medicine,* 350, 211-212.

Lemley, M.A. (2004). 'Ex ante and ex post justifications for intellectual property', *University of Chicago Law Review,* 71, 129.

Lichtman, D. & Picker, R.C. (2003). 'Entry policy in local telecommunications: Iowa utilities and Verizon', *Supreme Court Law Review,* 41, 53.

McConathy, E.H. & Conte, L.B. (2002). 'March-in rights to federally-funded inventions', *University Licensing,* p. 23.

Pharmaceutical Research and Mfrs. of America v. Walsh. (2003). 538 U.S. 644.

Posner, R.A. (1969). 'Natural monopoly and its regulation', *Stanford Law Review,* 21, 518-518.

Public Citizen's Congress Watch, *America's Other Drug Problem: A Briefing Book on the Rx Drug Debate.* [Online]. Available at: www.citizen.org/rxfacts.

Relman, A.S. & Angell, M. (2002). 'America's other drug problem: How the drug industry distorts medicine and politics,' *The New Republic,* 227 (25), 27-41.

Robinson, J. (1935). 'A fundamental objection to laissez-faire', *The Economic Journal,* 45, 580-582.

Saul, S. (2007, August 8). 'More generics slow the surge in drug prices', *New York Times.*

Rovner, J. (2004, March 11). 'Health- McLellan Answers Questions, Nomination Hold Remains', *Congress Daily.*

Snow, C.P. (1959). *The Two Cultures and the Scientific Revolution.* Cambridge: Cambridge University Press.

Verizon Communications v. Federal Communications Commission. (2002). 122 US 1646.

Viner, J. (1960). 'The intellectual history of laissez-faire', *Journal of Law and Economics,* 3, 45-69.

Global Drug Innovation in a World of Financial Finitude:
Retailing Virtue to Promote Capital Formation and Profit

Michael A. Rie
University of Kentucky College of Medicine

I. Introduction

Drug innovation in medicine is an interdependent element of globally non-prioritized individual health care budgeting by individuals and governments. People live longer lives and science discovers more options to expand diagnostic and therapeutic possibilities for drugs and other modalities that provide increasing numbers of niche markets. With this tremendous progress in the 20th century, price resistance to healthcare costs is rising in all the nations of the developed world. Cost increases for those who pay often shield patients from personal payment for drug purchase and result in no restraint in drug usage by patients. However, the decision in the United States to create a multi-tiered system of direct patient co-payments for drugs in the ambulatory sector, coupled with emerging implicit rationing prioritization in the hospital sector (Engelhardt, 1986; Engelhardt, 1988; Rie, 1995; Rie, 1997; Rie, 2003: Rie, 2007) have resulted in a consumer rebellion that is likely to spread

H.T. Engelhardt, Jr. and J. Garrett (eds), *Innovation and the Pharmaceutical Industry* (pp. 128–152).

to the other more socialized centrally command and control democracies of the West. This essay addresses the moral realities of the global drug innovation non-market and potential solutions to recapturing a robust capitalist market morality in the global market of patentable drugs.

What is a free and unfettered capitalist market? If ever a non-market capitalist economy existed, it is best described by the present state of pharmaceutical innovation in the world of developed nations. According to Milton Friedman (2002), the true benefits of the market system rely on competition and freedom of choice, for both those who sell and those who purchase. Contrast a trip to the local farmer's market for the purchase of fresh produce with the complexity of Eli Lilly Corporation's sale of Xigris® for the treatment of life threatening septic shock in the intensive care units of hospitals. Tomatoes are easily appreciated as green, ripe, rotten, small or large and of a flavor subjectively of value to the purchaser. The purchaser buys directly from the producer's agent and pays for the transaction with private funds, uniquely in his/her possession. Whether other consumers can find access to comparable quality and quantity of tomatoes on a given day is not assured. If demand exceeds supply, prices will rise. Farmers will cultivate more crops and the market will re-equilibrate or excess production will pose a liability for farmers. Unless the successful tomato merchant is uniquely involved in agricultural research to create the perfect tomato, there are no questions of long term research and development costs for the tomato and no claims regarding the price and relationship to such a process are made in the marketplace. However, the merchant selling a particularly tasty, robust tomato is likely to command a higher price than other merchants might command for their less desirable product.

By contrast, let us consider the scientific, industrial development, patenting, retailing and long term profitability of recombinant human activated protein C (Xigris®) created by Eli Lilly and Company for the treatment of severe septic shock. As is often the case, basic scientific discoveries preceded the decision to enter into the industrial development. In the case of Xigris® depicted in figure 1, we see Seeger's basic scientific discovery of activated Protein C's anticoagulant activity was described in 1960. This finding lay fallow in the scientific literature until the 1970s when a group of researchers in Dr. Stenflo's laboratory in Sweden were able to purify and report the amino acid sequence of the molecule. Another fundamental scientific discovery occurred in

Figure 1

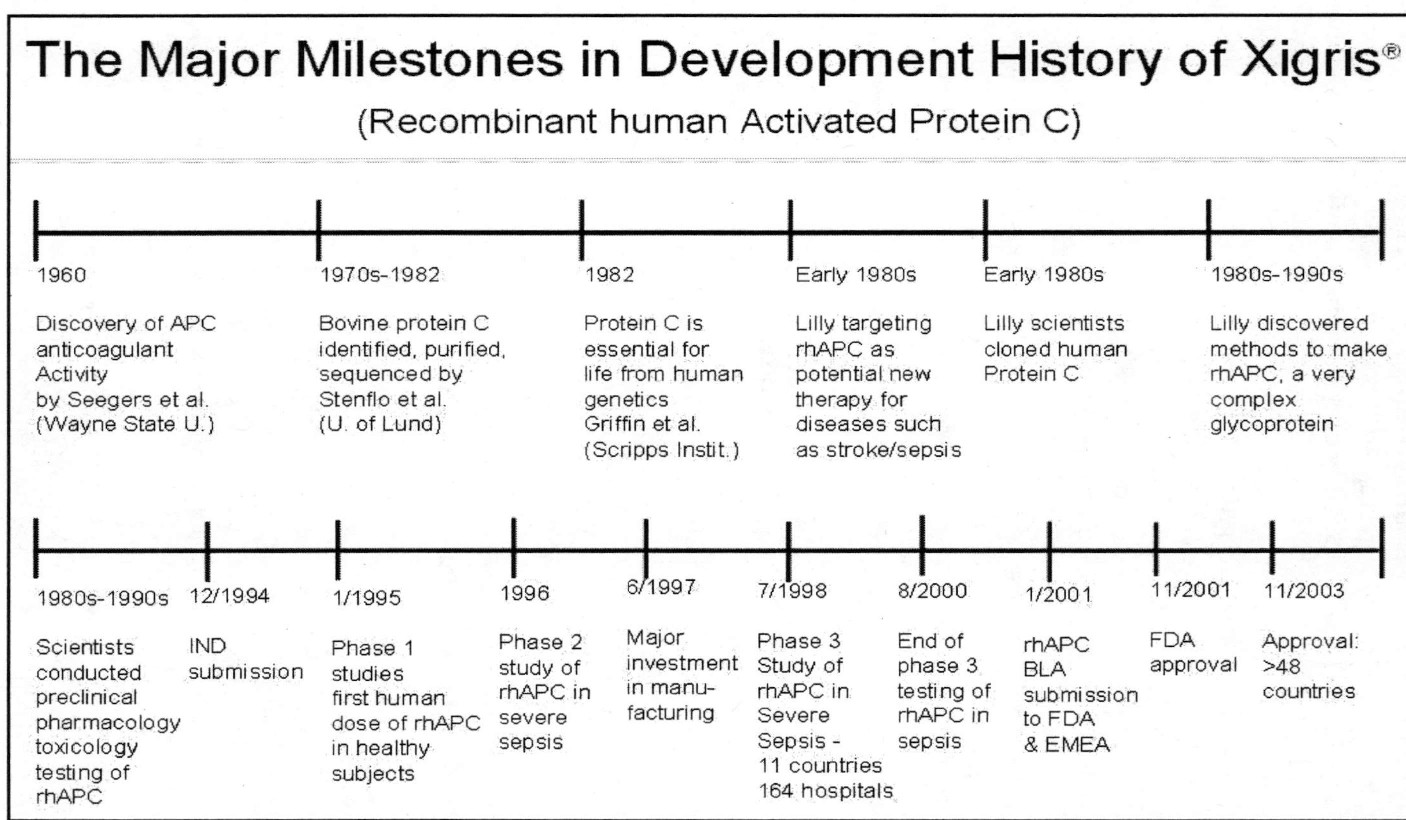
The Major Milestones in Development History of Xigris®
(Recombinant human Activated Protein C)
1960
Discovery of APC anticoagulant Activity by Seegers et al. (Wayne State U.)
1970s-1982
Bovine protein C identified, purified, sequenced by Stenflo et al. (U. of Lund)
1982
Protein C is essential for life from human genetics Griffin et al. (Scripps Instit.)
Early 1980s
Lilly targeting rhAPC as potential new therapy for diseases such as stroke/sepsis
Early 1980s
Lilly scientists cloned human Protein C
1980s-1990s
Lilly discovered methods to make rhAPC, a very complex glycoprotein
1980s-1990s
Scientists conducted preclinical pharmacology toxicology testing of rhAPC
12/1994
IND submission
1/1995
Phase 1 studies first human dose of rhAPC in healthy subjects
1996
Phase 2 study of rhAPC in severe sepsis
6/1997
Major investment in manu-facturing
7/1998
Phase 3 Study of rhAPC in Severe Sepsis - 11 countries 164 hospitals
8/2000
End of phase 3 testing of rhAPC in sepsis
1/2001
rhAPC BLA submission to FDA & EMEA
11/2001
FDA approval
11/2003
Approval: >48 countries

1982 which sparked the imaginative attention of scientists at Eli Lilly Company. This was namely that genetic Protein C deficiency resulted in lethal failure of human fetuses to develop through lack of the gene for the expression of Protein C. This led scientists at Eli Lilly to target activated Protein C as a potentially new and genetically identified therapy for diseases such as stroke and sepsis. Then followed a fortuitous scientific course in which the Lilly Corporation was among the first to clone a human protein (Insulin) which permitted further therapeutic cloning and production of Drotrecogin Alfa (Xigris®). Ten years of additional research and development were required inside the Lilly Corporation to invent secret methods to fuse long and complex protein chains together to form the complex glycoprotein. This synthetic production is unique as it is approximately 10 times the size of a human insulin. However human insulin now replaces animal insulin in standard therapy. It was not until 1995 (approximately 15 years after Lilly began to study the application of Protein C to human disease) that Phase 1 studies were conducted in normal, healthy, human subjects. By 1996 Phase II study was completed in severe sepsis. It should be understood that by the late 1990s approximately 13 other molecules that might be useful in the common condition of sepsis had been tried and failed in animals or humans. Lilly undertook its Phase III study on a massive scale involving 11 countries, 164 hospitals and required approximately 1690 patients before the randomized, controlled, placebo trial demanded by the FDA yielded a clear 13% diminution in death rate for a vast array of patients with a high mortality. By the time FDA approval was granted in November 2001, approximately $900 million dollars of corporate investment had been made and the intellectual property rights secured under the Lilly name. Xigris® entered the global marketplace at a price of approximately $6,800.00 per treatment episode for all countries. It was projected by the pharmaco-economists that this drug might eventually reach sales of one billion dollars per year. Unfortunately, sales ran far below that. This issue of market resistance has been summarized (Eichacker, 2006). Such writings implicate weak penetration of the pharmaceutical market as justification to prohibit a drug manufacturer's resources from either armslength funding of medical education or professional guidelines creation by medical professionals for the early diagnosis of severe sepsis (The FDA approved indication for Xigris®.)

II. The Clash of Human Desire to Fight Death and Financial Finitude

How could the economists have guessed so wrongly about a drug's marketing potential? In this case, the nature of human disease and end of life circumstances are carefully interwoven with a high number of patients that present with septic shock in hospitals and communities around the world. There are only four ways by which a human can die in a hospital that are not preventable. These are: cardio-respiratory failure, hemorrhage, uncontrolled infection and death of the whole brain. Protein C is a native substance of the body. When it is recreated and infused in the body it acts as an anticoagulant (substance that promotes bleeding). It was not surprising to see that creation of this therapeutic advance also carried significant risk. When people of advanced age or systemic disease become septic with infections, there are risks of bleeding, particularly in the human brain that make life salvage remotely possible and if so, with a markedly diminished quality of life.[1] Sepsis is also a common end of life circumstance for those who are immuno-compromised, totally incapacitated or living in nursing homes or extended care facilities and in which reasonable medical and personal decisions could opt against aggressive medical therapy. This segment of the sepsis universe is partially addressed by what is now a robust clinical movement of comfort and hospice care in hospitals. Patients are electing to forego treatment of fatal sepsis as an acceptable method of dying (Petersen, 2004, D-1).

This type of calculus to forego treatment at the end of life and in the face of global healthcare financial constraint requires new thinking and extreme moral sensitivity on the part of pharmaco-economists and the ethical accountability of marketing departments within pharmaceutical companies. The industry has long helped to promote the contemporary mystique that death may be optional or avoided if something new might offer even a small potential benefit. Coming to terms with end of life biology confronts physicians, hospitals and pharmacy and therapeutics (P&T) committees, health plans and formulary consultants on a daily basis. Tough decisions must be made as to how limited dollars are spent. To spend for one service item is to have less to spend on another. This leads to erratic and non systematic choices particularly in life threatening conditions in ICUs where defined individual patients compete for a finite number of beds (access) with differing probabilities of successful outcomes (Engelhardt & Rie, 1986).

The Wall Street Journal covered the surface of these policy and ethical problems that have existed for at least 25 years but which were catapulted into further public exposure when Lilly decided to support an unrestricted $1.8 million research grant to a group of physician researchers called "Values, Ethics, and Rationing in Critical Care Taskforce (VERICC)" (Regalado, 2003, A-1). Several VERICC task force members continue to be supported by Eli Lilly clinical grants and other mandated post marketing grants related to Xigris®. VERICC reported their results and findings in a peer reviewed article (Truog, 2005). Far from marketing a pharmaceutical these authors offered a thoughtful general taxonomy of various types of implicit rationing of healthcare occasioned by budgetary pressure in the ICU environment where Xigris® is consumed by patients. The authors offered no opinions about cost and moral choices in limited budget allocation (Rie, 2007). Several of the members of this taskforce were and are supported by Xigris® clinical grants and other FDA mandated post-marketing grants related to Xigris® (Eichacker, 2006). This has not stopped accusations in the medical and lay press that pharmaceutical "Businesses are Buying the Ethics they want" (DeVries, 2004, B-02).

The subject of drug rationing for a lethal human condition is clearly raised by this history. Sepsis remains a common human condition calling for the medical and human instinct to "fight death and rescue the dying patient". However, Xigris is only another double edged weapon in the high cost marginal rewards of ICU medicine in some patients with sepsis. One percent of the gross domestic product of the United States is consumed in ICU care and ICUs consume about 40% of hospital budgets. Some patients who may successfully thwart death are left to "technology dependent lingering limbo existence" in which they can be maintained with technologic support but not made to be independent of it (Engelhardt, 1986; Rie, 1995). Thus we now have patients who may receive repetitive doses of Xigris in this limbo before they finally succumb to death.

III. What Are the Ethical Profit-Making Opportuninies for Drug Makers in This Kind of Enviroment?

A. Price Resistance Defines the Market Morality of Human Finitude

If Xigris® has met its market resistance level, what can others take home from the case history? This drug was introduced with a high risk to reward ratio for a new unique best-in-class therapy. The FDA and the medical community read the PROWESS publication (Bernard, Vincent, Laterre, LaRosa, & Dhainaut, 2001) carefully and adopted drug usage criteria directly from the study's design. After nearly six years on the market there has been no compelling indication to expand the usage through off label indications. For a genetically recombinant protein this is not surprising and older biotechnology molecules are not easily finding evidence based market expansion. Rather, intensity of therapy and earlier identification of the indications have been medically accepted with positive outcome data with small marketing investments and increased drug sales.

Though Lilly never conceived that human insulin would find universal utility in intensive care units, the results of intensive insulin therapy decreasing infections, inflammation, length of ICU stay and increased survival are among the greatest advances in critical care medicine since 2001 (Van den Berghe et al., 2001). Today insulin infusions are used daily for non diabetic patients and ICU performance and efficiency is now measured by how tight blood sugar levels are controlled with insulin infusions. In 2008 American hospitals will be graded in their outcome performance by the Medicare federal payment system. How well the hospital meets the goal will be tied to hospital payment for care of the entire population of patients on a per case basis.

Similarly, modest unrestricted grants to the American and European intensive care professional societies to better summarize and define the septic syndrome in its earliest stages and severity are slowly increasing the awareness of earlier diagnosis and treatment with little fanfare and attention from the lay media (Dellinger et al., 2004). Whether this educational cultural approach will improve human survival as Xigris® usage criteria are earlier appreciated remains to be evaluated. However, sepsis will confront critically ill humans for the long term and its treatment will remain a cornerstone of critical care medicine.

Can it be that the intellectual property right for Xigris® will not erode after the American patent expires? There is substantial difficulty for a generic manufacturer to recreate giant complex proteins (Mathews, 2004, A-1). Lilly has made known to the world the molecular description of Xigris® but may not be required to divulge its secret methods of assembling the multiple segments of the molecule to produce the biologically active drug. Xigris® might not be a short-term "blockbuster" but could be a long-term steady bread winner for its maker. While antibiotics come with promise, their utility fades with time as bacteria become resistant to them. But will a biotechnology engineered molecule that recreates and enhances the body's own function succeed in this manner over the long term? If indeed this is true, then the production methods of a large protein molecule remain secret and expensive for new entrants into the marketplace. Lilly may find itself in the long term manufacture and sales of Xigris® or other complex protein molecules with a steady profit margin. Indeed the FDA and other national regulatory bodies are at a loss to describe standards of generic comparability of "look alike products" and may find it necessary to require new randomized trials of the generic product before displacing the "first in class" approved drug.

B. Drug Consumer Rebellions Need Resolution before Drug Industry Implosion

The contemporary public disdain of drug companies is based on American prices being substantially higher than those in Canada and all other developed world countries except Japan (Danzon & Furukawa, 2003; Kanavos & Reinhardt, 2003; Kanavos, 2004). When American managed care companies saw their ambulatory drug purchase costs rising faster than their hospital costs in the late 1990s, a near universal decision to shift costs to a multi-tiered co-payment methodology with patients ignited public awareness of drug costs directly. Medicare recipients were aware of these rising costs as they were always paying out of pocket. Thus began the classic consumer driven market ethic for competitive purchase from Canadian (cheaper) pharmacies and an unending consumer thirst for comparable drug at lower prices.

For half a century drug companies had adjusted to national regulatory bodies linking safety considerations to de-facto trade barriers (Jenkins, 2004). The industry accommodated to this "nation by nation" marketing and regulatory pricing. As long as companies could control their own prices in the largest (American) national market, sales abroad could still yield additional incremental profits through volume sales at reduced profit margins. American consumers would, by default, pay for worldwide research and development of new pharmaceuticals. As other countries have recently implemented consumer co-pays and reference pricing, additional pressure on American prices was needed to keep net revenues increasing with the costs of doing business (Fleming, 2003; Kanavos & Reinhardt, 2003; Kanavos, 2004).

The present industry methods of rationing supplies to Canadian pharmacies that resell inventory to American purchasers is likely to further accentuate the present consumer movement. As John Graham has stated (Graham, 2004), parallel track re-importation is not free trade and is likely to diminish the North American corporate desire to invent new pharmaceuticals both in America and globally. Rationing Canadian drug inventory is a stop gap industrial measure that will fuel an uncontrollable secondary resale movement of other global purchasers to Canada and directly to American consumers. Such activity will not be controllable by the industry unless it chooses to become a "pharmaceutical OPEC" and restrict the availability of drugs globally. European payment systems to drug manufacturers already have price-volume tradeoff provisions that limit profit through volume sales tied to pre existing unit price controls.

To succeed in the long run requires a moral commitment of the entire industry to a unitary global pricing strategy in much the way oil, coffee and sugar are traded in world commodity markets. To achieve such ends will require short term discipline and corporate sacrifice of all drug companies in countries that propose to protect intellectual property rights generally. The United States has succeeded in being home to research and development laboratories of the major drug firms because FDA approval carries the highest single market return on investment. Unfortunately the industry must seek globalization and its own brand of "get tough" policy towards the Eurocentric governmental "reference pricing" of consumer drug co-payments in favor of the Xigris® form of unitary drug pricing for global markets (Danzon & Furukawa, 2003; Kanavos & Reinhardt, 2003).

Global pricing carries with it a potential benefit to other countries. They may be able to attract drug companies to invest in research and development operations in their countries if they are loyal to globalization and further the goals of the International Conference on Harmonization (ICH). The market's invisible hand is likely to raise a series of options for all players not presently contemplated in the global non-market of today. Whether the industry can ignite the global market strategy without recourse to governmental trade policy seems to be as seminal to drug manufacturers in 2007 as the arrival of DRGs and managed care was 20 years ago to healthcare providers in the United States and now in France and Germany. Survivors of this transition will be those with a real earned reputation for outcomes, quality, excellence and end consumer satisfaction – unknown parameters in today's drug sales markets.

Globalization of prices will be morally and politically easier to accept before nation to nation trade wars, protectionism, and other national policy interests complicate the policy implementation. For example, a large Israeli pharmacy web site (www.MagenDavidMeds.com) advertises directly to American Jewish women in the *Hadassah Magazine* for common ambulatory drugs to be purchased by mail order from Israel. The drugs mentioned include several with American patents as well as generics. The Israelis offer discounts greater than Canadian websites and assure purchasers that the drugs are in tamper resistant blister packs with the date, location, and manufacturer and specifically they are permitted importation into the United States via a 1985 bilateral treaty between Israel and the United States. Whether such a treaty is valid for such a direct consumer purchase remains politically and legally debated. American history informs that when consumers overwhelmingly desired alcohol, federal prohibition failed and a constitutional amendment was needed, further complicating the interpretation of the Commerce Clause to this day. Should this importation portal grow, drug companies could rapidly find themselves at odds with the federal government's Middle Eastern foreign policy during the global war on terrorism. Needless animosities of no concern to drug manufacturers will be linked to global drug prices and trade. All such uncontrollable market risks would be diminished, if not eliminated by a global pricing strategy which will in itself require multinational moral choices of what drugs to buy and how much at the global price. One way or another, patients around the globe will be forced to participate directly in the purchase of their drugs and the anti-competitive governmental price caps will be partially eroded as people will have to decide for themselves what the marginal value of their drug purchases are worth to them individually. The preventive outcome effects of some drugs on costly morbidities will inspire larger insurer coverage of whatever source. Market efficiency will permit new drugs to be developed, companies to remain economically viable and pharmaco-economics and marketing employees to be held accountable for upholding an unfettered market morality.

C. Compliance Leveraging®: Turning the Sarbanes-Oxley Compliance Deadweight to Virtuous Venture Capital Advantage

There are fewer major drug manufacturers globally in 2007 than existed in 1980. Biotechnology and other securities investment were wildly speculative in the 1990s and investors were financially devastated when the market bubble burst. Europe realized after the fact that many of its major drug producers moved to the United States because excessive regulation made new drug development less profitable in Europe. Simultaneously corporate mergers have occurred globally because of the increasing costs of capital to fund the new brand of genomic research that is yielding miraculous scientific advancement at ever increasing costs. The liquidity and risk of venture capital availability for expensive early stage research is now generating new methods of developmental risk measurement that may lead to the "retailing of virtue" (Engelhardt, 1992) as a determinant of pricing capital's cost. The general wave of corporate financial turpitude (e.g. ImClone, Tyco, Enron, Worldcom) has created a new breed of risk-averse investors who are turning the very meaning of legal compliance requirements and corporate accounting into a market advantage for those who "do it right" with morally marketable fiscal transparency.

The Sarbanes-Oxley Act (2002) is lengthy, detailed and attempts (through the tedious law of corporate accounting and auditing) to toughen legal standards for regularly issued corporate financial reports. The pharmaceutical industry is capital intensive and the investment risks of research and development, as well as "creative marketing" represent an increasing "valuation black hole" for skittish public and private financial placements. Furthermore, the penalties levied against the Pfizer Corporation for more than $400 million (in relation to Pharmacia's unlawful and unethical promotion of off-label clinical indications of Neurontin) now opens the door to whistle-blower corporate employees in the marketing division who see personal profit as *Qui Tam* relators under the federal False Claims Act by documenting corporate attempts to defraud the federal government purchaser.

The casual response of company management may well be to hire more lawyers to monitor the policies and practices of their marketing and research departments. This is perhaps an excessive expense that is post hoc but not preventive through better operational policies and procedures. Another approach was conceptually published by Platt and Guyton (Platt & Guyton, 2002). They carefully point out that financial controls and reporting requirements are only one portion of the Sarbanes-Oxley Act and which covers "internal controls" both for *financial and non financial* activities. While most corporate lawyers and accountants initially gravitated to Section 404 of the law, Platt and Guyton point out that Section 302 holds CEOs, CFOs, and corporate boards responsible to certify full disclosure of "adequate" internal controls that evaluate non financial operational and regulatory risks material to the company's business.

Herein lies a moral opportunity for forward thinking companies to quantify their "standardized" non-financial risks to their investors and in turn be rewarded for such pre-hoc transparency in the venture capital markets. Attorneys will observe a dichotomy of thinking on the subject from their clients. In the end, as it has been in medicine and biomedical research, the ethical proposition of "doing it right" today becomes the "litigation nightmare" of tomorrow for clients who did not see the moral valuation of capital acquisition of yesterday.

IV. Retailing Virtue and the Financial Valuation of Compliance Leveraging®

Following the Platt and Guyton paper an unusually creative Compliance Leveraging® project team was created inside the Ernst and Young Accounting and Auditing firm (Watkins & Platt, 2002). These investigators have developed and registered the trademark of Compliance Leveraging®. This product is defined by its creators as follows:

"A groundbreaking system for automatically measuring, monitoring, evaluating, reporting, regulatory and contract compliance risk exposures and actions for the life sciences research industry and other related industries. The system is designed to be minimally intrusive to every day business operations and to foster an environment of continuous quality improvement."

Compliance Leveraging® as an all encompassing methodology of investment valuation in biotechnology in the pharmaceutical industry begins with the overarching view of "a march towards excellence" and that quality of research activities and marketing methods will become the driving determinant of how capital seeks out quality performers in the industry. The all encompassing nature of Compliance Leveraging® is laid out schematically in figures 2-6. Figure 4 gives a bar graph demonstration of how a numerical score attached to various modules of a corporation's operations would receive a relevant investment quality score based on best practices or standards of performance from professional societies regarding research ethics and general principals of how research projects should proceed. Figure 5 lays out the risk profile of an organization's regulated exposures during the Compliance Leveraging® process. From this diagram we can see that much will depend on the willingness of drug manufacturers to engage in sometime sensitive survey instruments conducted by outsiders in a corporation's operation. Confidentiality and protection of intellectual property rights will be a constant source of concern. What will determine the nature of cooperation will be the extent to which a Compliance Leveraging® reporting system will prove of benefit to internal operations of corporations and the advantage of that informational

Figure 2

Market Uses for Compliance Leveraging®

- Establish fair market values for a company's intellectual property using Compliance Leveraging®
- Potential to create pools of royalties tied to Compliance Leveraging® -vetted company intellectual property. These pools would be traded on Wall Street.
- Investors can use Compliance Leveraging® as a key quality differentiator among companies
- Companies can use Compliance Leveraging® as a key quality differentiator among research and products

Figure 3

Pharma 2003 And Beyond: Strategic Challenges and Solutions

The Pharmaceutical Industry Environment Is Affected By

- Risks from compliance uncertainties (e.g., regulatory inspection and enforcement) for new drug development
- Heightened regulatory and public (i.e., watchdog, media) standards and scrutiny
- Threats to free market pricing in the U.S.
- Delays of EMEA/FDA product approvals
- Higher drug development costs
- Increased regulatory scrutiny and potential legislation
- Increased post-marketing scrutiny and litigation

This means that company and industry valuations and growth are at risk

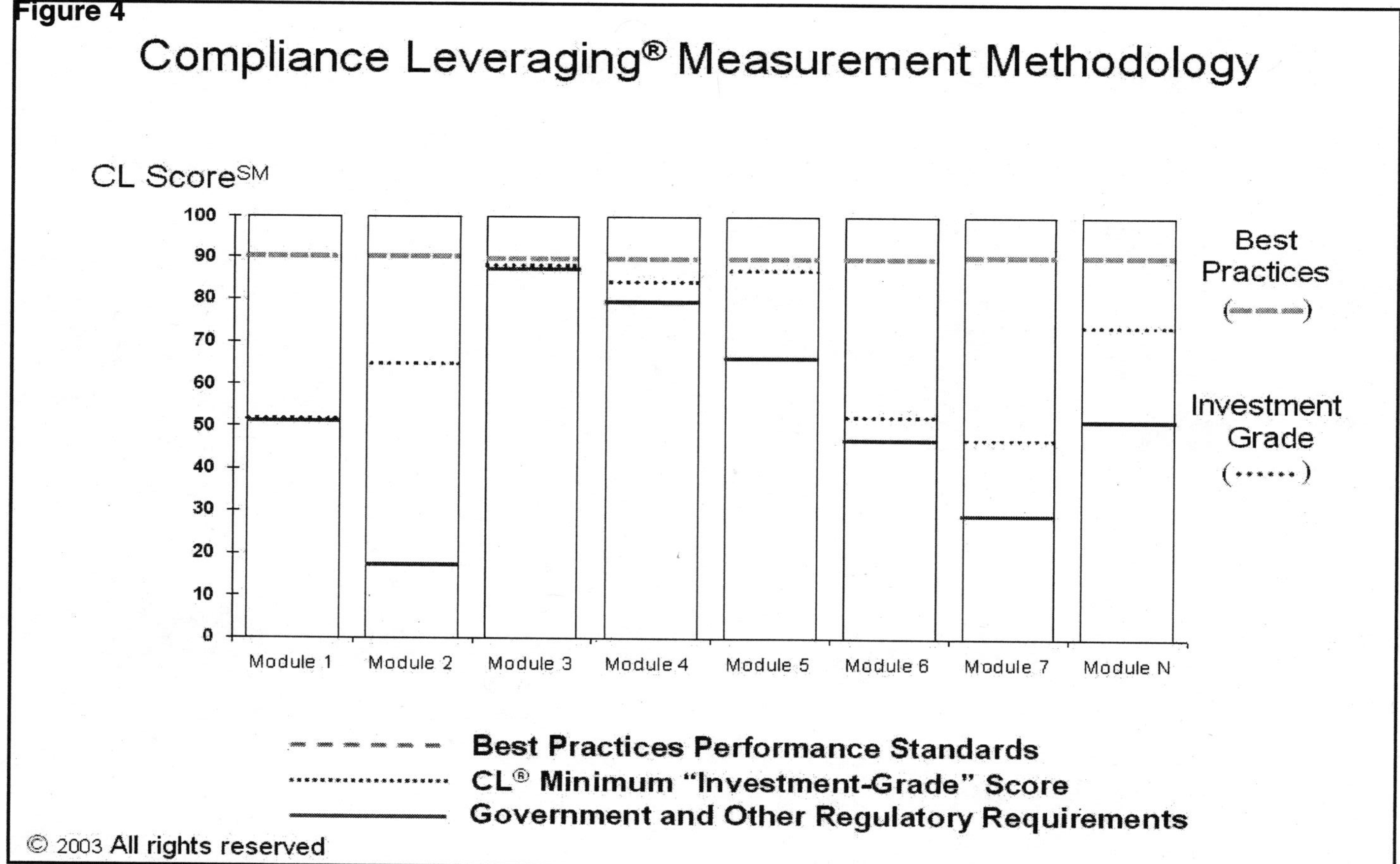
Figure 4
Compliance Leveraging® Measurement Methodology
CL Score℠
100
90
80
70
60
50
40
30
20
10
0
Module 1
Module 2
Module 3
Module 4
Module 5
Module 6
Module 7
Module N
Best Practices
Investment Grade
Best Practices Performance Standards
CL® Minimum "Investment-Grade" Score
Government and Other Regulatory Requirements
© 2003 All rights reserved

Figure 5

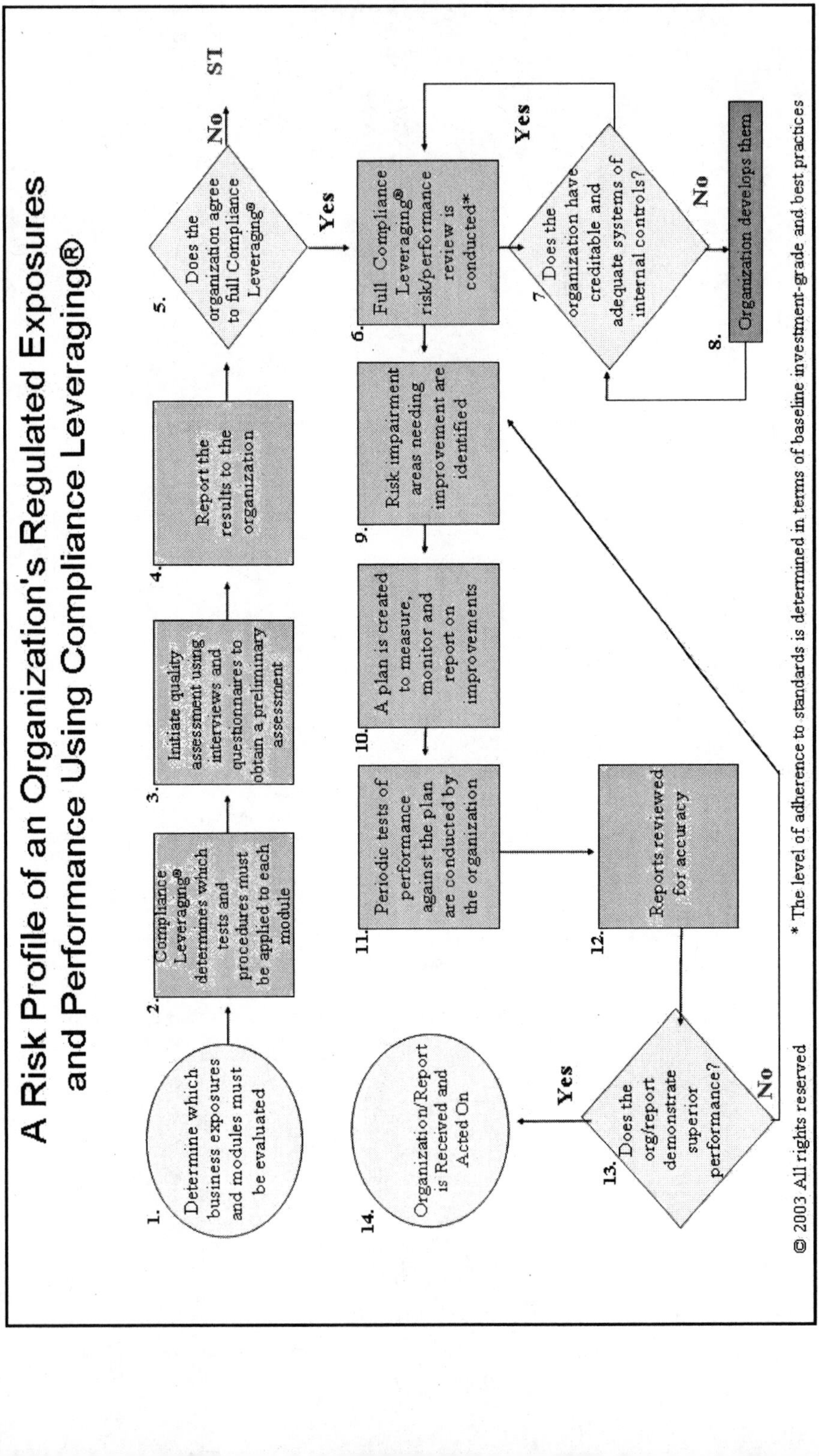

A Risk Profile of an Organization's Regulated Exposures and Performance Using Compliance Leveraging®

1. Determine which business exposures and modules must be evaluated
2. Compliance Leveraging® determines which tests and procedures must be applied to each module
3. Initiate quality assessment using interviews and questionnaires to obtain a preliminary assessment
4. Report the results to the organization
5. Does the organization agree to full Compliance Leveraging® — No → ST; Yes →
6. Full Compliance Leveraging® risk/performance review is conducted*
7. Does the organization have creditable and adequate systems of internal controls? — Yes → 6; No →
8. Organization develops them
9. Risk impairment areas needing improvement are identified
10. A plan is created to measure, monitor and report on improvements
11. Periodic tests of performance against the plan are conducted by the organization
12. Reports reviewed for accuracy
13. Does the org/report demonstrate superior performance? — Yes → 14; No → 9
14. Organization/Report is Received and Acted On

* The level of adherence to standards is determined in terms of baseline investment-grade and best practices

Figure 6

Compliance Leveraging®

Examples of Modules

- Good Manufacturing Practices (GMPs)
- Good Clinical Practices (GCPs)
- Good Laboratory Practices (GLPs)
- Adverse Event Reporting
- Protection of Research Volunteers (e.g., IRB and Informed Consent)
- Intellectual Property Protection (e.g., Material Transfer Agreements, Patent Filings, Licensing Agreements)
- Advertising and Promotion Standards & Adherence
- Regulatory Inspection Results
- Corporate Governance Standards

dissemination to the investment community of the world. While large drug manufacturers may feel presently content in their abilities to secure venture capital as needed, they will gravitate to such a mechanism more slowly than those primary research startup operations that are in developmental stage and have no products for sale in the world's markets. For those players, the advantages of Compliance Leveraging® in securing funds from nervous investors will play out more quickly in operation. If successful in practice, the early research companies will have greater corporate valuations when their single products are ready for broad market manufacture.

Interestingly, Platt and his group have devoted significant attention towards bringing the Compliance Leveraging® methodology to start up research operations outside the United States. Platt gave an extensive presentation at the Gene Forum in Tartu, Estonia in September 2003 entitled, "Rewarding Medical Research for Doing What is Right." Figure 6 lays out for medical researchers around the globe what the Compliance Leveraging® team believes to be those areas of research that should be rewarded for best practices and ethical behavior. It is apparent that some of these rely on cultural transformation of corporate behavior to affect the ethos of continuous quality improvement and transparent disclosure of research and its output to investors and ultimately the populations who will be consuming the drug product.

As Compliance Leveraging® is in its infancy, both pharmaceutical manufacturers, medical researchers, investment bankers and other speculators will be watching with interest to see if the area of medical research and development of drugs will eventually pursue a pathway of "transparent virtuous development" as a market driven ethos.

V. Research Ethics and Drug Innovation: Governmental Abuse of the Common Rule for Clinical Drug Trials and Healthcare Cost Containment

Nowhere in ethics and research are the opportunities for positive change and profit greater than in redefining the structure and meaning of research ethics for the protection of human subjects. Repetitive scandals in the clinical research universe of the United States have resulted in paralyzing regulatory strictures, incomplete measures and an outward migration of clinical trials to other nations that are quite pleased with acquisition of the trials and the funds that go with them (Kolata, 2004). Medical research, like capital, will move freely across the globe to where opportunities present themselves. The vast concentration of medical research laboratories created and funded by drug companies as exist in the Boston and Cambridge, Massachusetts area presently reflect the ability of the profit motive in the global drug industry to historically concentrate these resources in the USA. But can the research ethic scandals that are causing reflex regulation and paralysis of operations throughout the American research system continue as they are without migration of capital and laboratory operations elsewhere?

The legal problems for American medical research have been singularly affected by the scandal that occurred at Johns Hopkins University culminating in the Grimes vs. Kennedy Krieger Institute judgment (Grimes, 2002). In that opinion the Maryland Court of Appeals became the first American court to rule that the Nuremburg Code of Ethics and its successors would have legal standing in American legal disputes. The Johns Hopkins University was found to have participated in research that had no therapeutic purpose and posed risks to the subjects of the research without disclosure of the risks to the subjects. Such a legal finding has major implications for the conduct of governmental support in research universities as the Code of Federal Regulations requires such institutions to maintain oversight of research subject protections for patients receiving federal funds (See revised Note 2). The "common rule" is a regulatory extension of this federal legislation which implies that all research conducted in such institutions, whether it be paid for by governmental or private funds, shall adhere to the general ethical norms established through the Nuremburg Code of Ethics, the Declaration of Helsinki and those guidelines laid out in the Belmont Commission Report of the 1970s (See historical summary) (Rie, 2007). The common rule asserts federal control over a health care institution's freedom to freely contract privately for morally appropriate but politically proscribed research. This could be construed as an unconstitutional governmental taking of private property by eminent domain (Epstein, 1985).

Until the Grimes opinion (Grimes, 2002) no legal actions had been forthcoming. However, since that ruling a long series of federal reviews, rebukes and ultimately litigation in courts has occurred attempting to challenge and litigate against institutions for not sufficiently protecting the interests of research volunteers (Mello, 2003; Federman, 2003). A contemporary example of this was the trial and ultimately, vindication of the Fred Hutchinson Cancer Research Center at the University of Washington upholding the ethical correctness of entering research subjects into a twenty year old high-risk cancer chemotherapy protocol which was largely unsuccessful (Heath & Timmerman, 2004). The protocol involved early experiences in bone marrow transplantation for patients who had nearly universal risk of death. While the verdict upheld the notion that one should proceed to undertake hazardous research for fatal diseases or situation in which the prospect of success is remote, the verdict further supports the notion that informed consent of patients that enroll in research projects will remain a central cause of legal risk both for researchers and those who support the projects.

While this example is a clear and obvious one concerning the hazards and the risks of pursuing that which is new and original, other aspects of research ethics suggests that the cost contained health care institutions have been negligent in conflating health care cost containment activities with population based research. By keeping these activities outside the purview of research ethics they could avoid Institutional Review Board scrutiny. Greg Koski (the first director of the Office of Human Research Protections (OHRP) with the Department of Health and Human Services) stated that such was a common form for researchers to avoid the increasing frictions and difficulties of getting projects approved through IRBs (Koski, 2003). Koski also notes that, as is typical of a compliance-centered governmental regulatory culture, researchers look upon such activity as additional deadweight and resource consumptive activity without adding to the value of their science. He therefore advocates a switch from a regulatory culture to a culture of research responsibility. But to have such a responsibility culture requires the means with which to do it and some form of reward for those who "do it right." Thus, the concept of Koski may well find expression in the Compliance Leveraging® method for the drug industry (Engelhardt, 1992).

Compliance in industry is also regarded as deadweight to augment the costs of doing business and is not embraced as a driving form of cultural corporate policy. It therefore seems that wedding a cultural revolution in medical research ethics with one in drug innovation and manufacture are destined to be mutually interdependent because of the tight interplay of basic scientific research funded by governments that then flow into new and innovative ideas for the development of drugs and human disease treatments. The history of such a wedding dates back to the Bayh-Dole Act and has been summarized in some detail by Blumenthal (Blumenthal, 2003; Taurel, 2003; Moses, Braunwald, Martin, & Their, 2002; Crowley et al., 2004).

Kofke and Rie have summarized the history of research ethics and the law of health care system quality improvement as a conflict of cost containment and quality in medical care for patients (Kofke, 2003: Rie, 2007). They suggest widespread and systematic Nuremburg Code violations were occurring under the guise of quality assurance activities within the healthcare system. Particularly those activities that produce risk to patients without any benefit to the subjects and have a direct hypothesis and end point of reducing costs are likely to be regarded as both unethical and illegal activities that could well serve as the subject of human rights violations in American health care law. These activities are rarely brought to light unless outcome analysis of cost containment initiatives is undertaken with the view of reporting both positive and negative outcomes of the activities. But if such reports do occur, even from non-progenitors of the hypothesis, they meet the federal requirement of being research as they fall under the definition of "generalizable knowledge" in the Code of Federal Regulations.[2] Moral and legal analysis of this dilemma has been summarized (Kofke, 2003; Rie, 2007). A federally commissioned report (Hastings Center Report 2006; Hastings Center Report, 2007; Lynn, 2007) was recently submitted to the United

States Congress attempting to contain quality improvement activities in healthcare (and their implications for human subject protection) within the Code of Federal Regulations. It has been argued that such an approach conflates cost containment with population based negative outcome risks while threatening professional integrity of healthcare professionals and preventing disclosure of risks to patient populations (Grady, 2007; Rie, 2007).

Deciding when cost containment activities constitute research on human subjects is something of vital interest to the pharmaceutical industry (Grady, 2007). It is important that ethical issues of corporate process of care in the hospitals or the health system and health insurers, not be conflated with the sanctity and purity of scientific research and clinical trials in the development of new pharmaceuticals (Slutsky & Lavery, 2004; Steinbrook, 2002). It is apparent that the cost containment system has resulted in budget pressures to inadequately fund Institutional Review Boards (IRBs) in health care institutions where drug trials are occurring (Burman et. al., 2002). It is no longer morally appropriate for drug manufactures to assume that "indirect cost payments" are being wisely appropriated by health care institutions. Researchers feel constrained because they are facing the onerous burden of the common rule in a world where the financial court of public opinion has switched from primarily governmental finance to an industrial finance system of research funding (Crowley, 2004). Indeed, in American health care institutions engaged in research, the predominance of industrial financing over governmental financing has now resulted in a series of morally difficult questions, for the National Institutes of Health, the drug industry, the health equipment development industry, health care institutions and their researchers and OHRP regulators.

One of the areas where the pharmaceutical industry might take charge of this could be requiring independent IRBs that are not under the corporate purview of the institutions themselves, but are kept at arms length both from health care institutions and the pharmaceutical manufacturers.

The drug industry has been accused by Relman and Angell (Relman & Angell, 2002; Angell, 2000) of manipulating educational funds to the point that the American medical establishment must decide whether it can survive without those funds and develop some ethical norm acceptable to the American public (Hensley, 2004). Clearly the ethic of selling virtue and Compliance Leveraging® are a work in progress. Criticism of the industry should not be permitted to imply that governments have a legal right to expropriate private assets for non funded governmental "egalitarian" mandates (Epstein, 1985).

This tension is clearly visible in the writings of William Crowley (Seminara, Messager, Chatzidaki, Thresher, & Acierno, 2003; Landau, 2003; Crowley, 2004). Dr. Crowley is a distinguished researcher at the Massachusetts General Hospital that finds itself in the middle of a moral reformation of research ethics as a part of the Harvard Medical School. Harvard Medical School has decided, in a landmark institutional policy decision (Smallwood, 2004b), to develop an institute for therapeutic cloning research that will be totally separate from all federal funds and thus not directly constrained by the common rule. It is not the common rule that is on trial but rather the insertion of federal administrative moral pronouncements that seek to interfere in the legitimate ethics of medical and scientific research to advance human health. The pronouncements of the present federal administration of President Bush have injected a specific moral vision into the federal policies that now leaves the world of private sector research and drug development to develop a scientifically based ethos which will be fundamentally at variance with federal policy (Smallwood, 2004a; Kass, 2004). Whether federal policy will change in time is irrelevant to the question of whether science should pursue its aims in an ethical manner that divorces itself from governmental political control that violates public wishes and trust.

It has been the case in history before that scientists had to risk much for their ideas. William Harvey pursued a study of the anatomy of the circulatory system at a time that he was accused of being a grave robber seeking cadavers. Other researchers have come under criticism for developing vaccines or drugs by using themselves as research subjects so as not to expose others to the risks.

The quest for scientific truth and a medical ethos of research devoid of specific political moral views obstructing medical progress is presently much in the forefront of this discussion (Shapin, 1995; Horton, 2004). The recent death of the 40th President of the United States, Ronald Reagan, and the strong advocacy of his widow to advance therapeutic cloning research for the treatment of Alzheimer's Disease clearly champions the thirst for medical truth and health care progress over a historically reactive moral and religion based obstruction of science in secular pluralist societies. This long book has not yet been written to its conclusion but the issue of opportunity in this area for the drug industry and its legal component is visible. Developing a policy of funding independent IRBs devoid of governmental restriction (imposed by the common rule's political application to private funds) will do much to clarify the confusion that exists in medical research, ethics, cost containment and medical publication ethics. The ferocity with which critics and politicians have attacked the private use of funds in the drug industry's funding of medical education and research borders on a political expropriation of privately owned money. This may be an unconstitutional taking antithetical to the best interests of the citizenry (Epstein, 1985). How the industry chooses to structure its future in this arena will be the new reformation of research ethics and financial finitude in the care of patients.

Notes

1. Drug trials refer to this risk as the "Number Needed to Harm." For Xigris® it is 0.2%. This means that the drug will need to be infused into 500 patients before one patient develops a drug induced brain hemorrhage.
2. A recent example may be found in an article by Suarez and an editorial by Heros in the *Journal of Neurosurgery* (Suarez, 2004; Heros, 2004).

   Briefly, a hospital chose to prohibit the use of human albumin infusions for treatment of patients with ruptured cerebral arterial aneurysms as part of a general formulary restriction in the use of albumin. Albumin had being part of professional standards of care for more than 25 years. However, Type I scientific evidence in support of this moderately costly treatment was lacking despite a generation of animal research supporting the hypothesis for its use. The matter came to publication when physician investigators sought industrial research funds to conduct a retrospective analysis of the hospital's experiment in medicinal formulary restriction.

   IRB approval was required and granted for retrospective review of this practice for a one year period with a comparison of the prior year's practice when albumin was available to the physicians. The published results were negative for this population based intervention. The hospital subsequently reinstated the permissibility and availability of albumin for this patient population.

   The ORHP reviewed the matter and declared the proscription of albumin by the hospital to NOT be research. The OHRP concluded its investigation without any action. Subsequent to the Suarez publication the NIH changed its research funding priorities in the area of stroke and other acute ischemic neurological conditions. Suarez was funded to pursue this work prospectively and the NIH awarded a multi center trial of albumin to improve outcomes in stroke (*See Suarez Matter*) (Rie, 2007).

Acknowledgments

Christopher Marrone and Thane Wettig of the Eli Lilly Company generously supplied industrial developmental history and global pricing information concerning Xigris® global marketing.

Leslie Platt and Philip Cyr and Joshua Berlin provided information to present the Compliance Leveraging® project and its details from the Ernst and Young organization for this presentation and publication.

However, the views expressed herein about Compliance Leveraging® and related matters are solely those of the author.

References

Angell, M. (2000). 'The pharmaceutical industry: To whom is it accountable?', *The New England Journal of Medicine,* 343(19), 1415–16.

Baily, M.A., Bottrell, M., Lynn, J., Jennings, B. (2006). 'The ethics of using QI methods to improve health care quality and safety', *Hasting Center Report.* [Online]. Available: http://www.thehastingscenter.org

Bernard, G.R., Vincent, J.L., Laterre, P.F., LaRosa, SP., & Dhainaut, J.F. (2001). 'Recombinant human protein C worldwide evaluation in severe sepsis (Prowess) study group,' *The New England Journal of Medicine,* 344, 699-709.

Blumenthal, D. (2003). 'Academic industrial relations in the life sciences', *The New England Journal of Medicine,* 349(25), 2452-2459.

Bok, D.C. (2003). *Universities in the Marketplace: The Commercialization of Higher Education.* Princeton, NJ: Princeton University Press.

Burman, W.J., Reeves, R.R., Cohn, D.L., & Schooley, R.T. (2001). 'Breaking the camel's back: Multicenter clinical trials and local institutional review boards', *Annals of Internal Medicine,* 134(2), 152-157.

Code of Federal Regulations, Title 45. (2001). Protection of human subjects. Department of Health and Human Services. National Institutes of Health. Office for Protection from Research Risk, part 46. [Online]. Available: http://ohrp.osophs.dhhs.gov/humansubjects/guidance/45cfr46.htm

Crowley, W.F., Sherwood, L., Salber, P., Scheinberg, D., Slavkin, H., Tilson, H., Reece, E.A., Ctanese, V., Johnson, S.B., Dobs, A., Genel, M., Korn, A., Reame, N., Bonow, R., Grebb, J., & Rimoin, D. (2004). 'Clinical research in the United States at a crossroads: Proposal for a novel public-private partnership to establish a national clinical research enterprise', *Journal of the American Medical Association,* 291(9), 1120-1126.

Danzon, P.M. & Furukawa, M.F. (2003). 'Prices and availability of pharmaceuticals: Evidence from nine countries', *Health Affairs* (On-line), w3, 521-536.

Dellinger, P.R., Carlet, J.M., Masur, H., Gerlach, H., Calandra, T., Cohen, J., Gea-Banacloche, J., Keh, D., Marshall, J.C. Parker, M.M., Ramsay, G., Zimmerman, J.L., Vincent, J., & Levy, M. (2004). 'Surviving sepsis: Campaign guidelines for management of severe sepsis and septic shock', *Intensive Care Medicine,* 30, 536-555.

DeVries, R. (2004, February 8). 'Businesses are buying the ethics they want', *The Wall Street Journal,* B-02.

Eichacker, P. Q., Natanson, C., & Danner, R.L. (2006). 'Surviving sepsis-practice guidelines marketing campaigns and Eli Lilly', *The New England Journal of Medicine,* 355 (16), 1640-1642.

Engelhardt, H.T. & Rie, M.A. (1986). 'Intensive care units, scarce resources and conflicting principles of justice', *Journal of the American Medical Association,* 253, 1159-1164.

Engelhardt, H.T. & Rie, M.A. (1988). 'Morality for the medical industrial complex: A code of ethics for the mass marketing of health care', *The New England Journal of Medicine,* 319, 1086-1089.

Engelhardt, H.T. & Rie, M.A. (1992). 'Selling virtue: Ethics as a profit maximizing strategy in health care delivery', *Journal of Health and Social Policy,* 4(1), 27-35.

Epstein, R.A. (1985). *Takings: Private Property and the Power of Eminent Domain.*

Cambridge, MA: Harvard University Press.
Federman, D.D. (2003). 'Minimizing risk in clinical research', *Annals of Internal Medicine,* 139(1), 71-72.
Fleming, C. (2003, November 17). 'Europeans face health cuts: Insurers are reluctant to fill gaps left by cuts in government benefits', *The Wall Street Journal.* [Online]. Available: http://www.wsj.com/article/0,,SB106902036177290500,00html
Friedman, M. (2002). *Capitalism and Freedom.* Chicago: University of Chicago Press.
Grady, C. (2007). 'Quality improvement and ethical oversight', *Annals of Internal Medicine,* 146, 677-678.
Grimes vs. Kennedy Krieger Institute. (2002). Maryland Court of Appeals, 366MD.29, 782 A2D, 807.
Graham, J. (2004). 'Bitter medicine: US – Canada prescription drug black market is not free trade', *The National Review* [Online]. Available: http://www.nationalreview.com/comment/graham200403290856.asp
Heath, D. & Timmerman, L. (2004). 'Jury finds Hutch not negligent in 4 deaths', *Seattle Times.* [Online]. Available: http://www.seatletimes.nwsource.com/html/local-news/2001899403_hutchverdict0
Hensley, S. (2004, April 19). 'Doctors continuing education needs prescription for change', *The Wall Street Journal.* [Online]. Available: http://www.wsj.com/documents/accme.pdf
Heros, R. (2004). 'Fluid management,' *Journal of Neurosurgery,* 100, 581-582.
Horton, R. (2004). 'The dawn of McScience', *The New York Review of Books,* LI(4), 7-9.
Jenkins, H.W. (2004, April 28). 'Why not import drugs from fantasyland?', *The Wall Street Journal,* A-17.
Jennings, B., Baily, M.A., Botrell, M., & Lynn, J., (2007). 'Health care quality improvement: Ethical and regulatory issues', The Hastings Center. [Online]. Available: http://www.thehastingscenter.org
Kanavos, P. & Reinhardt, U. (2003). 'Reference pricing for drugs: Is it compatible with US healthcare? *Health Affairs,* 22(3), 16-30.
Kanavos, P. (2004). 'Pharmaceutical regulation in Europe', (Manuscript in preparation) *Health Affairs.*
Kass, L. (2004, March 3). 'We don't play politics with science', *The Washington Post.* [Online]. Available: http://www.irbforum.org/user/mail
Kolata, G. (2004, March 5). 'Companies facing ethical issues as drugs are tested overseas', *The New York Times.*
Koski, G. (2003). 'Research regulations and responsibility: Confronting the compliance myth – A reaction to Professor Gatter', *Emory Law Journal,* 52(1), 404-416.
Kofke, W.A. & Rie, M.A. (2003). 'Research ethics and law of healthcare system quality improvement: The conflict of cost containment and quality,' *Critical Care Medicine,* 31[Suppl.], S143–S152.
Landau, M. (2003). 'Protein pegged to onset of puberty', *Focus News from the Harvard Medical Dental & Public Health Schools,* November.
Lynn, J., Baily, M.A.., Buttrell, M., et al, (2007). 'The Ethics of Using Quality Improvement Methods in HealthCare', *Annals of Internal Medicine,* 146, 666-673.
Matthews, A.W. & Hamilton, D. (2004, February 18). 'FDA takes steps toward allowing generic versions of biotech drugs', *The Wall Street Journal,* A-1.
Moses, H., Braunwald, E., Martin, J.F., & Their, S.O. (2002). 'Collaboration with industry: Choices for the academic medical center', *The New England Journal of Medicine,* 347(17), 1371-1375.

Peterson, A. (2004, April 13). 'Designing a better place to die: Long focused on sustaining life at all costs, some ICUs add hospice-like services', *The Wall Street Journal,* D-1.
Platt, L.A. & Guyton, O. (2003). 'A recipe for returning investor confidence: Zeroing in on non-financial risk exposures', *The Journal of Biolaw and Business,* 6(2), 2-4.
Regalado, A. (2003, September 18). 'To sell pricey drug, Eli Lilly fuels debate over rationing', *The Wall Street Journal,* A-1.
Relman, A.S. & Angell, M. (2002). 'America's other drug problem: How the drug industry distorts medicine and politics', *The New Republic,* 227(25), 27-41.
Rie, M.A. (1995). 'The Oregonian ICU: Multi-tiered monetarized morality in health insurance law', *The Journal of Law, Medicine and Ethics,* 23(2), 149-166.
Rie, M.A. (1997). 'Rationing critical care services in the United States', *Current Opinion in Critical Care,* 3, 329-333.
Rie, M. A. (2003). 'Respect for human life in the world of intensive care units: Secular and Reform Jewish reflection on the Roman Catholic view.' In H.T. Engelhardt and M.J. Cherry (Eds.), *Allocating Scarce Medical Resources: Roman Catholic Perspectives* (pp. 43-52). Washington, DC: Georgetown University Press.
Rie, M.A. & Kofke, W.A. (2007). 'Nontherapeutic quality improvement: The conflict of organizational ethics and societal rule of law.' *Critical Care Medicine,* 35[Suppl.] S66-S84.
Sarbanes-Oxley Act. (2002). Public Law 107-204.
Seminara, S.B., Messager, S., Chatzidaki, E.E., Thresher, R.R., & Acierno, J.S. (2003).
'The GPR54 gene as a regulator of puberty', *The New England Journal of Medicine,* 349(17), 1614-1627.
Shapin, S. (1995). *A Social History of Truth.* Chicago: University of Chicago Press.
Slutsky, A.S. & Lavery, J.V. (2004). 'Data safety and monitoring boards', *The New England Journal of Medicine,* 350(11), 1143-1147.
Smallwood, S. (2004a, March 1). 'Bush drops two supporters of embryo research from bioethics panel', *The Chronicle of Higher Education.* [Online]. Available: http://chronicle.com/daily/2004/03/2004030103n.html
Smallwood, S. (2004b, March 1). 'To avoid restrictions, Harvard will create a stem-cell center with private funds', *The Chronicle of Higher Education.* [Online]. Available: http://chronicle.com/daily/2004/03/200403015n.html
Steinbrook, R. (2002). 'Improving protection for research subjects', *The New England Journal of Medicine,* 346(18), 1425-1430.
Suarez, J.I., Shannon, L., Zaidat, O.O., Suri, M.F., Singh, G., Lynch, G., & Selman, W.R. (2004). 'Effect of human albumin administration on clinical outcome and hospital cost in patients with subarachnoid hemorrhage', *Journal of Neurosurgery,* 100, 585-590.
Taurel, S. (2003, November 3). 'Hands off my industry', *The Wall Street Journal.* [Online]. Available: http://online.wsj.com/article/106782096631988000.00html
Troug, R.D., Brock, D.W., Cook, D.J., Danis, M., Luce, J.M., Rubenfield, G.D. & Levy, M.M. (2006). 'Rationing in the Intensive Care Unit', *Critical Care Medicine,* 34, 958-963.
Van den Berghe, G., Wouters, P., Weekers, F., Verwaest, C., Bruynincx, F., Schetz, M., Vlasselaers, D., Ferdinande, P., Lauwers, P., & Bouillon, R. (2001). 'Intensive insulin therapy in critically ill patients', *The New England Journal of Medicine,* 345, 1359-1367.
Watkins, W.D. & Platt, L.A. (2002). 'Translating research quality into greater global investment', *Partners with Vision: Global Pharmaceutical Report: Ernst and Young Accountants Annual Report,* December 23-25.

Time, Money and the Market for Drugs[1]

John C. Goodman
National Center for Policy Analysis, Dallas

I. Introduction

Americans spent about $275 billion a year on prescription drugs in 2006.[2] When over-the-counter remedies are added the total of legally purchased chemical entities climbs to nearly $300 billion. Although the expense is a small part of our nation's $2.1 trillion health care bill, the dollars involved are substantial, amounting to more than $2,600 per household per year.[3]

Given the enormity of it all, one would expect a robust, well-functioning market for drugs, especially those that are consumed by large numbers of people. In fact, what we find is a market with many anomalies. Consider that:

- Millions of Americans who did not even have arthritis took such arthritic pain relief medicines as Vioxx and Bextra (since removed from the market) and Celebrex (still on the market) when less risky, less expensive over-the-counter remedies would have been more appropriate.[4] The fact that these drugs require a doctor's prescription suggests that millions of patients were getting poor advice from their physicians.[5]
- While Americans over-consume some drugs, such as Ritalin and antibiotics (and in the later case degrade the effectiveness of the

H.T. Engelhardt, Jr. and J. Garrett (eds), *Innovation and the Pharmaceutical Industry* (pp. 153–183).

drugs for society as a whole), we under-consume other drugs. In fact, for such conditions as diabetics, hypertension, asthma, obesity and high cholesterol, our use of effective drug therapies appears to be a small fraction of what it should be (Kleinke, 2004).

- While there has been a rising chorus of complaints in recent years over the high cost of prescription drugs, the vast majority of patients overpay for their drugs—in part because they fail to employ shopping techniques they routinely use when they purchase other goods and services and in part because they do not even know about therapeutic or generic substitutes (Herrick, 2004a).
- Whereas lawyers and other professionals routinely communicate with their clients by phone and by email, it is very rare for physicians to communicate with patients that way—even for routine prescriptions (Liebhaber & Grossman, 2006).[6]
- Whereas the computer is ubiquitous in our society and studies show that electronic medical records systems have the capacity to improve quality and greatly reduce medical errors (including 200,000 adverse drug events), no more than one in five physicians or one in four hospitals have such systems (Hillestad, 2005).
- Despite the fact that many new drug therapies are less expensive and more effective than competing therapies, many health insurance plans (especially Medicaid and Medicare) do not cover them.
- Whereas lawyers routinely advertise in search of former Vioxx users who can serve as plaintiffs in lawsuits against drug manufacturers, doctors and doctor groups almost never advertise to attract patients with arthritis or, for that matter, any other chronic illness.

Interestingly, virtually all of these features of our health care system are the direct result of the way in which we pay for health care, especially the way we pay doctors. That is, we compensate physicians in ways that are different from the way we pay for other professional services and those differences create problems in the medical marketplace that do not arise in other markets. The principal payment methods, moreover, are not the natural result of free market forces. They are instead the product of distortions created by public policies. And in most cases, mistakes embedded in the public policies and in the payment mechanisms reflect a failure to understand the economics of time.

II. Time as a Rationing Device

Many Europeans believe that in America health is rationed by price, whereas in Europe it is generally made available for free. In fact, health care is almost as free at the point of consumption in America as it is in Europe.

On the average, every time Americans spend a dollar on physicians' services, only 10 cents is paid out-of-pocket; the remainder is paid by a third party (an employer, insurance company or government) (CMS, 2006). From a purely economic perspective, then, our incentive is to consume these services until their value to us is only 10 cents on the dollar. Moreover, millions of Americans do not even pay the 10 cents. Medicaid enrollees, Medicare enrollees who have medigap insurance, and people who get free care from community health centers and hospital emergency rooms pay nothing at the point of service. Most members of HMOs and PPOs make only a modest copayment for primary care services. Clearly we are not rationing health care on the basis of price.

But if not price rationing, how do we ration physicians' services? We ration the same way other developed countries ration care. We force people to pay for care with their time.

The services of physicians are a scarce resource and a valuable resource. So at a price of zero (or at a very low out-of-pocket price) the demand for these services far exceeds supply. Unable to bring supply and demand into balance with money prices, our system does that next best thing. We ration by waiting.

Like money, time is valuable. So the higher the time cost to patients, the lower will be the demand for physicians' services. If we think of market wages as a proxy for the opportunity cost of time (the next best use of time), then the cost of an hour of time is higher for a high-income patient than a low-income patient. Accordingly, in high-income areas shorter waiting times will be needed to ration the same amount of care than in low-income areas. The longest waiting times of all will tend to be in inner-city hospital emergency rooms, where the money price is usually zero and people have a very low opportunity cost of time.

Some may object that the real demand for physicians' services is not determined by time or money but by the amount of sickness in society. Yet this view is surely wrong.[7] Consider that 12 billion times a year Americans purchase over-the-counter (OTC) drugs and suppose that on their way to these acts of self-medication all of the purchasers stopped to get professional advice. To meet that demand, we would need 25 times the number of primary care physicians we currently have (Rottenberg, 1990, pp. 27-28)!

Now suppose that instead of physically going to a doctor's office, purchasers of OTC drugs could get professional advice by means of telephone or email. The same problem would arise. The demand for advice would far exceed the ability of physicians to supply it.

In general, patients cannot have the best of both worlds. If they communicate with doctors the way they communicate with lawyers, they will have to be charged money prices for the use of the doctor's time (the way they pay legal fees). Health care cannot be both easily accessible and free. It must be one or the other. Waiting is not an accidental byproduct of modern health care delivery. It is an essential ingredient.

Forcing patients to pay for health care with their time is not the only form of non-price rationing. An alternative is to reduce demand through quality degradation. The classic example is the "Medicaid mill," where patients spend very little time with physicians and receive very little health care. Instead, the doctor-patient contact is a legal necessity in order for the patient to acquire a prescription or such devices as syringes and asthma inhalers—all of which can be resold on the street (Passley, Brodt, & Jones, 1993; Levy & Luo, 2005).

There is also evidence that physicians have responded to Medicare's attempts to ratchet down their fees by reducing nonprice amenities, spending less time with patients and scheduling more follow up visits (Herrick, 2002; Hawryluk, 2002). On the whole, however, it appears that most physicians prefer to reduce nonhealth amenities and lower the quality of care only very reluctantly.

We know that when price has been artificially constrained in other markets, quality can be observed to change in order to equate supply and demand. Before airline fares were deregulated, the Civil Aeronautics Board kept prices artificially high—thus creating excess supply. Unable to attract customers by lowering prices, the airlines responded with such quality improvements as more frequently scheduled flights, more seat space and other amenities (Dolan & Goodman, 1995). Rent control laws, by contrast, lead to excess demand. Unable to raise rents, landlords find that they can spend less on maintenance and allow other quality deterioration and still lease their housing units (Tucker, 1990).

Why don't we see more quality deterioration in medicine? It may be that professional ethics, professional pride or perhaps the threat of malpractice litigation prevents doctors from doing things that are clearly in their financial self-interest. Unfortunately, these same motivations do not seem to work in the opposite direction, however. As we shall see, there are major quality improvements that are not being made because they are not in the physician's financial self-interest.

There is nothing normal or natural about rationing by waiting. The exterior offices of lawyers, accountants, architects and other professionals are called "reception areas," not "waiting rooms," and very little waiting actually goes on. The reason: waiting is a wasteful way to allocate resources. In markets for other goods and services, the consumer's cost is typically the producer/seller's income. But when people pay for goods with their time, their waiting cost is not someone else's income. It is a net social loss.

To try a back-of-the-envelope calculation, let us assume that a roundtrip doctor visit (door-step to door-step) takes about 1-1/2 hours. Assuming an hourly wage of $20 and five doctor visits per person per year, the annual cost of waiting for the country as a whole is close to $45 billion. That sum of money, judiciously spent, could insure every (long-term) uninsured person in America.

Rationing by waiting is not only socially wasteful, it is a poor way of delivering health care. Under such a system, there is no way to insure that those who need care the most get it first, or even get care at all (Goodman, Musgrave, & Herrick, 2004). Human resource experts estimate that one-quarter of physicians visits are for conditions that patients could easily treat themselves (Powell, 2003). Balanced against these "unnecessary" visits are all of the potential visitors who choose not to seek care. Undoubtedly, many of those are "necessary" but unrealized visits; and, hence, the patients go without professional treatment.

The fact that patients cannot consult with physicians by telephone or email leads to two bad consequences. First, the unnecessary visitors (say, patients who have a cold) expect at least a prescription in return for their investment of waiting time and all too often the drug will be an antibiotic. For physicians, these prescriptions may be thought of as a convenient way of maintaining a patient clientele (Soumerai & Lipton, 1995). Were telephone consultations possible, the physician would more likely recommend an OTC remedy, thus avoiding the cost of waiting for the patient and the cost of degrading the effectiveness of antibiotics for society as a whole.

The second bad consequence is that rationing by waiting imposes disproportionate costs on patients who need more frequent contact with physicians. Because the chronically ill need more interactions with their doctors, they face above-average waiting costs. This may be one reason why so many are not getting the one thing they most need from primary physicians and the thing that is most likely to prevent more serious and costly health problems later on—a prescription. Kleinke (2004) estimates that:

- If the National Heart, Living and Blood Institute (NHLBI) guidelines were followed, the number of Americans receiving drug therapy for hypertension would more than double—rising from 20 million to 43 million.
- If NHLBI guidelines were followed for asthma patients, the number of asthma medications would increase from two-fold to ten-fold.
- If the guidelines were followed for the treatment of obesity, the number of Americans treated with drugs for obesity would be 12 times the current number.
- If the guidelines were followed for the treatment of high cholesterol levels, the number of Americans taking statin drugs (such as Lipitor) would be 10 to 15 times its current level (Kleinke, 2004, p. 37).

The ability to consult with doctors by telephone or email could be a boon to the chronically ill. Face-to-face meetings with physicians would be infrequent, especially if patients learned how to monitor their conditions and manage their own care. Remote consultations could be used to change a drug prescription or determine whether an office visit was needed.

So why don't we see physician entrepreneurs exploiting the opportunity to meet the unmet needs of the chronically ill? The reason: under current payment practices physicians would be financially worse off if they tried to do so.

III. The Failure to Use Time as a Reimbursement Device

In the United States, there is probably a conference being held on some aspect of health care every week. At the many conferences organized and attended by third-party payers, a recurring topic is: how can we get doctors to change what they are doing? The irony is that doctors in general do what third-party payers pay them to do. If we want to change doctor behavior, we must start by changing third-party payer behavior.

Lawyers are typically paid hourly fees and the fee is the same regardless of how the hour is spent. That is as it should be. Suppose it were not so. Suppose a lawyer got paid $200 an hour for preparation and delivery of jury summations but only $10 an hour for jury selection. Clients would tend to get great summations of their cases, all presented to the wrong set of jurors.

If you are a client, you want your lawyer to allocate her time so that the last hour spent on any one aspect of your case contributes just as much to a legal victory as the last hour spent on any other aspect of your case. Only if your lawyer's time is allocated that way will you maximize the probability of success for a given input of time. To make sure that the attorney's incentives are to do just that, every hour of the attorney's time must be compensated at the same rate.

Unfortunately, this common sense principle is routinely ignored in medicine. It is ignored by the federal government in Medicare, by state governments in Medicaid and by almost all private payers as well. In general, fee-for-systems pay doctors different fees for different services. So, for example, a physician may get paid at one rate for a hour spent on task A, a lower rate for an hour spent on task B, and perhaps nothing at all for an hour spent on task C—even though C may be better for the patient than either A or B.

Why do doctors avoid telephone and email consultations? The short answer is: they do not get paid for these types of consultations (Herrick, 2007).[9] Medicare does not pay for these types of consultations, nor does Medicaid or most private insurance. In general, doctors only get paid to see patients in their offices. Doctors paid under capitation arrangement would seem to have different incentives. But, as discussed below, HMO doctors ration their time by waiting as well.

Why are most medical records still stored on paper? Why aren't they instead stored electronically, where they can be used to coordinate care, measure quality and reduce medical errors? Again, the short answer is: there is no financial incentive to do these things. For the most part, we collect, manage and distribute most medical information by means of "pen, paper, telephone, fax and Post-it note" because doctors cannot get compensated for making an investment in computer technology (Kleinke, 2005). Even those who argue that computerized systems are potentially profitable admit that all the benefits of quality improvement redound not to the doctor, but to patients and insurance companies (Miller, West, Brown, Sim, & Ganchoff, 2005).

Why do doctors so often prescribe brand name drugs and fail to tell patients about generic, therapeutic and over-the-counter substitutes? Why do they typically not know the price of the drugs they prescribe or the costs of alternatives? The short answer is: they do not get paid to know these things.

Learning about drug prices is not a simple exercise. As explained below, there is a national market for drugs, and prices vary radically. Knowing the current best price, knowing where the patient can obtain that price, and knowing all the prices and availabilities of all the alternatives is demanding and time consuming. Moreover, for the doctor it is time that is not compensated.

A related question is: why do doctors not spend more time helping their patients find the most appropriate drug therapy? Before it was removed from the market, most of the patients taking Vioxx did not have arthritis and were taking an inappropriate pain remedy. Further, the best predictor of whether a patient was taking Vioxx was whether a third-party payer was paying the bill (Doshi, Brandt, & Stuart, 2004). As noted, we can infer that a lot of patients were getting a lot of bad advice. Unfortunately, the doctor's incentives are to practice medicine the way other doctors practice medicine and patients are unlikely to ask many questions if someone else is paying the bill.

What about entrepreneurship? Could a physician gain a competitive advantage by being better informed about drug therapies and their appropriateness and their prices? Probably. But the real question is not whether these additional patient-pleasing services would attract more patients; it is whether these activities would increase the physician's income. Time spent researching drugs is time not spent with patients. In the language of other professions, these are "non-billable hours." Further, time spent on these activities is time not spent on activities that are billable. All too often, the incentives are to avoid uses of time that are not compensated.

One consequence of rationing by waiting is that the time of the primary care physician is usually fully booked, unless she is starting a new practice or working in a rural area. This means that almost all the physician's hours are spent on billable activities. Further, there is very little incentive to compete for patients the way other professionals compete for clients. The reason: neither the loss of existing patients nor a gain of new patients would affect the doctor's income very much. Loss of existing patients for example, would tend to reduce the average waiting time for the remaining patients. But with shorter waiting times, those patients would be encouraged to make more visits. Conversely, a gain of new patients would tend to lengthen waiting times, causing some patients to reduce their number of visits. Because time, not money, is the currency we use to pay for care, the physician doesn't benefit (very much) from patient pleasing improvements and is not harmed (very much) by an increase in patient irritations.

This insight may explain why doctors in some areas now refuse to take any new Medicare patients.[10] Assuming that retirees have a lower opportunity cost of time, odds are they are willing to out-wait the nonelderly patients. And since Medicare pays at a lower rate than private insurance, such crowding out actually lowers the physician's income. Medicaid typically pays even less than Medicare and since Medicaid patients also tend to have a lower-than-average opportunity cost of time, small wonder that many doctors refuse to see any new Medicaid patients.[11]

The special characteristics of a market in which services are rationed by time may help explain another phenomenon: Why does the atmosphere of a typical doctor's office more resemble a Department of Motor Vehicles than a typical private sector firm? In one recent survey, only 38 percent of people in telephone contact with their physicians office, (e.g. to make an appointment or renew a prescription) said they were treated courteously.[12] This is an amazing statistic. It is doubtful that a for-profit firm could survive in any other competitive market if more than half its customers were not treated courteously.

The treatment of the chronically ill is especially interesting in this context, since in almost all cases optimal treatment involves drug therapies. Numerous studies have shown that chronic patients can manage their own care, with lower costs and as good or better health outcomes than with traditional care. Diabetics, for example, can monitor their own glucose level, alter their medication when needed and reduce the number of trips they make to hospital emergency rooms (Benjamin, 2002).[13] Similarly, asthmatics can monitor their peak airflow, adjust their medications and also reduce the need for physician and emergency room services.[14]

The problem is: to take full advantage of these opportunities, patients need training; and they rarely get such training. An emergency room doctor can save herself and future doctors the necessity of a lot of future emergency room care if she takes the time to educate the mother of a diabetic or asthmatic child about how to monitor and manage the child's health care. But time spent on such education again, is not billable. And since activities that reduce emergency room visits eventually will probably lower overall future doctor incomes, there is no economic incentive to engage in them.

Further, if primary care physicians attempted to specialize in the treatment of the chronically ill they would likely attract a preponderance of "hard" cases. This would not be a problem if they were compensated by the amount of time they spend on each case. But since they typically are compensated based on procedures, rather than time, they lose money on hard cases (which take more time) and try to make up for the losses with the gains from the easy cases (which take less time). Thus, physicians who attract an above-average number of difficult-to-treat cases will experience a reduction in their hourly income.

Would physicians practice medicine differently if they were paid differently? There is ample evidence that the answer is: yes. Surprisingly, however, the predominant forms of compensation currently used throughout the developed world do not seem to matter very much.

Consider general practitioners working in four different settings: (1) a U.S. HMO, (2) Britain's National Health Service, (3) Canada's Medicare, and (4) U.S. private practice. Since the first two arrangements are capitated, physicians get no extra income for an additional visit. Since the last two are fee-for-service, physicians in these systems get extra income for additional visits. Despite these very different sets of incentives, HMO and fee-for-service doctors in the United States have very similar practice patterns—at least in terms of the time spent with patients.[15] And the practices of Canadian and British doctors are more similar to each other than to their capitated and fee-for-service counterparts in the United States. Relative to the U.S. average, British and Canadian patients see their doctors slightly more often, but there is less time spent with the doctor on each visit (Goodman, Musgrave, & Herrick, 2004). Note that relative to private practice physicians, HMO doctors may be less free to prescribe certain drugs and order expensive tests; and this is even more true for doctors in Britain and Canada.

In all four settings it appears that physicians act as though they are paid to engage in face-to-face contact with as many patients as demand their services. To equate supply with demand, in all four cases the primary form of rationing is rationing by waiting. However, because there is no money price in Britain or Canada, compared to modest copayments in the United States, the rationing problem is greater and physicians respond to that problem in part by reducing average time spent with patients. Note that what is missing in all four settings is any opportunity for doctors and patients to eliminate wasteful waiting time by changing the nature of the financial transaction.

To find radically different physician behavior, one must look at markets where third-party payers are not involved at all, such as the markets for cosmetic and lasik surgery. Unlike other forms of surgery, the typical cosmetic surgery patient can (a) find a package price in advance covering all services and facilities, (b) compare prices prior to the surgery and (c) pay a price that is lower in real terms than the price charged a decade ago for comparable procedures—despite the considerable technological innovations in the interim (Herrick, 2006).

Ironically, many physicians who perform cosmetic surgery also perform other types of surgery. The difference in behavior is apparently related to how they are paid. A cosmetic surgery transaction has all the characteristics of a normal market transaction in which the seller has a financial interest in how all aspects of the transition affect the buyer. In more typical doctor-patient interactions, doctors are not paid to be concerned about all aspects of care and therefore typically ignore the effects on the patient of the cost of time, the cost of drugs and other ancillary costs. Note, this holds for HMO doctors as well as fee-for-service doctors and what is true for U.S. doctors in general is also true of doctors who practice in the government-run health systems of other developed countries.

The idea that physicians mainly do what they get paid to do may strike some readers as a criticism. It is not meant to be so. Most people in most trades, professions and jobs do what they get paid to do. If they did not, the world would be a chaotic place in which to live.

IV. Time as a Valuable Patient Resource

As noted, patients must spend both time and money to access the health care system; and for most, the time cost is higher than the monetary cost at the time the care is received. Time is also important in another way. The principal way that Americans find out about options in the medical marketplace is by investing their time. The payoff is in terms of health and money. Patient-initiated research can lead to better health outcomes and less expensive care. But if there are no financial rewards, patients will have reduced incentives to make such investments. In economic terms, with weak incentives to acquire information, patients will be "rationally ignorant."[16]

In a fascinating study for the National Center for Policy Analysis, Devon Herrick showed that patients can reduce the cost of their pharmaceuticals—in some cases by as much as 90 percent—by employing the same techniques they use when they shop for other goods and services (Herrick, 2004a). To take but one example, the *New York Times* compared the U.S. and Canadian prices of ten drugs in order to show how much cheaper drugs are in Canada. Yet Herrick showed that in eight of the ten cases, U.S. patients could beat the Canadian price by careful shopping ("NCPA: Drug Re-Importation," 2003). Here are a few examples of smart shopping:

- *Buying in Bulk:* Just as the unit price is lower when people buy larger quantities of cereal and laundry detergent, the same principle works for most drugs. That is, a three month supply is typically cheaper (per pill) than a one month supply.
- *Pill Splitting:* Because of the peculiar way drugs are typically priced, a 50 milligram pill often costs about the same as a 100 milligram pill. So purchasing the larger dose and cutting the pill in half has the potential to cut the overall pharmaceutical cost in half.[17]
- *Comparison Shopping:* Prices for the same prescription can vary radically among drugstores within a few blocks of each other, allowing savings as much as 80 percent or more.[18]
- *Shopping on the Internet:* Patients need not confine their search to local markets. There is a national market for drugs, and by using the Internet, patients can compare prices at AARP, all the major retail chains and other outlets as well.
- *Generic Substitution:* Patients need not be completely reliant on physicians and pharmacists to learn about opportunities for generic substitution. There are web sites to help them out.
- *Therapeutic Substitution:* There are also web sites that will inform patients about opportunities for therapeutic substitution.

How often do patients use smart shopping techniques to lower the cost of their drugs? More often than might be supposed. A study of Medicare patients found that patients without insurance coverage for drugs paid about the same price as patients with insurance (Rettenmaier & Wang, 2003). Apparently, people can be quite resourceful when the money they spend is their own.

Unfortunately for third-party payers, most of the time when people buy drugs they are spending someone else's money rather than their own. As noted, smart shopping for drugs is a time consuming effort. Accordingly, it is an effort unlikely to be made unless the patient expects to realize economic gain. How likely is a Medicaid patient to buy in bulk or split pills in order to save money for Medicaid? How likely is a senior citizen to search for generic or therapeutic substitutes in order to save money for a medigap insurer? How likely is an employee to comparison shop on the Internet in order to save money for an employer?

Our system of third party payment not only leads to economic waste, it can have harmful health consequences as well. Take patients with arthritic pain. Vioxx and Bextra (before they were taken from the market) and Celebrex cost about $800 more over the course of a year than such over-the-counter remedies as ibuprofen (Herrick, 2004a, Table 3). Let us concede that for some patients the brand name drug is superior. Are the extra benefits of a brand drug worth $800 a year in addition to the risk of side effects?

Drugs affect different people differently. Moreover, different people have different attitudes toward risk. So it is virtually impossible for one person to make such a choice for another. When people are spending their own money, presumably they will reveal their preferences through their actions. But as noted, most of the patients who were taking Vioxx (and should not have been) were not spending their own money. Third-party payers were paying the bill. And most of those insurance plans probably did not cover the cost of ibuprofen.

Another example is the prescription drug Clarinex, used by allergy sufferers. Some scientists claim that the over-the-counter drug Claritin is chemically the same (Schieber, 2004). Yet a year's supply of the former costs about $1,144, compared to only $280 for the latter and less than $19 for an OTC generic equivalent.[19] As in the case of arthritic pain relief, many insurers will cover the cost of brand name drug but not the OTC alternatives—inducing patients to opt for the drug with the highest social cost.

Again it is logical to ask: why doesn't entrepreneurship solve this problem? The ideal solution in these examples is to avoid third-party payment altogether. Instead, deposit funds in a patient Health Savings Account (HSA) and allow patients to make their own (unbiased) choices.[20]

The problem is that (until recently) deposits to HSAs were subjected to income and payroll taxes, whereas third-party insurance premiums could be paid (by employers) tax free. As of 2004, nonelderly Americans have access to tax free HSA accounts, at least in principle, but the conditions to qualify are quite restrictive (Goodman, 2005). A second problem is that the law requires employers to make the same deposit to every employee's account—despite the fact that actual health care costs vary radically from employee to employee. This means that employers cannot set up special accounts for arthritis suffers or for employees who suffer allergies (Goodman, 2005).

A third problem is that the law virtually forces employees to use their HSAs in a way that piggybacks onto the current payment system rather than fundamentally challenge it. That is, even if the patient saves money by buying an OTC drug rather than a prescription drug, the expenditure does not count towards satisfaction of the deductible unless the drug is covered by the plan. With conventional coverage, for example, the OTC drug would not be covered.

Similarly, using HSA money to pay for telephone or e-mail consultations may result in savings for the employee. But unless these services are covered by the health plan, the spending doesn't count toward satisfaction of the deductible. (These and other needed changes in the law governing HSAs are discussed below.)

There is also a third problem: the interest of the employee/patient and the employer/insurer are not always the same.

V. Time Horizons and Third-Party Payers

In a genuinely free market for health insurance, one would expect people to form long-term relationships with their insurers. This follows from the nature of the insurance contract. In the very act of joining an insurance pool, people necessarily cede to the managers of the pool the power to make a great many decisions (often not well specified in advance) about what will be covered and what will not. Whereas individuals on their own can choose between health care and other uses of money when the amounts of money involved are small, these decisions often must be delegated to insurers when the amounts involved are large.[21]

Ideally, insurance administrators will make the same kinds of tradeoffs individuals would have made on their own. But this is likely to happen only if the relationship is long term. In general, we want decision makers to consider all the costs and all the benefits in making coverage decisions. But many costs borne today will produce health benefits only in future years. So if the relationship is of short duration, the insurer will tend to overly discount future health benefits relative to current health costs (Kleinke, 2001).

In contrast to the ideal, virtually all insurance contracts today are of 12 month duration. With respect to drugs, this means that insurers like drugs that produce quick (less than 12 months) economic payoffs and dislike drugs with long-term (more than 12 month) economic payoffs. Some of the chronic conditions mentioned above are good examples (Kleinke, 2004).

- By making a bigger effort to treat patients with hypertension with drug therapy, an insurer with a long term contract will avoid the much higher costs of treating strokes and cardiovascular disease.
- By more aggressive treatment of obesity, the insurer could avoid some of the consequential costs of cancer, diabetes, heart disease, depression and stroke.
- By making a greater effort to treat high cholesterol, the insurer could avoid some of the higher consequential costs of stroke and heart disease.

But since insurance contracts are not long-term, the insurer who engages in aggressive preventive measures today is likely to be lowering some *other* insurer's costs tomorrow, rather than its own. Interestingly, a well-known method for evaluating the value of drugs and other therapies is cost effectiveness analysis (CEA). This method takes into account all economic costs, all health benefits and all of the time periods in which they are realized (Tengs et al., 1995). Yet despite the prevalence of this measure in medical journal articles, virtually no third-party payers are basing coverage decisions on CEA today (Kleinke, 2001).

It might be supposed that since employers have long term relationships with their employees, the employer will take the long view with respect to health insurance. Unfortunately, there are other regulations that distort the employer's incentives. Although federal tax law encourages employers to provide health insurance (as an alternative to paying additional taxable wages), employee benefits law requires employers to accept all enrollees at community-rated premiums. Since this means that employers will lose money on employees (and their dependents) who have high health costs, employers have an economic interest in attracting employees who are healthy and avoiding employees who are sick. Although they cannot legally discriminate against employee applicants on the basis of their health conditions, employers can pursue their self-interest in a different way: they can sponsor health plans that attract healthy employees and repel sick employees by over-providing to the healthy and under-providing to the sick.[22]

There is a third distortion that affects employer behavior. Viewed in very narrow economic terms, employers can gain in two ways when they spend money on employee health care: (a) they can avoid high future health care costs by treating a problem when it is less costly and (b) they can reduce days of missed work due to sickness. Yet there are many benefits that employees (and their dependents) get from health care that do not fall into these categories. Relief from allergies is one example. Sildenafil citrate (Viagra) is another. The treatment of mild obesity, sever acne, toenail fungus and overactive bladder are other examples. In each of these cases, the benefit is realized by the employee. There is small, if any, impact on work. Thus the employer has weak incentives to cover the costs. Many employers also fail to pay for and administer flu vaccines, believing (perhaps falsely) that the pay back (in terms of fewer missed days of work) is small (Kleinke, 2001).

It might be thought that government is a solution to the problem addressed here. For example, unlike a private insurer or an employer, the government's relation with Medicare enrollees is by definition long-term, lasting until the senior's death. Additionally, many people (including nursing home residents) have long-term relationships with Medicaid. It turns out, however, that government health insurance is not better with respect to these issues. If anything, it is far worse.

When Medicare and Medicaid were created in 1965, the benefit package in both programs basically aped the standard Blue Cross/Blue Shield benefits common at the time (Goodman & Musgrave, 1992, Chapter 5). Since Blue Cross did not cover drugs, Medicare did not cover them either. Drug coverage was left as an option under state-administered Medicaid programs. In the years since then, new and innovative drug discoveries not only have allowed medical breakthroughs in terms of curing diseases and saving lives, they have also in many cases substituted for more expensive, alternative therapies (Lichtenberg, 1996; Lichtenberg, 2001).

In fact, new drug therapies are generally thought to be a central factor in the long-term decline in hospital admissions and hospital lengths of stay in the United States ("Outlook 2001"). For that reason almost all private insurance today, including all Blue Cross plans, cover drugs. Yet while private insurance has changed in the intervening years, Medicare and Medicaid have not changed, with the exception of a highly unusual optional drug benefit that is offered under Medicare.

It is both ironic and unfortunate that basic Medicare insurance (Part A & Part B) will pay to amputate the leg of a diabetic, but will not pay for the drugs that would have made the amputation unnecessary in the first place. Similarly, Medicare will pay for the hospital care of a heart attack or stroke victim, but will not pay for the drugs that would have prevented the heart attack or stroke to begin with.

In Medicaid, practice varies from state to state. But because drug coverage is an optional benefit, the temptation on the part of state governments is to limit access to drugs in order to control growing Medicaid costs. The states have succumbed to this temptation repeatedly, even though there is evidence that doing so ultimately raises, rather than lowers, total Medicaid costs. For example, one study found that a Medicaid program's restriction of reimbursement to three drugs led to an increase in emergency mental health visits, hospitalizations in community mental health centers and entry into nursing homes—at a cost well above the drug cost savings (Soumerai & Lipton, 1995).[23]

Why does government insurance underperform private insurance, even when the time horizon for the government is so much longer? One reason is that the time horizon that counts is not that of the government in the abstract but that of elected officials; and typically the relevant horizon for politicians does not extend longer than the next election. Another reason is that vested interests coalesce around Medicare and Medicaid spending and it is in their self interest to resist changes that would reduce their compensation (say, because of reduced hospital or nursing home stays) because of increased compensation for producers of drugs.

VI. The Challenge for Entrepreneurs

Whenever there is waste and inefficiency in a market, there is an opportunity for entrepreneurs to make profits by eliminating that waste and inefficiency. The health care market is no exception. What makes entrepreneurship difficult in health care is that in order to eliminate waste and inefficiency, the entrepreneurs must step outside of the normal payment mechanisms. This means that patients who take advantage of these services often must pay out-of-pocket for what theoretically should be covered by their insurer.

The entrepreneurial activities we have identified tend to have two characteristics: (a) they allow patients to economize on time and (b) they step outside the normal reimbursement channels, usually asking for payment at the time of service. Here are some examples:

- *MinuteClinics.* These are walk-in clinics located in selected Target and Club Food stores and some CVS Pharmacies, and Wal-Mart has signaled its interest in providing a similar service through its stores nationwide. They are staffed by nurse practitioners. No appointments are necessary and most office visits take only 15 minutes. Most treatments cost around $59. In contrast to standard physician practice, medical records are stored electronically and prescriptions are also ordered that way (Freudenheim, 2006).

- *TelaDoc.* This service offers medical consultations by telephone. A doctor usually returns patients' calls within 30 to 40 minutes. If the call is returned later than 3 hours the consultation is free. Access is available around the clock. Registration for the service costs $18. Phone consultations are $35 each, with a monthly membership fee ranging from $4.25 to $7.[24]
- *Doctokr.* This is the Virginia medical practice of Dr. Alan Dappen. Although he offers in-office appointments, he encourages most patients to have either an e-mail consultation or a phone consultation. Dappen charges based on the amount of time required. A simple consultation generally costs less than $20.[25]
- *CashDoctor.com.* This is a loosely-structured network for doctors across the country that are "cash friendly." Practice styles and fee schedules are available online.[26]

An example of opportunities seized and opportunities missed is a software package called MyChart, produced by Epic Systems of Madison, Wisconsin, and made available to about 300,000 patients nationwide by such large health centers as the Cleveland Clinic, UT Southwestern and Harvard Vanguard Medical Associates. MyChart has the potential to allow doctors and patients to communicate online, but in practice its use is more limited. UT Southwestern patients, for example, can use the system to:

- Check results of lab tests.
- View summaries of previous doctor appointments, physicians' instructions and dates of future appointments.
- Review their allergies, immunizations and other medical records.
- Check their prescriptions history and order refills.
- Navigate to other sites with relevant medical information.

Neither patients nor third-party payers currently pay for this service, however. So why do health centers incur the cost to make it available? In part, the service may help them compete for patients. But in helping their patients the centers also help themselves. Note that the services provided to patients are services that otherwise are normally provided to patients over the phone by doctors and nurses, using up time on non-billable hours. What patients cannot do, by contrast, is ask questions and get answers about their health condition as an alternative to a face-to-face physician meeting.

MyChart, economizes on time for doctors and their patients. But it does so in a way that substitutes for non-billable time without cutting into billable time. Patients gain in the process, but not nearly as much as they could gain if the system's full potential were realized.

Drug companies are also trying to exploit inefficiencies in the market with direct-to-consumer (DTC) advertising. Although the practice is controversial and some manufacturers have suspended their DTC programs, these activities reflect commonsense economic principles.

Why is it that manufacturers advertise some drugs directly to consumers and not others? Products that are advertised tend to have three characteristics: (a) the price of the drug is not regulated or artificially depressed by government policies, thereby allowing the manufacturer to profit from the DTC activity; (b) the drug is often not covered by insurance, thereby bypassing traditional payment systems; and (c) the advertising helps patients economize on time by conveying information that might not otherwise be obtainable except through costly search.

Examples of drugs that are not advertised are childhood vaccines and flu vaccines, despite the social value of these remedies. The reason: their price tends to be regulated or heavily influenced by the government.

Under the Vaccines for Children program, the government uses its purchasing power to negotiate discounts for vaccines and distributes them to physicians and various health agencies for free or at a reduced price, essentially creating a children's vaccine entitlement. As a result, more than half the supply of childhood vaccines is purchased by government at deep discounts. Many firms have left the market, given the low profit margins, and less than two percent of drug company revenue is derived from vaccines (Herrick, 2004b).

Like children's vaccines, more than half of flu vaccines are directly purchased by the government, or indirectly reimbursed by the government at discounted prices. In a market where government is the dominant buyer, exercising monopsonistic power, the price may be driven so low that the producer's profit is slim or nonexistent. The exposure to legal liability lowers profitability even more. Thus many manufacturers have dropped out of the vaccine market altogether (Herrick, 2004b).

By contrast, drugs that are advertised tend to be drugs that are not covered by insurance (such as Viagra) or drugs which employers and insurers have weak incentives to cover or encourage because there are no perceived benefits for third-party payers or because of their long payoff periods (Kleinke, 2001).

A different type of entrepreneurship is occurring among third-party payers. Recognizing that physicians have weak incentives to improve quality and reduce the patient's non-physician costs, the paying entities are trying to directly change those incentives.

Take the choice between brand name drugs and generics for example. Doctors receive about one billion branded drug samples each year—more than three for every person in the country. These are handy to give to patients at the time of a consultation and they increase the chances of compliance. Also, once started on a branded drug, the tendency is to write a prescription for the same drug. To counteract that incentive, Aetna is placing an ATM-style dispenser of generic drugs in doctors offices, making it easy for the physicians to give away a 30 day supply of the medication (as opposed to only a week or so for the branded samples) (Hensley, 2005).

An even more radical idea is "pay for performance," which is the all the rage among cost control experts. Medicare, for example, has several pilot programs underway to pay additional compensation for specific behavior (Connolly, 2003). Many private insurers are doing the same (Rosenthal, Frank, & Epstein, 2005). These experiments may produce positive payoffs. They are, however, crude attempts to accomplish by artificial means what markets are supposed to do naturally. In what other market for a good or service do we find buyers telling sellers how to produce? Or paying the producer to produce one way rather than another? The fact that we do not see such arrangements in any other market suggests that there are reasons to be pessimistic about how well they will work in medicine.

Undoubtedly, we will see more examples of entrepreneurship in the future. But to take full advantage of the possibilities, we need changes in public policy.

VII. Needed Change in Public Policy

Why do third party payers use payment systems that cause health care to be delivered in an inefficient way? The short answer is that through the years government policies have encouraged the current payment systems. Of those policies, the most important is the tax law.

Since the end of World War II, employer payments for health insurance have been excluded from the taxable income of employees. This is a valuable tax subsidy. An average-wage worker facing a 15 percent income tax also pays a 15.3 percent payroll (FICA) tax (employer and employee shares combined) and perhaps a 5 percent state income tax. Through the tax system, therefore, government is effectively "paying" more than a third of the cost of the insurance. For higher-income employees (the decision-makers on employee benefits), government effectively pays half the cost.

Yet while tax policy generously encourages third-party insurance, it harshly penalizes self-insurance through a savings account designated for potential health expenses. With recent exceptions discussed below, every dollar the employer deposits in such an account faces federal and state income taxes in addition to the payroll tax. In this way, tax policy encourages all of us to pay all medical bills through third-party payers.[27]

The result of these tax law incentives is a health insurance system in which insurers pay for many expenses that would be better paid by patients themselves. To try and control these expenses, third-parties impose a great many constraints, which are often crude attempts to reduce wasteful spending. Since insurers are not parties to the physician consultations, they try to enumerate procedures they will pay for and tend to limit those to the physician's office. Since insurers cannot directly observe the effects of drugs on patients, they try to limit drug expenses by such unwieldy devices as drug formularies.

In general, insurers will find it in their self-interest to limit payments for services they cannot monitor very well. Since they cannot measure very well the benefits of computerized patient records (especially that part of the benefit that accrues to their own insurers), they have weak incentives to pay for the cost. The same principal applies to reimbursement for physician-initiated efforts to help patients control their drug costs. Drug formularies are easier and (perhaps cheaper) to implement.

In order to have a workable, well-functioning market for drugs, we need to fundamentally change the way we pay for health care, including the way we pay doctors.

A step in the right direction is the creation of Health Savings Accounts (HSAs). Instead of an employer or insurer paying all the medical bills, about 12 million people are managing some of their own health care dollars through these accounts and Health Reimbursement Arrangements (HRAs).[28] Instead of relying solely on third-party insurance, people can now partly self-insure in this way.

How can patients spending their own money expect to pay the rock bottom prices for physician services and prescription drugs that large insurers negotiate using their huge buying power leverage? Part of the answer is that HSAs are always combined with high deductible insurance and HSA holders usually pay the same discounted physician fee that the insurer pays. The same principle can, and should, apply to drugs. That is, in purchasing a prescription drug from an HSA, the patient should get her insurer's drug discount.

Another part of the answer is that patients can often do better than a third-party insurer. That is, by using minute clinics, call-a-doc services, and by buying drugs and arranging for tests over the Internet, many patients will find that they can pay less than their insurer would have paid under a traditional arrangement.

In an ideally constructed HSA insurance plan, patients will not spend a dollar on care unless they get a dollar's worth of value (Pauly & Goodman, 1995). Incentives under the new law are far from ideal, but they are better than under traditional insurance.[29]

Despite their many advantages, HSAs can be made even better. Two changes in particular are needed and both have the potential to fundamentally change health care for the chronically ill: (1) employers need to be able to make different contributions to the HSAs of different employees, depending on their health status and (2) there is a need for complete flexibility with respect to the setting of deductibles and copayments.

The chronically ill are responsible for an enormous amount of health care spending. In fact, almost half of all health care dollars are spent on patients with five chronic conditions (diabetes, heart disease, hypertension, asthma and mood disorders) (Druss et al., 2001). This is where HSAs have the greatest potential to reduce costs and improve the quality of care.

Healthy people tend to interact with the health care system episodically. Once in awhile they go to an emergency room or take a prescription drug. On these occasions, they gain knowledge that improves their skills as medical consumers. But it may be several years before they use that knowledge again, by which time it may be obsolete.

The chronically ill are different. Their treatments are usually repetitive, involving the same procedures and medicines, week after week, year after year. Consequently, cost-saving discoveries by these patients are not one-time events. Rather, they pay off indefinitely. Suppose a diabetic patient learns how to cut the costs of her drugs in half, by comparing prices, shopping online, bulk buying, pill splitting or switching to a generic brand. Such a discovery could be financially very rewarding to a patient who must pay these costs out-of-pocket.

As noted, numerous studies have found the chronically ill can reduce costs and improve quality by managing their own care. But health care management is difficult and time consuming. To encourage the effort, patients should reap both health rewards and financial rewards from making better decisions. Employers should be able to create specialized HSA accounts for patients with differing chronic conditions. They should be able to adjust the account's funding to fit specific circumstances. A typical Type II diabetic, for example, might receive one level of HSA deposit from an employer; a typical asthmatic patient another.

The problem is: The HSA law requires employers to deposit the same amount in each employee's HSA account, irrespective of medical condition. This is a strange requirement, given that employers who give employees choices of health plans are risk-rating their premium payments whether they are aware of it or not. If the sickest employees all choose Plan B and the healthiest choose Plan A, then the employer will invariably pay more premiums per employee to Plan B. Yet although employers risk-rate their premium payments, they are not allowed to risk-rate HSA deposits.

The second needed change relates to the deductible. Not all medical services are the same. Patients can exercise discretion for many of their health care needs, and it is *appropriate* for them to do so. Take arthritic pain relief. None of us can determine for another individual whether any particular tradeoff between cost and pain relief is worthwhile. So it is appropriate and desirable for people to make these decisions themselves, and reap the benefits and bear the costs of their decisions.

By contrast, a semiconscious patient on a gurney is not in a position to make choices about alternative treatments. Even if he could, discretion in this setting is typically *inappropriate.* Or consider the case of a diagnosed schizophrenic. He may choose to stop taking his prescribed medication; but it is in society's self-interest to make sure he is not encouraged to do so.

Unfortunately, the HSA law treats all these cases the same. It requires a high, across-the-board deductible and requires the patient to bear the costs of purchases below the deductible amount. A better approach would allow insurers to design plans so that different deductibles (and copayments) apply to different medical services. Where patient discretion is possible, and appropriate, the deductible should be high. Where patient discretion is more difficult, and in any event inappropriate, the deductible should be low or nonexistent.

An even more fundamental change would be to carve out whole categories of services for which the patient is responsible for payment. There would be no need for a deductible with respect to these services and HSA spending on them would not count toward a deductible. Under the current system, the distinction between covered and uncovered services frequently distorts patient incentives. As noted above, for example, e-mail and telephone consultations (as an alternative to face-to-face encounters) are typically not covered. Similarly, OTC purchases (as an alternative to brand drugs) are typically not covered. A better approach is to erase the distinction between covered and uncovered services—freeing the patient to discover the most efficient options.

Freed from the strictures of conventional health insurance, the market would then be free to offer products that reduce time as well as money costs in patient-pleasing ways.

Under the current system, HSA plans with deductibles and copayments are an extension of the current payment system and reinforce it rather than challenge it. Under the current HSA rules, if a patient pays for care with dollars, those dollars count toward a deductible and move the patient closer to the point when a third-party will pay all remaining financial costs. But if a patient pays for care with time, this does not count toward the deductible. Further, under most HSA plans, time-saving innovations are typically not covered expenses. In these ways, most HSA plans are tacked on to the existing payment system, rather than an alternative to it.

The current HSA law's primary problem is that decisions the market should make have been made by the tax-writing committees of the U.S. Congress instead. What is the appropriate deductible for which service? How much should be deposited in the HSAs of different employees? How can we use these accounts to meet the needs of the chronically ill? In finding answers, markets are smarter than any one of us because they benefit from the best thinking of everyone. Further, as medical science and technology advance, the best answer today may not be the best answer tomorrow.

South Africa's experience with HSAs (called Medical Savings Accounts) provides an interesting contrast.[30] These accounts emerged in the 1990s under Nelson Mandela's presidency and have now captured more than half the market for private health insurance there. Since the South African government never passed a law imposing an HSA design, their plans developed in a relatively free market. The South African "free-market HSAs" are different, and in some ways more attractive, than what we have in the United States. For example, one of the most popular plans there offers first-dollar insurance coverage for most hospital procedures, on the theory that hospitalized patients have little opportunity to make choices, and discretion is not appropriate in that setting in any event. A high deductible applies to "discretionary" expenses, however, including most services delivered in doctors' offices.

South Africa's more flexible approach also allows more sensible drug coverage. While a high deductible applies to most drugs, a typical plan pays from the first dollar for drugs that treat diabetes, asthma and other chronic conditions. The reason is obvious: It would be counter-productive to encourage patients to skimp on drugs that prevent more expensive-to-treat conditions from developing.

Although most recent legislation has unwisely restricted the ability to use HSAs in South Africa, including restrictions on their use to meet the needs of chronic patients, the country's experience can be a useful guide to policymakers in the United States. Ideal reform in this country would allow unlimited contributions to HSAs and permit such accounts to wrap around any third-party insurance—paying for any expense the insurance plan does not pay. Barring that, we should at least allow flexible deductibles and risk-rated deposits to HSAs.

Notes

1. The author would like to thank Devon Herrick for help in the preparation of this manuscript and Gerald Musgrave for useful comments.
2. Estimate based on "IMS Health Reports U.S. Prescription Sales Jump 8.3 Percent in 2006, to $274.9 Billion," IMS Health, March 8, 2007.
   Health care expenditure is estimated to top $2.1 trillion in 2006. See Centers for Medicare and Medicaid Services, U. S. Department of Health and Human Services (2007).
3. According to the Consumer Healthcare Products Association, over-the-counter drug sales in 2006 was $15.4 billion, excluding Wal-Mart.
4. One study found that two-thirds of patients on Cox-2 inhibitors were not at risk for gastrointestinal conditions like ulcers or bleeding and most of them had not tried cheaper alternatives. See Cox, Motheral, Frisse, Behm, & Mager (2003). See also *Drug Cost Management Report (2003).*
5. Not all experts agree that Cox-2 Inhibitors are more risky than older nonsteroidal anti-inflammatory drugs (NSAIDS) such as ibuprofen and naproxen. For instance, John Calfee, a scholar with the American Enterprise Institute points out that between 10,000 and 20,000 people die annually of complications from taking older NSAIDS. See Calfee (2005).
6. There are exceptions. It is common for people to get test results by phone and to get refills on prescriptions by phone conservations with doctors and nurses. What is rare is an actual telephone consultation. Only about 24 percent of patients exchange

e-mail with their physicians for clinical issues. Center for Studying Health System Change (Liebhaber & Grossman, 2006).

7. That consumers are responsive to health care prices, and for some services very responsive is well established in health economics. For a useful review of the literature, see Morrisey (2005). Some credit the work of three economists—Mark Pauly, Martin Feldstein and Joseph Newhouse—for introducing the economic way of thinking into health care. See Pauly (1971), Newhouse (1993), Feldstein & Friedman (1977). For a comprehensive (but critical) review of this literature, see Melhado (1998).
8. Take the Resource-based Relative Value Scale (RBRVS), used to pay physicians by Medicare, Medicaid and many private insurers. This system pays a fee for a physician visit but does not compensate for pre- and post-encounter work, including coordination of care, research on drugs and drug prices, and supervising nurses and physicians assistants. Nor does it pay for telephone or email communication with patients. The RBRVS also tends to pay a fixed rate for a visit, ignoring differences in the complexity of cases and the time needed to treat them. See Johnson & Newton (2002).
9. Among health plans that do pay, some will not compensate doctors for e-mail exchanges unless the patient has first been examined in an office. Other insurers reimburse less for e-mail exchanges than for in-person visits. See Freudenheim (2005). An exception is, Blue Shield of California, which pays physicians the same for an e-mail consultation ($25) as it does for an office visit. See Koenig (2003). The American Medical Association has created a reimbursement code for online consultation patients, making it easier for physicians to get paid.
10. According to a Center for Studying Health System Change survey, about 27 percent of physicians limit the number of new Medicare patients they will accept—or do not accept Medicare patients at all. See "Physician Acceptance of New Medicare Patients Stabilizes in 2004-05," (2006).
11. According to a recent survey by the Center for Studying Health System Change, nearly 48 percent of physicians refuse to accept any new Medicaid patients (Cunningham and May, 2006).
12. By contrast, 59 percent of dental offices (when payment is more likely to be out-of-pocket) passes the courtesy text. See Boswell (2003).
13. Also see Norris, Engelgau, & Narayan (2001).
14. A Dutch study comparing self-management to usual care found that those monitoring their own asthma achieved a savings of about 7 percent the first year and a 28 percent savings the second year, compared to those in standard care with a primary physician. A recent study of asthma patients trained to perform in-home asthma telemonitoring found that the results of self-testing were consistent with established guidelines. Moreover, participation in telemonitoring did not require that patients have extensive computer knowledge. See Wang, Zhong, & Wheeler (2005), and Finkelstein & Cabrera (2000).
15. A 1998 editorial by the editor-in-chief of the *New England Journal of Medicine* argued that capitated payment systems would force doctors to reduce the time spent with each patient and, thus, lower the quality of care. See Kassirer (1998). The following year, this view was echoed in Kenneth Ludmerer (1999). However, two subsequent studies found that over the 1990s (the decade of managed care) the average time doctors spent with patients actually increased. See Mechanic, McAlpine, & Rosenthal (2001), and Luft (1999).

16. On the economics of rational ignorance, see Caplan (2001).
17. Note: not every pill can be split (e.g., time release capsules), but many can; pharmacists will often split pills for customers and patients can purchase pill splitting devices to do it for themselves
18. In a Missouri survey conducted for the Heartland Institute, prudent shopping saved consumers almost 10 percent on branded drugs and 81 percent on generics, on the average. Moreover, prices within a single city differed by 3 percent to 16 percent for brand-name medications and by 39 percent to 159 percent for generic medications. See Public Issue Management (2002).
19. Prices for Clarinex and Claritin are for packages of 30 doses from Walgreens.com. The price for the generic version of Claritin (Loratadine) is for Sam's Club. All prices surveyed fall 2006.
20. Health Savings Accounts (HSAs) sometimes called Medical Savings Accounts (MSAs) is an idea developed by the National Center for Policy Analysis. It got considerable attention as a result of Goodman & Musgrave (1992).
21. See Goodman (2004).
22. See the discussion on the economics of "managed competition" in Goodman, Musgrave, & Herrick (2004).
23. Another study of HMO enrollees found that the more restrictive a drug formulary, the greater the total health care costs for five major drug-intensive diseases—again swamping any savings on the cost of the drugs. See Horn et al., (1996).
24. Information taken from TelaDoc.com Web site. Also see "'Doctor on Call' Redefined," (2005).
25. Information taken from Doctokr.com Web site. Also see Norbut (2003).
26. Information taken from CashDoctor.com Web site.
27. The tax treatment of out-of-pocket expenses has varied over the years. Currently, tax payers can only deduct from their income, out-of-pocket medical expenses that exceed seven percent of their adjusted gross income. As a result, few Americans receive any tax subsidy for out-of-pocket payments. The only way most workers can pay out-of-pocket expenses tax free is by depositing money into a flexible spending account to pay incidental medical bills. However, since these accounts are use-it-or-lose-it, they encourage wasteful spending. Some economists have argued that reliance on third-party payment would be reduced if out-of-pocket spending were completely deductible. See Cogan, Hubbard, & Kessler (2004). However, the alternative to third-party-insurance is not out-of-pocket spending. The alternative to third-party insurance is self-insurance. In general, people who have third-party insurance have economic incentives to overconsume health care. If they can, in addition, deduct their out-of-pocket copayments and deductibles, the incentives to overconsume become even worse.
28. Estimate by William Boyles, Consumer Driven Market Report, 2007. For a brief discussion of how HSAs compare to HRAs and FSAs, see Cannon (2003).
29. Money withdrawn from an HSA before age 65 faces ordinary income taxes plus a 10 percent penalty. So a taxpayer in the 15 percent bracket losers 25¢ on every dollar withdrawn. This means a dollar of health care trades against 75¢ of other goods and services. That's far from perfect, but much better than trading against 10¢ under the traditional insurance.
30. See Matisonn (2002) and Matisonn (2000).

References

Benjamin, E. M. (2002). 'Self-monitoring of blood glucose: The basics,' *Clinical Diabetes,* 20(1) Winter, 45–47.

Boswell, S. (2003). 'How you fit in the big health-care picture', *Dental Practice Report,* March 2003.

Calfee, J. (2005). 'The Vioxx fallout', *American Enterprise Institute for Public Policy Research, Health Policy Outlook,* September-October.

Cannon, M. (2003). 'Three avenues to patient power', *National Center for Policy Analysis,* Brief Analysis No. 430.

Caplan, B. (2001). 'Rational ignorance versus rational irrationality', *Kyklos,* 54(1), 3-26.

Centers for Medicare and Medicaid Services, U. S. Department of Health and Human Services (2007). 'National Health Expenditure Accounts, 2006 highlights.' [Online] Available at: http://www.cms.hhs.gov/NationalHealthExpendData/downloads/highlights.pdf Accessed January 28, 2008.

Cogan, J.F., Hubbard R.G., & Kessler, D.P. (2004, December 8). 'Brilliant deduction', *Wall Street Journal.*

Connolly, C. (2003, July 11). 'Pilot test will pay hospitals for quality; Government hopes care will improve', *Washington Post.*

Cox, E., Motheral, B., Frisse, M., Behm, A., & Mager, D. (2003). 'Prescribing COX-2s for patients new to cyclo-oxygenase inhibition therapy', *American Journal of Managed Care,* 9(11), 735-42.

Cunningham, P.J., Staiti, A., & Ginsburg, P.B. (2006, January). 'Physician Acceptance of New Medicare Patients Stabilizes in 2004-05,' Center for Studying Health System Change, Tracking Report No. 12.

Cunningham, P.J. & May, J.H. (2006, August). 'Medicaid Patients Increasingly Concentrated Among Physicians', Center for Studying Health System Change, Tracking Report No. 16.

Dolan, E.S. & Goodman, J.C. (1995). 'Flying the deregulated skies: Competition, price discrimination, congestion', in: E.S. Dolan & J.C. Goodman (Eds.), *Economics of Public Policy,* 5th ed. (pp. 143-159). St. Paul: West Publishing Company.

Doshi, J.A., Brandt, N., & Stuart, B. (2004, February 18). 'The impact of drug coverage on COX-2 inhibitor use in medicare', *Health Affairs,* Web Exclusive. [Online]. Available at: http://content.healthaffairs.org/cgi/content/full/hlthaff.w4.94v1/DC1.

Drug Cost Management Report. (2003, November 21). 'A new study from express scripts, Inc. indicates that patients are being prescribed expensive Cox-2 inhibitor drugs even when they have no increased risk for gastrointestinal events.' [Online]. Available at: http://www.findarticles.com/p/articles/mi_m0NKV.

Druss, B.G., Marcus, S.C., Olfson, M., Tanielian, T., Elinson, L., & Pincus, H.A. (2001). 'Comparing the national economic burden of five chronic conditions', *Health Affairs,* 20(6), 233-241.

Feldstein, M.S. & Friedman, B.S. (1977). 'Tax subsidies, the rational demand for health insurance, and the health care crisis', *Journal of Public Economics,* 7(2), 155-178.

Finkelstein, J. & Cabrera, M.R. (2000). 'Internet-based home asthma telemonitoring', *Chest,* 117(1), 148-155

Freudenheim, M. (2005, March 2). 'Digital Rx: Take two aspirins and e-mail me in the morning', *New York Times.*

Freudenheim, M. (2006, May 14). 'Attention shoppers: Low prices on shots in clinic', *New York Times*.

Goodman, J.C. & Musgrave, G.L. (1992). *Patient Power: Solving America's Heath Care Crisis*. Washington, DC: Cato Institute.

Goodman, J.C., Musgrave G.L., & Herrick, D.M. (2004). *Lives at Risk: Single-Payer National Health Insurance Around the World*. Lanham, MD: Rowman and Littlefield Publishers.

Goodman, J.C. (2004). 'Designing health insurance for the information age', in: R.E. Herzlinger, (Ed.), *Consumer-Driven Health Care: Implications for Providers, Payers and Policymakers*. San Francisco, CA: Jossey-Bass.

Goodman, J.C. (2005). 'Making HSAs better', *National Center for Policy Analysis*, Brief Analysis No. 518.

Hackbarth, G.M., Reischauer, R.D., & Miller, M. (2002, March 3). '2002 survey of physicians about the Medicare program', *Medicare Payment Advisory Commission*.

Hawryluk, M. (2002, October 21). 'Physician payment crunch: Medicare cuts hit medicaid access,' *American Medical News*.

Hensley, S. (2005, October 12). 'Generic drugs sampled freely in Aetna Test', *Wall Street Journal*.

Herrick, D.M. (2002). 'Is Medicare too stingy?,' *National Center for Policy Analysis*, Brief Analysis No. 421.

Herrick, D.M. (2006). 'Update 2006: Why are health costs rising?,' *National Center for Policy Analysis*, Brief Analysis No. 572.

Herrick, D.M. (2004a). 'Shopping for drugs: 2004', *National Center for Policy Analysis*, NCPA Policy Report No. 270.

Herrick, D.M. (2004b). 'What's behind the flu vaccine shortage', *National Center for Policy Analysis*, Brief Analysis No. 493.

Herrick, D.M. (2006). 'Shopping for drugs: 2007', *National Center for Policy Analysis*, NCPA Policy Report No. 293.

Herrick, D.M. (2007, November 28). 'Convenient care and telemedicine,' *National Center for Policy Analysis*, NCPA Study No. 305.

Hillestad, R. (2005). 'Can electronic medical record systems transform health care? Potential health benefits, savings and costs', *Health Affairs*, 24(5), 1103-1117.

Horn, S.D., Sharkey, P.D., Tracy, D.M., Horn, C.E., James, B., & Goodwin, F. (1996). 'Intended and unintended consequences of HMO cost-containment strategies: Results from the managed care outcomes project', *American Journal of Managed Care*, 2(3), 253-264.

Hughes, B. (2005, March 9). 'IMS reports 2004 global pharmaceutical sales grew seven percent to $550 billion', *IMS Health*.

Hughes, B. (2004). 'Tracking thirteen key global Pharma markets: 12 months to December 2004', *IMS Retail Drug Monitor* (IMS Health).

Johnson, S.E. & Newton, W.P. (2002). 'Resource-based relative value units: A Primer for academic family physicians', *Family Medicine*, 34(3), 172-176.

Kassirer, J. P. (1998). 'Doctor discontent', *New England Journal of Medicine*, 339(21), 1543-1545.

Kleinke, J.D. (2001). 'The price of progress: Prescription drugs in the health care market', *Health Affairs*, 20(5), 43-60.

Kleinke, J.D. (2004). 'Access versus excess: Value-based cost sharing for prescription drugs', *Health Affairs*, 23(1), 34-47.

Kleinke, J.D. (2005). 'Dot-gov: Market failure and the creation of a national health information technology system', *Health Affairs* 24(5), 1246-1262.

Koenig, D. (2003, December 21). 'A few doctors seeing patients online', *Akron Beacon Journal.*

Levy C. & Luo, M. (2005, July 18). 'New York Medicaid fraud may reach into billions', *The New York Times.*

Lichtenberg, F.R. (1996). 'Do (more and better) drugs keep people out of hospitals?', *American Economic Review,* 86(2), 384-388.

Lichtenberg, F.R. (2001). 'The benefits and costs of newer drugs: Evidence from the 1996 medical expenditure panel survey', *National Bureau of Economic Research,* Working Paper 8147.

Liebhaber, A. & Grossman, J.M. (2006, September). 'Physicians Slow to Adopt Patient E-mail,' Center for Studying Health System Change, Data Bulletin No. 32.

Ludmerer, K. (1999). *Time to Heal: American Medical Education from the Turn of the Century to the Era of Managed Care.* New York: Oxford University Press.

Luft, H. (1999). 'Why are physicians so upset about managed care?' *Journal of Health Politics, Policy and Law,* 24(5), 957-66.

Matisonn, S. (2000). 'Medical savings accounts in South Africa', *National Center for Policy Analysis,* Policy Report No. 234.

Matisonn, S. (2002). 'Medical savings accounts and prescription drugs: Evidence from South Africa', *National Center for Policy Analysis,* Policy Report No. 254.

Mechanic, D., McAlpine, D.D., & Rosenthal, M. (2001). 'Are patients' office visits with physicians getting shorter?' *New England Journal of Medicine,* 344(3), 198-204.

Melhado, E.M. (1998). 'Economists, public provision, and the market: Changing values in policy debate', *Journal of Health Politics, Policy and Law,* 23(2), 215-263.

Morrisey, M. (2005). 'Price sensitivity in health care: Implications for health care policy', National Federation of Independent Business.

National Center for Policy Analysis. (2003, July 24). 'NCPA: Drug Re-Importation Not Needed', Press Release.

National Health Expenditure Web Tables, National Health Expenditure Data, Centers for Medicare and Medicaid Services, U.S. Department of Health and Human Services, Table 7, Physician and Clinical Services Expenditures Aggregate, Per Capita Amounts, and Percent Distribution, by Source of Funds: Selected Calendar Years 1970-2005, 2006. Available at: http://www.cms.hhs.gov/NationalHealthExpendData/downloads/tables.pdf. Access verified, June 28, 2007.

Newhouse, J. (1993). *Free for All? Lessons from the RAND Health Insurance Experiment.* Cambridge, MA: Harvard University Press.

Norris, S.L., Engelgau, M.M., & Narayan, K. (2001). 'Effectiveness of self-management training in type 2 Diabetes', *Diabetes Care,* 24(2), 197-201.

Passley, M., Brodt, B., & Jones, T. (1993, October 31-November 9). 'Medicaid: system in chaos', (a series in nine parts), *Chicago Tribune.*

Pauly, M. (1971). *Medical Care at Public Expense: A Study in Applied Welfare Economics.* New York: Praeger.

Pauly, M. & Goodman, J.C. (1995). 'Tax credits for health insurance and medical savings accounts', *Health Affairs,* 14(1), 125-129.

'Physicians payment crunch: Medicare cuts hit Medicaid access', *American Medical News,* October 21, 2002.

Powell, D.R. (2003, September). 'Implementing a medical self-care program', *Employee Benefits Journal,* International Foundation of Employee Benefit Programs.

Public Issue Management. (2002). '2002 Missouri prescription drug pricing survey', Heartland Institute.

Rettenmaier, A.J. & Wang, Z. (2003). 'Who pays higher prices for prescription drugs?' *National Center for Policy Analysis,* NCPA Policy Report No. 265.

Rosenthal, M.B., Frank, Li, Z., & Epstein, M. (2005). 'Early experience with pay-for-performance: From concept to practice', *Journal of the American Medical Association,* 294(14), 1788-1793.

Rottenberg, S. (1990). 'Unintended consequences: The probable effects of mandated medical insurance', *Regulation,* 13(2), 27-28.

Schieber, S.J. (2004). 'Why coordination of health care spending and savings accounts is important', unpublished manuscript.

Soumerai, S.B. & Lipton, H.L. (1995). 'Computer-based drug-utilization review—risk, benefit, or boondoggle?', *New England Journal of Medicine,* 332(24), 1641-1645.

Tengs, T.O., Adams, M.E., Pliskin, J.S., Safran, D.G., Siegel, J.E., Weinstein, M.C., & Graham, J.D. (1995). 'Five-hundred life-saving interventions and their cost-effectiveness', *Risk Analysis,* 15(3), 369-390.

Tucker, W. (1990). *The Excluded American: Homelessness and Housing Policies.* Washington, DC: Regnery Gateway.

Tufts Center for the Study of Drug Development. (2001). *Outlook 2001.* Boston: Tufts University.

Wang, L.Y., Zhong, Y., & Wheeler, L. (2005). 'Direct and indirect costs of asthma in school-age children', *Preventing Chronic Disease* [Online]. Available at: http://www.cdc.gov/pcd/issues/2005/jan/04_0053.htm.

Perils of Parallel Trade: Reimporting Prescription Drugs from Canada to the US

John R. Graham
Pacific Research Institute, San Francisco

I. Introduction

Within the last decade, a gray market trade has risen between Canada and the United States: the diversion of prescription drugs meant for Canadian patients to Americans who want prescriptions at Canadian prices, which are often much lower.

Currently, US law makes it illegal for anyone but the manufacturer or his appointed agent to import prescription medicines into the United States (unless the Secretary of Health and Human Services allows it, which he has not yet done). Nevertheless, the growing price difference for prescription drugs between Canada and the United States has created an opportunity for Canadian entrepreneurs to export prescription drugs from Canada to the United States. Because the warehouses are outside the US, they exploit a loophole that (many agree) allows individual US residents to import 90-days worth of drugs for personal use.

II. Free Trade Versus Parallel Trade

The illegal shipment of prescription drugs from Canada to the United States is an example of "parallel trade", the subject of a useful economic and legal literature. "Parallel trade occurs when differences in

H.T. Engelhardt, Jr. and J. Garrett (eds), *Innovation and the Pharmaceutical Industry* (pp. 184–192).

national economic, social, legal or regulatory regimes result in different prices among countries, creating opportunities for arbitrage" (Barfield & Groombridge, 1999, p. 185). When a country's exchange rate appreciates, so do parallel imports (Barfield & Groombridge, 1999, p. 245 and references). The deteriorating value of the Canadian dollar was a major cause of the pressure to allow pharmaceutical parallel trade, but the recent rise in that currency has not erased the price differences (Graham, 2007).

The key difference between parallel trade and free trade is that free trade occurs with the voluntary participation of all parties. Parallel trade, on the other hand, opposes the interests and wishes of the affected manufacturers. For this reason, it is defined as a "gray market" (Ruff, 1992, p. 120).

This is important to understand because some proponents of pharmaceutical parallel trade incorrectly criticize efforts to stop it as anti-competitive. If GlaxoSmithKline, a British-headquartered company, was lobbying to prevent an American drug maker, such as Pfizer or Eli Lilly, from selling its products in the United Kingdom, that would violate the principles of free trade. Efforts by GlaxoSmithKline to secure its own distribution are not.

Parallel trade can only take place if governments prevent manufacturers from negotiating vertical restraints with distributors—that is, asking them to conform to limits on their reselling. Laws and regulations regarding parallel importing have become increasingly complicated and technical (Rothnie, 1993, p. 471). Some governments, such as the European Union (EU), favor parallel trade, because they believe (incorrectly) that using vertical restraints to maintain price differences is negative for social welfare. Anti-trust law often prevents manufacturers from imposing vertical restraints on distributors. For example, the doctrine of "first sale" prevents patent (or copyright) owners from stopping secondary sales (Barfield & Groombridge, 1999, pp. 196-199).

However, analysis going back to the 1960s shows that many vertical restraints favor competition, and a small literature on the benefits of price differentiation and discouraging parallel trade has been written in the last two decades (Danzon, 1997; Elzinga & Mills, 1997; Hausman & MacKie-Mason, 1988; Malueg & Schwartz, 1994; Scott Morton, 1997a; b). To summarize (and risk over-generalizing), these scholars point out that if the law forces manufacturers to charge only one price, that price is more likely to be the higher price than the lower price. This will ensure that prospective buyers who could have bought the good for the lower price are shut out of the market.

This analysis has influenced American law, which has traditionally restricted parallel imports, although parallel trade for trademarked goods (such as luxury-branded handbags) increased significantly during the 1980s. In a 1997 decision, the US Supreme Court decided on a "rule of reason" standard for judging vertical restrictions by manufacturers over distributors, reflecting economic thinking that recognized the value of voluntarily negotiated restraints for efficiency (Barfield & Groombridge, 1999, pp. 196-199; Malueg & Schwartz, 1994, p. 168; Ruff, 1992, p. 121).

Perhaps the most important thing to understand about trade in patented medicines is that usually only a small share of the sales price is accounted for by marginal costs of manufacturing and distribution. Because patents prevent competitors from making exact copies, the original manufacturer can charge what appears to be a high price. However, the extra profit goes to pay a return on the R&D. If this were not permitted, investors would not be interested in financing expensive R&D. However, it also means that manufacturers will be happy to sell their products at lower prices to customers who cannot pay the standard price, as long as the low-priced sales earn a little more than they cost to manufacture and distribute. However, the manufacturer must have a means to keep the two buyers separate, because the high-income buyers would also like to pay a lower price (Danzon, 1997).

The technical term that describes the reach of patent-holders' rights after the first sale of their protected products is *exhaustion.* Under *national exhaustion,* a patentee can prevent parallel importation of his product from a foreign country. Under *international exhaustion,* the patentee loses the right to control further trade in his product after he has first sold it abroad, thus facilitating parallel importing. *Regional exhaustion* is a middle ground between the two. (For example, the European Union has regional exhaustion, and American politicians who support the cross-border trade in prescription drugs from Canada but no other country implicitly support regional exhaustion.)

The North American Free Trade Agreement (NAFTA) and the World Trade Organization's Agreement on Trade Related Intellectual Property Rights (TRIPS) are silent on the question of whether countries should enforce national or international exhaustion of patent rights. Although some American judges have favoured arguments supporting parallel importing, the United States has traditionally respected national exhaustion. It was US negotiators who succeeded in putting the "right of importation" into the TRIPS Agreement, which lets countries give patentees the right to stop parallel importing (Barfield & Groombridge, 1999, pp. 190-199; Rothnie, 1993, pp. 170-185). This makes proposed American legislation in favor of re-importing quite remarkable. They completely reverse the US' position on the question of exhaustion. As we shall see, this has considerable consequences for the validity of US patents.

III. Problems of Parallel Trade Between Canada and the US

The first problem of parallel trade from Canada to the United States is that it violates patent laws in both countries. The inventor of a patented good is meant to be free from competition from equivalent, identical products (Barfield & Groombridge, 1999, p. 233).

Patent laws are national, and patents for many drugs expire on different dates in Canada than they do in the US. As well, the mechanism for introducing generic competition against branded medicines is different in Canada than the United States. Furthermore, the United States provides for six months of exclusivity for the first generic manufacturer to successfully challenge a patent. This was a feature of the Hatch-Waxman Act of 1984 that was meant to give an incentive to the first generic competitor to successfully challenge an innovator's patents. Nothing similar exists in Canada. As well, the United States extends exclusivity for patented products in certain circumstances, especially if the drug is a so-called "orphan" (that is, has a small potential market), or is tested specially for use on children ("pediatric exclusivity"). As well, the US restores the terms of patents devalued by the time that the FDA takes to approve a medicine for safety and efficacy. The patent term is restored by the time it takes for the FDA to approve a medicine, by up to five years, for a total of no more than 14 years from the time the FDA approves until the patents expire. Canada has no similar provision to protect intellectual property from regulatory encroachment.

Regulations governing the introduction of competing generic products are periodically reviewed in both countries. By allowing parallel importing, legislators are allowing foreign laws to trump their own decisions regarding intellectual property. This is not to say that legislatures should shake the confidence of inventors by changing patent laws arbitrarily, but any legislative decisions with respect to patent laws should be made explicitly and deliberately, with full regard to all consequences.

For example, Hillary Clinton demanded lower US drug prices during her 2000 Senate campaign, and presented a list of six US patented drugs and their prices in the two countries. One of those drugs was Nolvadex® (tamoxifen), for which she reported a price of $390 (US), compared to Canadian tamoxifen, at $50 (US) (Clinton, 2000). However, there had been no patent on the drug for many years in Canada.[1] The fact that she compared the patented drug in the US to a generic version in Canada magnified the savings. Obviously, importing a generic drug into a country where a patent is in force violates the patent, but Mrs. Clinton did not explain why she thought that US patents on Nolvadex® should be repealed. Indeed, if the other five drugs on her list had not been patented in Canada, she probably would have compared Canadian generic prices to US patented ones for those drugs as well.

Another problem with parallel importing is that it can only thrive with government intervention that prevents drug makers from imposing certain conditions of sale on wholesalers and pharmacies. Because this intervention devalues the assets of foreign investors in Canada, it invites scrutiny under the international trade agreements to which Canada is a signatory, the most important being the North American Free Trade Agreement (NAFTA). It seems possible that the Canadian and Manitoban governments' tolerance of parallel importing is a violation of certain NAFTA provisions.

Article 1110 states that: "No Party may directly or indirectly nationalize or expropriate an investment of an investor of another Party in its territory or take a measure tantamount to nationalization or expropriation of such an investment..." The actions of the Canadian and Manitoban Industry Ministers plausibly fall into this category. One of the achievements of Canada's strengthened patent law, which was firmed up in order to be in accordance with international trade agreements, was a significant increase in capital investment by multinational, including American, research-based drug makers. Prior to 1987, Canada had poor patent protection for pharmaceuticals and pharmaceutical R&D in Canada was $106 million (Cdn). As early as 1993, investment had increased to $504 million (Cdn), and it has continued to grow to over $1.2 billion (Cdn) in 2002 (McArthur, 1999, p. 96; Pazderka, 1999; Patented Medicine Prices Review Board, 2007, p. 39). The governments' bushwhacking these companies, by allowing parallel trade for the benefit of local intermediaries certainly appears "tantamount" to expropriation.

Article 1105 states that: "Each Party shall accord to investments of investors of another Party treatment in accordance with international law, including fair and equitable treatment and full protection and security." Through allowing parallel trade, the governments of Canada and Manitoba are certainly not giving foreign-owned manufacturers "fair and equitable treatment and full protection and security", rather, they are destroying the value of their investments in Canada.

This weakening of intellectual property rights also means that inventors can neither prevent parallel traders from debasing the quality of their products, nor deter counterfeiting. Strong intellectual property rights give innovators and distributors an incentive to invest in marketing, service, and quality guarantees (Maskus, 2000, p. 155). This does not imply that consumers should not have the right to assume as much risk as they want, but parallel importing is less safe than free market distribution of prescription drugs because it threatens to prejudice manufacturers' interests in the safety of their medicines, as well as their ability to guarantee safety. Furthermore, parallel trade is actually more expensive than free trade, because it adds unnecessary costs of transportation and administration (Danzon, 1998, p. 299). There is no natural competitive advantage for Canadian warehouses in distributing mail-order prescriptions to American patients. If a free market solution can be implemented to solve the problem of American patients who cannot afford their prescriptions, it will be safer and more efficient than illegal shipments from Canada.

The pharmaceutical parallel trade between Canada and the US is also likely unsustainable in a practical sense, because those who manufacture the medicines will not tolerate its growth. The current level of pharmaceutical parallel trade from Canada to the US is a trivial share of the US market. The ultimate consequences of parallel trade depend upon how much this grows, how the drug makers respond to it, and how governments react in turn.

If all the prescriptions going to the US from Canada were for patients who are not able to buy their medicines at US prices, parallel importing would be a win-win scenario. Patients would get their drugs and manufacturers would gain some revenue that they would not otherwise have earned. However, this is not the case. By its very nature, parallel importation means that the drug makers have no idea who is buying their products; and millions of medically uninsured Americans are high-income earners (Irvine & Zelder, 2002).

The willingness of the research-based drug makers to cut off supplies to Canada is conditioned by a couple of factors. Firstly, their ability to manage their supply chains to prevent the parallel trading. Secondly, the risk that the Canadian government would allow generic manufacturers to make copycat versions of patented drugs under compulsory licenses (which is permitted for emergencies) if the research-based drug makers stop supplying Canada. The more confidence they have that Canadian law will support the integrity of their distribution into Canada, the less likely they will be to restrict supplies. Unfortunately, Canada's inaction to date gives little confidence in this regard. The real question then becomes the degree to which research-based drug makers will risk Canada's returning to a regime of compulsory licensing, which depends on whether the US government would then allow Canadian generic medicines to be parallel traded into the United States, thereby completely abolishing US patents. Despite Senator Clinton's apparent willingness to do so, it is this author's opinion that such a drastic step by the US government would be unlikely. Therefore, it is very real possibility that research-based drug makers will close up shop in Canada if this parallel trade is not stopped.

Nevertheless, another approach might not create an "emergency" that would allow Canada to impose compulsory licensing without running afoul of international trade law. This would be for the drug makers to raise prices in Canada to the US level. This cannot be done easily with drugs already sold in Canada, because Canada's Patented Medicine Prices Review Board does not generally allow price increases greater than the annual change in the Consumer Price Index (CPI). However, Canadian prices of patented medicines have usually risen less than the change in the CPI. We should not expect this to continue.

For newly introduced breakthrough drugs, Canadian prices are set with regard to those in the United Kingdom, France, Germany, Sweden, Switzerland, and Italy, as well as the United States. We should expect the drug makers to raise prices of medicines in those first six countries to US levels, so that Canadian prices can be set similarly high. Indeed, as a general rule, we should expect one, global price to evolve for each patented medicine—a price similar to the one currently in the US—in response to broadening the scope for parallel trade from foreign countries into the US.

IV. Conclusions

Wholesale parallel trade in prescription drugs from Canada to the United States is not a solution to the challenges that a small but significant number of Americans have in paying for prescriptions.

Furthermore, parallel trade is illegal: It violates the patent laws of both countries; and it may put Canada in violation of certain articles of NAFTA.

As well as being illegal, parallel trade has little to recommend it: It is a less safe method of getting prescriptions to patients than the free market; and manufacturers are likely to restrict or eliminate their supplies to Canada, or raise their Canadian prices, if the law normalizes parallel trade.

Note

1. Nolvadex® (tamoxifen) was patented in the United States until February 2003, and generic competition started there in March.

References

Barfield, C,E. & Groombridge, M.A. (1999). 'Parallel trade in the pharmaceutical industry: Implications for innovation, consumer welfare and health policy', *Fordham Intellectual Property, Media & Entertainment Law Journal*, X, 1, 185-265.

Clinton, H. (2000). *Hillary Clinton Receives Endorsement of Nurses—Announces New Proposal to Make Prescription Drugs Affordable.* Campaign speech (February 8). New York, NY: Hillary Rodham Clinton for U.S. Senate Committee.

Danzon, P.M. (1997). 'Price discrimination for pharmaceuticals: Welfare effects in the US and the EU', *International Journal of the Economics of Business*, 4(3), 301-321.

Danzon, P.M. (1998). 'The economics of parallel trade', *Pharmacoeconomics*, 13(3), 293-304.

Elzinga, K.G. & Mills, D.E. (1997). 'The distribution and pricing of prescription drugs', *International Journal of the Economics of Business*, 4(3), 287-299.

Graham, J.R. (2007). 'US prescription drug prices: persistent pressure for piracy', *Fraser Forum*, June, 13-14.

Hausman, J.A. & MacKie-Mason, J.K. (1988). 'Price discrimination and patent policy', *RAND Journal of Economics*, 19(2), 253-265.

Irvine, C. & Zelder, M. (2002). *Medically Uninsured Americans: Evidence on Magnitude and Implications.* Public Policy Source No. 58. Vancouver, BC: The Fraser Institute.

Malueg, D.A. & Schwartz, M. (1994). 'Parallel imports, demand dispersion and international price discrimination', *Journal of International Economics*, 37(3/4), 167-195.

Maskus, K. (2000). *Intellectual Property Rights in the Global Economy.* Washington, DC: Institute for International Economics.

McArthur, W. (1999). 'Intellectual property rights and the pharmaceutical industry: The consequence of incomplete protection', in O. Lippert (Ed.), *Competitive Strategies for the Protection of Intellectual Property* (pp. 85-104). Vancouver, BC: The Fraser Institute.

Morton, F.S. (1997a). 'The strategic response by pharmaceutical firms to the Medicaid most-favored customer rules', *RAND Journal of Economics*, 28(2), 269-290.

Morton, F.S. (1997b). 'The interaction between a most-favored customer clause and price dispersion: An empirical examination of the Medicaid rebate rules of 1990', *Journal of Economics & Management Strategy*, 6(1), 151-174.

Pazderka, B. (1999). 'Patent protection and pharmaceutical R&D spending in Canada', *Canadian Public Policy XXV*, 1, 29-46.

Patented Medicine Prices Review Board. (2007, July 19). *Annual Report 2006*. Ottawa, ON: Patented Medicine Prices Review Board.

Rothnie, W.A. (1993). *Parallel Imports.* London: Sweet & Maxwell.

Ruff, A. (1992). 'Releasing the grays: In support of legalizing parallel imports', *UCLA Pacific Basin Law Journal*, 11(1) 119-154.

Risk, Responsibility, and Litigation[1]

Sandra H. Johnson
Saint Louis University School of Law and Center for Health Care Ethics

and

Ana S. Iltis
Saint Louis University Center for Health Care Ethics

I. Introduction

Humans face a wide range of threats from their environment and from the malfunctioning of their own bodies. On the one hand, there are risks of new SARS-like epidemics and multi-drug-resistant tuberculosis. On the other hand, the aging populations of the world are at significant risk of Alzheimer's, cardiovascular disease, and cancer. While traditional public health interventions are critical to lowering these risks, the hope for lowering these risks also is intimately tied to the possibility of innovation in pharmaceuticals and medical devices. Thus it is a reasonable public policy goal (1) to encourage innovation in the development of pharmaceuticals and medical devices in the hope of decreasing morbidity and morality risks for current and future persons. This is accomplished by establishing rules, regulations, policies, and practices that encourage such innovation and that are not likely to impede it. At the same time, public policy also must aim (2) to bring justice to persons injured by devices and drugs, and (3) deter the development and distri-

H.T. Engelhardt, Jr. and J. Garrett (eds), *Innovation and the Pharmaceutical Industry* (pp. 193–229).

bution of dangerous products. These three aims of public policy may not be pursued independently of one another.

Since the development of pharmaceutical and medical innovation requires the investment of considerable funds, one would hope to establish legal and public policy rules that encourage investment in these areas. Investors must take into consideration both the likelihood for profits as well as the possibility of costs, such as those incurred through products liability litigation. Venture capitalists, for example, when considering the likelihood of return on any investment, must ask whether such funds are better invested in the pharmaceutical and medical industry or in the production of video games and popular movies. At the same time, public policy should discourage negligence, including failure to test the safety of medical products, and deceit, particularly deceit that can lead to harm, such as the cover-up of known dangers. Individuals harmed by such practices must be compensated, and purveyors of defective products held accountable, particularly when their negligence resulted in the distribution of dangerous drugs or devices. In establishing a particular threshold for holding that companies have acted immorally, unethically, or improperly so as to be liable at law, one must be concerned with the balance between the interests of particular parties to be treated justly and the need to promote innovation that will lead to effective treatments for persons in the future.

There are instances in the history of products liability litigation in which the balance among the goals of public policy—encouraging innovation, bringing justice to the injured, and deterring the development and distribution of dangerous products—has been maintained and others in which it has been distorted. Cases in which judgments comport with science raise few questions. But the balance is distorted in cases in which multi-million dollar settlements or verdicts have been reached, even though the scientific evidence of product-caused injury at best has been unavailable or, at worst, has shown that the products in question did not cause the claimed injuries. This paper offers a framework for understanding how judgments that do not comport with scientific evidence and that result in imbalances that might threaten pharmaceutical and medical device innovation arise.

Much of the discussion focuses on the conditions that shape products liability litigation and influence outcomes. As one considers these issues and the broader public policy context within which they arise, it is important to recognize that public policy aims and the litigation process may be informed by ethical considerations. There are competing conceptions of corporate responsibility that may influence how persons judge corporations and assess damages.

There is a long-standing tradition in medicine of recognizing physicians as having special, fiduciary duties to their patients. More important for products liability litigation is a fundamental question of organizational ethics: do corporations that provide health care or sell health-related products have special duties to individuals and/or to society? Do such corporations have ethical duties, the breach of which may be relevant in making judgments and assessing damages? If so, what are these duties and how much should they influence litigation?

The dominant approach in health care organization ethics today is stakeholder theory. In contrast to a shareholder approach, which holds that corporations' ethical responsibility is to abide by the law and maximize the interests of those who are financially invested in them (Friedman, 1962 & 1967), stakeholder theory holds that corporations have ethical responsibilities to all who are affected by their decisions and actions. The stakeholders include investors, patients, the public, and clinicians. It is open to question whether stakeholder theory is an appropriate model for organizational ethics (Sternberg, 1999). But even if one adopts stakeholder theory, there is much room for debate, as stakeholder theory leaves a number of questions unanswered. Thus it should not be surprising to find different conceptions of corporate responsibility operating in products liability cases.

First, stakeholder theory offers no normative reason for ranking the stakeholders in any particular order. Many who have developed stakeholder theory for use in health care have stated that patients' interests must come first (e.g., Werhane, 2000, pp. 176-177; AMA, 2000), but this is not inherent in the stakeholder approach. One could argue, as utilitarians would, that it is more important to protect the interests of the majority than of specific individuals. In cases it which it is overall best for society that the relatively few patients harmed by a particular product not be compensated or be compensated less than they otherwise might be, utilitarians would argue that we should limit awards. Those individuals' interests should not trump the interests of society. A different account of the need to respect individual persons, particularly those who have been harmed, would generate a radically different recommendation.

Second, stakeholder theory does not tell us which interests of a given party should be taken into account or which of those interests a corporation has an obligation to fulfill or at least consider. Do persons who use a drug to treat rheumatoid arthritis made by Company X and who develop unrelated but coincidental health conditions have a claim on Company X to develop drugs to treat those other conditions? Does Company X's obligation increase if it has a large amount of money available for research and development? Does a company that produces a cholesterol lowering medication have an obligation to make exercise equipment available to those who use the drug, if it is thought that exercise will help lower their cholesterol even further? Should the company develop a financial assistance program for uninsured consumers in need of the drug?

Third, there is no single account of how one should rank competing interests among stakeholders of the same category. One can imagine that persons with a particular medical condition might be considered members of the same category. Consider a situation in which there is a new drug being developed to treat the condition. It is in the interest of those whose disease state is more advanced to have the drug become available quickly, just in case it works. Those who have the same condition but are not yet as sick as the other group have an interest in ensuring that the drug is well-tested in controlled clinical trials before they use it so that they can be sure it is safe and effective. Stakeholder theory itself does not move us toward a resolution of these competing claims.

Fourth, stakeholder theory cannot resolve substantive debates concerning what is in a person's or group's interest. Is it better for persons to be permitted access to a product that promises to relieve suffering but that poses significant risks, or is it better to prevent the dissemination of a product that would expose persons to those risks?

Tensions emerge at two levels in attempting to determine whether a corporation that provides health care or health products has special obligations to others and, if so, what those obligations are, what roles they should play in litigation, and the extent to which they should constrain public policy. First is the assessment of the extent to which a corporation has obligations to any particular party, a tension exemplified in the debate between stakeholder theory and shareholder theory proponents. Second, even if one can agree on the extent to which a corporation has duties to other parties, there is disagreement concerning how to rank and interpret those interests. This is exemplified by the multiple ways in which one might apply stakeholder theory. Those who make decisions in products liability cases are likely to hold varying views on these issues. Their underlying conceptions of corporate obligations and of how to balance properly the competing interests of various parties may shape their decisions.

What stakeholder theory can add, especially in the context of litigation defense, is a method for identifying a broad range of persons who have a stake in the work of the defendant entity in terms of benefit from the essential enterprise. From a plaintiff's perspective, stakeholder theory establishes a moral claim on the work of the corporation.

II. Product Liability Litigation

A. Science and Law: Convergence and Divergence

Demonstrating or attempting to establish the causal connection between the product and the alleged harm is critical to liability in products litigation. There are well-known cases in the history of products liability litigation in which there was medical evidence that the alleged injuries or harms were real and there was strong scientific evidence to support the causal connection between a device or drug and a harm, e.g., the Dalkon Shield increased the incidence of Pelvic Inflammatory Disease (Cox, 2003; Gareen, Greenland, & Morgenstern, 2000; Sivin, 1993; Snowden & Pearson, 1984; Kaufman et al., 1983; Lee, Rubin, Ory, & Burkman, 1983) and DES taken by women during pregnancy caused problems in the reproductive systems of their female fetuses (Senekjian, Potkul, Frey, & Gerbst, 1988; Jeffries et al, 1984; Kaufman, Adam, Binder, & Gerthoffer, 1980). However, there also have been large verdicts and settlements in cases in which the scientific evidence did not strongly support a plaintiff's claim that a particular product had caused the alleged harm. Sometimes it was not even certain that there was a harm at all. These include cases regarding Bendectin and silicone breast implants.

Bendectin, which was prescribed to treat morning sickness during pregnancy, was available in U.S. from 1956-1983. In 1969, a number of case reports began appearing in the medical literature describing birth defects, including limb deformities and reductions, abnormalities in the gastrointestinal tracts, and neural tube defects in babies born to women who had taken Bendectin during pregnancy (see Paterson, 1969 & 1977; Donnai & Harris, 1978; Menzies, 1978; Frith, 1978; Mellor, 1978; Fisher, Nelson, Allen & Holzman, 1982; Grodofsky & Wilmott, 1984). These reports of individual practitioners' experiences did not constitute sufficient evidence to determine that Bendectin caused the anomalies. Epidemiologic data evaluating the incidence of birth defects in children born to women who took Bendectin compared to that of the population in general was necessary to make that kind of assessment. Amidst the early case reports, epidemiologic studies were undertaken and some studies did suggest that there was a slight possibility that women who took Bendectin were more likely to give birth to babies with anomalies (Rothman, Fyler, Goldblatt, & Kreidberg, 1979; Golding, Vivian & Baldwin, 1983). However, the majority of epidemiologic studies examining the relationship between Bendectin and fetal anomalies have not confirmed a causal connection between Bendectin and birth defects (e.g., Elbourne, et al., 1985; Gibson, Colley, McMichael, & Harthshorne, 1981; Jick, Holmes, Hunter, Madsen, & Stergachis, 1981; Smithells & Sheppard, 1978; Fleming, Knox, & Crombie, 1981; Newman, Correy, & Dudgeon, 1977; Milkovich & van den Berg, 1976; MacMahon, 1981; McCredie, Kricker, Eliott, & Forrest, 1984; Aselton et al., 1985; Nelson & Forfar, 1971; Zierler & Rothman, 1985; Clarke & Clayton, 1981; Michaelis, Michaelis, Gluck, & Koller, 1983). The thousands of suits filed against Merrel National Laboratories (later Merrel Dow Pharmaceuticals), the maker of Bendectin, had mixed results. Nevertheless, in a significant number of cases, juries returned verdicts in favor of the plaintiff (Lasagna & Shulman, 1993). It is plausible that the discrepancies between epidemiologic studies and the disagreements among scientists led juries and judges to rule in favor of plaintiffs.

One of the most well-known examples of products liability litigation in which the scientific evidence and jury verdicts often seemed at great odds concerns silicone breast implants. Between 1980 and the mid-1990s, the American public was exposed to intense and sometimes dramatic discussions concerning silicone breast implants. Introduced in the U.S. in 1962, silicone breast implants became increasingly popular and it was estimated that by 1992 approximately 1 million American women had implants. By 1997, this number was estimated at somewhere between 1.5 and 1.8 million (Institute of Medicine, 2000, p. 2). Although in 1977 a woman from Cleveland was given $170,000 in a settlement from Dow Corning for pain and suffering allegedly caused by a ruptured implant, silicone breast implants first became the subject of public controversy in 1982 when a report came out of Australia that three women who had silicone implants also had connective tissue disease (Van Nunen, Gatenby, & Basten, 1982). Soon after, litigation began in the United States. In 1984, in *Stern v. Dow Corning Corp.* [Case No. C-83-2348-MMP(N.D. Cal 1984)], the plaintiff alleged that her systemic autoimmune disease had been caused by her implants. The jury concurred and awarded her $211,000 in compensatory damages and $1.5 million in punitive damages (Stewart, 2002, p. 6). The theory that silicone breast implants were causing connective tissue disease in women grew in popularity, more anecdotal reports emerged in the medical literature, more lawsuits were filed, and more plaintiffs were awarded millions of dollars in verdicts and settlements (Angell, 1996).

In December, 1990, Connie Chung interviewed on prime-time television women who had silicone implants and who claimed that their implants had caused them to suffer a litany of problems. Chung concluded on the air that these were dangerous devices that should not be marketed. Some have suggested that such a public event had a significant effect in solidifying in the minds of many lay Americans that silicone breast implants do in fact cause autoimmune disease. The American public became increasingly uneasy in the early 1990s and there was a tidal wave of pressure for the government to "do something." In 1992, the FDA banned silicone implants (with some exceptions for clinical trials involving patients who had undergone mastectomies and were having breast reconstruction) stating that they had not yet been proven safe.[2] The FDA did not say that they were dangerous, simply that they were not proven safe. But that fine distinction seemed to be lost on the public and the courts, and the FDA's action cracked the presumed safety that consumers afford products on the market. More lawsuits were filed against the makers of silicone implants and ultimately the makers of the silicone itself. Often manufacturers settled out of court, but in many of those cases that went to trial, jury verdicts were in the millions of dollars. Perhaps the most sensational case was *Johnson v. Medical Engineering Co, Johnson v. Bristol-Myers Squibb Corp., et al.,* [CN 91-21770 (TX Dist. Ct., 125 Jud. Dist. 1992)]. The plaintiff claimed that a variety of ailments, including respiratory and bladder infections, chronic fatigue, muscle and joint pain, headaches, and dizziness were the result of a ruptured implant. Even though the jury knew she was a heavy cigarette smoker, they decided that the implant was the cause of her alleged ailments and awarded her $25 million ($5 million in actual damages and $20 million in punitive damages) (Hersch, 2002). (Medical Engineering Corporation is a subsidiary of Bristol Myers Squibb.)

As progress was made toward a class action settlement with numerous implant manufacturers, the number of ailments particular women attributed to their implants grew, as did the number of women claiming to have been harmed. Everything from lupus, to neurological problems, to headaches, to pain was blamed on silicone implants. It was even alleged that a new "disease" had been caused by implants, silicone-induced autoimmune disease (Angell, 1996). All this while there was no conclusive scientific evidence linking silicone implants to any, let alone all, of these conditions (Gabriel et al., 1994; Sanchez-Guerrero et al., 1995).[3] In fact, a variety of expert panels were convened by the courts to assess the scientific evidence available. The panel established for *In re Silicone Gel Breast Implants* [793 F.Supp. 1098 (J.P.M.L. 1992)], for example, produced a report in November, 1998 in which all four experts, a toxicologist, immunologist, epidemiologist, and rheumatologist, agreed that the animal and human data available did not support the claim that the silicone in silicone breast implants was causally connected to the variety of ailments alleged by the plaintiffs. They reviewed the existing studies and found none of them compelling. The few studies that did suggest a link between the two were flawed, the experts held, in ways that made it impossible to accept their conclusions as definitive (Hooper, Cecil, & Willging, 2001). These flaws included a failure to verify patients' symptoms and reliance on a small sample size. For example, the Women's Health Cohort Study (Hennekens, Lee, Cook, et al., 1996) suggested that there is a slight possibility that women with implants may be at slightly higher risk for reporting certain conditions. But this study suffered from serious limitations, including the fact that the study was based on a questionnaire sent to women after there had been significant media attention given to the matter and no effort was made to verify the reported ailments. The results have not been confirmed by more rigorous studies (Institute of Medicine, 2000; European Committee on Quality Assurance and Medical Devices in Plastic Surgery, 1998).

What is most important for our discussion is that in all of the litigation and all of the pre-trial hearings and negotiations leading to the out of court settlements, no strong scientific evidence was offered showing that silicone implants had caused any kind of disease. In fact, in at least one case, the plaintiff's attorney urged the jury to set science aside and look at the case as one concerning ethics (*Gladys J. Laas, et al v. Dow Corning Corporation, et al* Cause No. 93-04266, Harris County, Texas). During the trial, the plaintiff had argued that the manufacturer had acted unethically because it had not done follow-up tests to determine what happened when silicone migrated in the body and that the manufacturer had tried to cover up evidence of the dangers associated with silicone. The implication was that even if there was no scientific evidence to support the causal connection between silicone breast implants and the alleged injuries, Dow Corning should be held liable for what the plaintiff called unethical conduct.

The plaintiffs in many of the silicone breast implant cases never provided independent verification that they were suffering from all the problems and harms they alleged. Many of them had been seen by the same series of physicians who had begun to "specialize" in treating women with implants. Plaintiffs' attorneys often referred women to these physicians, a circumstance which raised suspicions of false reporting (Angell, 1996; Kolata & Meir, 1995). Some women did have physical ailments, but it was not clear that any, let alone all, of their difficulties were the result of their implants. Virtually all the scientific evidence presented suggested no link. Numerous panels of experts have been convened in the United States and Europe to examine the evidence. There is to date no clear scientific evidence that silicone breast implants cause connective-tissue diseases (Institute of Medicine, 2000; European Committee on Quality Assurance and Medical Devices in Plastic Surgery, 1998 & 2000; Gott & Tinkler, 1994). The epidemiological data simply do not support the claim that there is a causal connection between implants and systemic disease.

Despite the fact that the preponderance of scientific evidence did not and does not support the plaintiffs' claims, large awards have made to plaintiffs in silicone breast implant litigation. How did this happen?

The goal of science is to attain a well-reasoned, accurate conclusion reached by an accepted methodology (Capron, 1996). However, the ability to revise prior theories, ideas, and conclusions perpetually exists. Science progresses with new information over periods of time and may be more appropriately explained as the continued refining of hypotheses that approach a highly probable truth (Cowell, 2000). Thus, science is not subject to a closed time frame. As scientists obtain new data, they revise and replace even well-established scientific theories (Feldman, 1995). Scientific theory never achieves finality and does not produce fixed, unassailable conclusions. In fact, finality and closure are not necessarily desirable in the scientific community. "The very nature of science incorporates a view of even generally accepted explanations of phenomena as tentative truths, not settled certainties" (Cheng, 2003).

The preferred method for establishing a link between an allegedly toxic substance and a human disease is epidemiological research (Henning & Berman, 2003; Green, 1992). Such research, which collects data from a large number of people over an extended period of time, can offer the "best" scientific guess there is (Wagner, 2003). However, epidemiological research is expensive and time consuming (Cheng, 2003); and these studies are generally not available prior to litigation (Cheng,

2003). Michael Green illustrates this point by noting that "[a]mong seventy-five chemicals found to be carcinogens in animals, only thirteen had been the subject of epidemiologic study" (Green, 1992). Even so, epidemiological research is not incontrovertible and is subject to the same reconsideration as are the other methods of scientific research (Golanski, forthcoming; Wagner, 2003; Cheng, 2003).

The law, on the other hand, has a very different time frame. It requires that time be frozen so that fact finders may assess responsibility at a given moment in time (Cowell, 2000). Courts take a case between two litigants and make the best decision out of whatever evidence is presented (Cheng, 2003). There is no requirement of absolute correctness in deciding particular cases. Edward Cheng observes that "to require certainty or even near-certainty [in law] would be impracticable and undesirable. The law thus compromises" (Cheng, 2003). Henry Hart and John McNaughton emphasize that the law does not require absolute assurance of the perfect correctness of particular decisions. While it is important that the court be right in its determinations of fact, it is also important that the court decide the case when the parties ask for the decision and on the basis of the evidence presented by the parties. A decision must be made now, one way or the other (Hart & McNaughton, 1958). Thus, the goal of accuracy gives way to the law's emphasis on expedient dispute resolution and finality (Cheng, 2003). Unlike scientific inquiry, the law does not reexamine decisions that are considered final (Cheng, 2003). Doctrines such as res judicata and collateral estoppel reflect the policy that the law prefers final judgments, even if these prior findings are later deemed incorrect.

Cheng also notes that a tension is created, therefore, when the law attempts to draw upon scientific data, especially that which is immature or incomplete. The law wants answers, but science is not ready (Cheng, 2003). The law, operating under a finite timeline, attempts to obtain answers from science, which has a potentially indefinite life cycle. The law's goal of resolution of the current dispute directly clashes with science's slow progression toward a consensus. Thus, the legal system ends up with the problem of changing scientific evidence (Cheng, 2003).

Statutes of limitations, which exist to protect defendants and to prevent the litigation of stale claims (*U.S. v. Kubrick*) compound this timing problem when there are questions surrounding general causation. In traditional tort cases, statutes of limitations make sense. Evidence is generated from a single incident, and from that point forward the value of evidence degrades: Memories fade; physical evidence may become lost; witnesses may become unavailable. Logic and judicial efficacy thus suggest that such claims should be brought in a timely fashion.

However, this limitations period does not produce such favorable results when there is uncertainty as to the cause of one's injury. Evidence about general causation typically improves, rather than degrades, over time (*U.S. v. Kubrick*). In contrast, time and further scientific inquiry may produce more conclusive data regarding the harmful effects of a certain product or substance (Cheng, 2003).

Under the discovery rule, the statute of limitations does not begin to run until the plaintiff discovers or reasonably should have discovered the injury, and in many jurisdictions, its cause (Cheng, 2003). While the discovery rule may relax the rigid constraints of statutes of limitations, it has not eliminated the timing problem between science and the law. Plaintiffs are required to bring claims within a time period from the point they "discovered or reasonably should have discovered" the injury and cause thereof. The problem here is that the law cannot pinpoint a time in which science yields sufficient data. Since science is constantly vulnerable to reexamination, an anomaly emerges when the law attempts to select a time at which a plaintiff "reasonably should have discovered" an injury. After all, even science is unwilling to identify such a point.

Thus, science may provide (or even compel) plaintiffs with data supporting causation that is determined sufficient under discovery rule standards, but this data may be inaccurate or in its infancy. The statute of limitations, both under the discovery rule and under a limitations period marked at the point when the injury occurred, may begin to run despite the absence of causation data sufficient for scientific or litigation standards. Plaintiffs are then left with a choice between not bringing a claim at all and brining one based on immature scientific support. Unsurprisingly, the latter is generally chosen. The legal system then picks up where it would have been absent the discovery rule- facing the problem of changing scientific evidence in a system that values timeliness over accuracy.

The remainder of our discussion analyzes the principal psychological, cultural, and social factors shaping and driving such cases. Much of the explanation for the disjunction between the evidence and the awards turns on the social construction of the concepts of trust, causation, proof, consent, fault, and responsibility.

B. Telling the Story: The Role of Narrative

Pleadings, motions, briefs, and opening and closing statements all aim to construct a social reality of medical intervention now subject to litigation. They tell a story of the expectations, relationships, disappointments, harms (real or imagined, feared or invented) claimed by the now-plaintiff patient, and the care or failings of the physician or manufacturer. An analysis of these narratives provides a tool for examining the social construction of consent, cause, proof, injury or harm, and fault. As our discussion will demonstrate, the social-legal construction of such concepts has dramatic implications for the costs likely to be imposed on companies attempting to develop new drugs and medical devices.

Before a lawsuit is a lawsuit, it's a story. The pleadings for most lawsuits typically are relatively devoid of the detail of human drama (Eastman, 1995). The job of both the plaintiff's and the defendant's attorneys is to make the case a story once again – to the judge, very definitely to the jury, and increasingly to the media and public at large.

The importance of establishing a narrative framework for presenting the case is prominent in practical advice from experienced litigators. For example, two attorneys from the defense bar advise plaintiffs' and defense attorneys, in relation to damages:

> All through the trial, tell the story behind the actual damages. The same narrative skills you employ in convincing the jury your client has been wronged should be used to show the jury how much your client has lost.
> . . .
> It is the personal impact that drives home the story of your client's damages far more dramatically than any damages expert can. . . .
> The defense lawyer, meanwhile, must tell the other side of the story in comparable dramatic fashion. . . . Dramatize the facts with fact witnesses before trotting out the cold, unrelenting economic data. (Frey & Orr, 2004)

Scholars who use narrative as an analytical tool have identified a particular "narrative framework" for litigation as a system or process. The narrative framework used in litigation contrasts with that used in other legal processes or relationships. For example, in litigation:

> [P]arties struggle against one another in order to convince a decision maker of the truth of "what happened." . . . The assumption that one party is right and one party is wrong is not open to question; litigation is based on a shared norm among all participants (litigants, judge, jury) that only one of the litigants is right about "what happened." (Rubinson, 2004)

Furthermore, Rubinson asserts that the narrative of the case must establish that the untoward event was attributable to human action that was somehow inappropriate, if not corrupt. In establishing what happened and identifying fault or blamelessness, trial lawyers aim at convincing the decision maker not only that a client's version of events, context, and significance is true, but that the decision maker has an important role to play in the story. The decision maker—judge or jury—is called upon to "vindicate goodness by identifying and rewarding the 'good' party and condemning and punishing the 'bad' party" (Rubinson, 2004). The decision maker determines how the story ends.

A comparison to mediation is useful in understanding the extent to which this narrative framework of one truth and righting wrongs defines litigation. The narrative framework for mediation, in contrast to litigation, does not view the parties as engaged in a struggle to prove the truth of what happened and culpability for the bad act that disrupted the ordinary and desirable pattern of life. Instead, mediation intentionally articulates a norm that stories of what happened are always determined by the particular perspective of the one providing the description. For this reason, mediation does not focus on the past as the basis for a decision, as does litigation, but rather focuses the parties on what arrangements would best serve them in the future (Rubinson, 2004).

There is evidence that juries recognize something as fact and organize and give significance to facts by using stories that they construct themselves, emerging from their own beliefs and their own experience (Pennington & Hastie, 1991). Litigators recognize this in their emphasis on jury selection and in their investment in constructing a story that will appeal to the specific panel they face.

There are many popular narrative frameworks in American culture that juries may bring to the interpretation of events in products liability and negligence litigation, including, for example, the David and Goliath story, but also Marcus Welby and the story of the accomplishments of pharmaceuticals in curing the conditions that killed or disabled juror's grandparents. Many assume that juries place any facts into a plaintiff-friendly narrative framework. In fact, research indicates that juries are "biased against plaintiffs, often blaming them for their fates," and failing to compensate them for their injuries (Podlas, 2004; Saks, 1992). Evidence also suggests that jury awards against business defendants are actually less than those against non-business defendants (Podlas, 2004).

This documented pattern gives some insight into the story that juries, as a whole, may actually bring to the table; and it is more complicated and more nuanced than some assume. Of course, despite the research showing a generalized bias against plaintiffs and in favor of defendants, individual episodes and anecdotal evidence provide a troubling counterweight. For example, several jurors for silicone breast implant trials have admitted that they simply did not care about the scientific and medical evidence (Breast Implants on Trial, 1996) and others that they awarded the plaintiff damages because they felt sorry for her even though they were not convinced that the implants caused her illnesses (Bandow, 1998).

Some scholars argue that judges approach deciding a case in exactly the same way that juries do (Rubinson, 2004). Comparing different courts' statements of the facts of what is supposed to be the same case, for example at different levels of review, easily proves that judges take care to present their decisions within a particular rendition of the facts that may differ significantly or subtly from the way that the previous court described "what happened." Such a comparison of judicial presentation of facts may indicate that judges also understand facts through a narrative lens.

The analysis of narrative in products liability and negligence litigation reveals an assumption that the process has to do with truth, fairness and justice and is essentially a normative process (Wells, 1990). Robert Cover, in the seminal work on narrative and law, observes that judges can do nothing else (Cover, 1982). The plaintiffs' bar clearly understands the importance of the morality tale at the center of litigation. Defendants' attorneys ignore the power of the normative narrative at their peril. Some scholars have even suggested that judges should consider presenting the rationale for particular decisions in common moral terms rather than in the less appealing terms of economics (Kaplow & Shavell, 2002).

Mathematical calculations and statistical analyses have to be set in a context, in a story, in order to be persuasive to the jury. Relying solely or even primarily on statistical evidence is dangerous for both plaintiffs and defendants. For plaintiffs, statistics will neither provide the link to careless or corrupt behavior that informs the litigation narrative nor embody the victim. For defendants, statistics can never outweigh the presence of a living individual plaintiff. This dynamic has been observed in decision making about risk generally, where decision makers tend to treat "statistical lives" differently from identified individuals, knowingly choosing courses of action that will produce a predictable number of deaths and injuries, but reversing course dramatically and usually suddenly when those "statistical lives" are identified and individualized, (Calabresi & Bobbitt, 1978)

The McDonalds coffee litigation, described below, provides an illustration. The defense, at least according to news reports, framed the corporate decisions and plaintiff's injuries in statistical terms arguing that the episode was statistically insignificant. Jurors, with the help of the plaintiff's narrative framework, viewed the defendant as saying that the plaintiff's injuries were insignificant. In characterizing the amount the jury should award in punitive damages, the plaintiff's attorney did not simply provide the numbers in relation to the overall corporate revenues, but rather set the amount as "two days sales of coffee."

Class action litigation is particularly affected by the narrative framework of litigation. In class action litigation, the plaintiffs are large in number and, although there has to be a basic and minimum commonality (Wright, Miller, & Kane, 2004), class members are diverse. If one accepts the power of narrative in litigation, either from a practical or a theoretical perspective, class actions present a particular challenge. Because of numbers, class actions are litigated upon the stories of a few of the members of the class. Plaintiffs are able to select the most appealing members of the class presenting the most compelling cases for relief. Other class members get the advantage of the strong current created by these signal cases. In addition, the sheer number of plaintiffs in a class action can provide an important element of the narrative: the defendant must have known what was happening.

Finally, lawyers are by training if not by personality predisposed to accept the power of narrative and the "social construction of reality" because these notions express the common experience in the law that different people see things differently. Lawyers are also accustomed to pluralistic values and policy goals. What may be harder to accommodate is the view that science itself is subject to rhetoric, social values, and institutional pressures. The fundamental nature of science is currently debated, with one extreme arguing that science "reports on natural reality" and the other extreme arguing that science is "a social, rhetorical, and institutional enterprise that only manages to convince us that it deals in natural reality" (Caudill & LaRue, 2003). Empirical evidence suggests that the public is "critically reflective" and "suspicious about the interests of scientists, and aware of scientific controversies, inconsistencies, and errors" (Caudill & LaRue, 2003). Certainly, common experience is replete with examples of scientific risk assessment and scientific advice that has turned in opposite directions on a dime.

Recent attention to financial conflicts of interest in research also suggests that scientists, in their work as scientists, can be influenced by scientifically irrelevant factors such as who sponsored the research. At least one meta-analysis of the results of drug studies suggests that the outcomes of the studies are influenced by the interests of the sponsor (Bekelman, 2003).

The tools of narrative can be applied to the problem of scientific evidence in products liability and negligence litigation. Realizing that the decision maker, whether jury or judge, brings a critical construct to the evidence presented borne of the experience of changeability in science over time should influence the context set for scientific evidence. The attorney would fashion a narrative of particular reliability or trust for this expert or this body of research; or, if on the other side of the expert testimony, telling a story of a habit of change, called "progress," as a characteristic of science or a story of "work for hire" in science generally as well as particularly in this case.

C. Trust

An additional factor to consider is the role of trust in litigation and the extent to which a party or witness' trustworthiness or perceived trustworthiness might influence a juror's assessment of the information. Health care is built on trust (Illingworth, 2002; Mechanic, 1998; Pellegrino, 1991; Potter, 1996; Zaner, 1991). Litigation evidences a breach of trust, at least from the perspective of the plaintiff. When finger-pointing begins, decision makers draw broadly in weighing credibility and fixing fault, including data, personal experience, and history. In cases in which there is conflicting evidence or in which conflicting stories are told, jurors must decide whom they will trust. When a jury considers a corporate defendant in the health care industry, what image and history provide the social context? The image of companies that have decreased morbidity and mortality through the development of insulin, antihypertensives, and broad-spectrum antibiotics? Or is the defendant corporation of the sort that brought us Enron, WorldCom, the Pinto, health care fraud, and thalidomide? The history of corporate scandals and fraud combined with the way this history has been portrayed in the media may very well predispose many jurors to distrust the corporate defendant and trust the plaintiff. In fact, there is evidence that many Americans do not trust corporations or their leaders. Recent corporate scandals, including misconduct among healthcare organizations, are likely to increase this lack of trust.

The history of corporate scandals and breaches of trust can do more than predispose jurors to see the defendant as untrustworthy and to find for the plaintiff, however. They can fuel outrage among jurors, and even when the corporate defendant's history is not tainted, the plaintiff's attorneys may be able to count on a general sense of outrage against corporate giants to win the jury's trust and sympathy. This may mean that there is a greater burden on corporations to prove that their products are benign and that their actions were appropriate.

Preconceptions concerning the obligation of healthcare providers to be trustworthy, to do good, and to avoid harm may shape how jurors understand and interpret plaintiffs' stories and defendants' explanations. The natural history of trust in health care, including the impact of law, is a topic of current discussion in health law and ethics. It is increasingly being suggested that not only individual practitioners have a duty to be trustworthy but that healthcare organizations, and we can include here manufacturers of medical devices and drugs, have similar duties of trustworthiness, beneficence, and non-maleficence (Buchanan, 2000; Dorr-Goold, 2001; Rhodes & Strain, 2000). If jurors share these assumptions regarding the obligations of healthcare providers, even if the assumptions are undisclosed and perhaps subconscious, they may find themselves thinking that manufacturers and physicians had a duty to make sure that no one was harmed by a device or drug and that perhaps they could have done something more to prevent the plaintiff's suffering. Even if they did not directly cause the harm, could they have stopped it? After all, no one is supposed to get hurt by going to the doctor! We will give further attention to the impact of perceptions regarding risk among patients and jurors.

The legal system seems to have built into it an important role for trust. In the case of *Daubert v. Merrell Dow Pharmaceuticals, Inc.* (1993), the Supreme Court held that scientific testimony admissible in court should no longer be restricted to that which the Frye standard, established in 1923, would allow. According to *Frye v. United States* (1923), only evidence that was the subject of scientific consensus was admissible. Over time, this came to mean information that had been subject to peer review and had been published in established scientific and medical journals. The Court held that this standard was no longer appropriate, in part because it sometimes required the exclusion of cutting-edge research. In *Daubert,* the Court laid out four considerations that should guide the use of scientific evidence:

(a) Is the expert's theory capable of being tested, and has it been tested?
(b) If the expert has applied a purportedly scientific test or method in arriving at his conclusions, does that test have a known error rate, and are there special controls or procedures necessary for its application?
(c) Has the expert's theory or methodology been the subject of peer-review and publication?
(d) Has the expert's theory or methodology been "generally accepted" in the relevant scientific community? (Worthington, Stallard, Price & Goss, 2002).

Expert testimony must meet these criteria for a judge to permit a jury to hear the testimony. But the criteria are flexible and are interpreted and applied at judges' discretion. This means that either judges themselves must be knowledgeable enough about science and medicine to serve as evidence gatekeepers, or they must enlist other experts to help them judge the testimony (Browne, Keele, & Hiers, 1998; Worthington, Stallard, Price, & Goss, 2002). The *Daubert* criteria do not, and are not intended to, eliminate the possibility of expert witnesses disagreeing and offering competing accounts. When persons are presented as expert physicians or scientists, there is some expectation that they will be knowledgeable and truthful. When such persons offer conflicting accounts, as they did in the silicone breast implant cases, jurors must decide whom to trust. To rely on an expert's professional status is insufficient in those cases, because all are presumed to be qualified and trustworthy. So other factors must be taken into account. These may include how well jurors understand their testimony, personal attributes, and jurors' overall assessment of the trustworthiness of the party on whose behalf the witness is testifying.

D. Science and Statistics

In addition to the influence of narrative and trust on jurors' assessment of the evidence, the fact that products liability litigation often involves complex scientific evidence also affects the extent to which jury decisions are commensurate with the evidence. Moreover, because scientific opinion changes over time, jurors may not consider science the most reliable source of information.

The understanding of basic science, statistics and statistical analysis, and the concept of risk most persons have are limited (Kovera, McAuliff, & Hebert, 1999; Lehman & Nisbett, 1990 cited in Worthington, Stallard, Price, & Goss, 2002). This allows the parties involved in the litigation to construct a reality for jurors that does not necessarily mirror the reality supported by the scientific evidence.

In products liability litigation, jurors are often presented with extensive scientific information, much of which they are likely to find difficult if not impossible to understand (Menon, 1995). In the case of breast implant litigation, much of the information concerned toxicology, immunology and rheumatology. To expect jurors to be able to assess this information with an appropriate level of understanding is unwarranted. But the problem extends beyond jurors not understanding the basic scientific issues at stake to their inability or limited ability to assess scientific studies and data in general. Without an understanding of statistics and statistical analysis, for example, jurors may not understand the importance of sample size and of controlling for variables. Without these distinctions they cannot appropriately differentiate between scientifically strong and weak studies. All they can know is what each party in the litigation claims regarding a study, and then their choices rest not on the evidence itself but on some other factor, such as the credibility of the witness or party in question, or the sympathy each party elicits in them. The limited understanding most jurors have of statistics and statistical analysis may leave them unable to appropriately assess the merit of the scientific evidence with which they are presented (Worthington, Stallard, Price, & Goss, 2002). Yet this is precisely what they must do when presented with conflicting information. Attorneys representing the party whose claims are not supported by the evidence can use this to their advantage; they may depict as real cause and effect relationships and correlations that are unsupported by scientific evidence (Riley, 1996; Worthington, Stallard, Price, & Goss, 2002).

There is some evidence to suggest that in those cases in which the scientific evidence does not support a plaintiff's claim, plaintiffs' attorneys are particularly keen to have the case heard by a jury whose understanding of science and statistics is limited. For example, in 1985 litigation consolidating nearly 1,000 Bendectin cases [*In re Richardson-Merrell, Inc. "Bendectin" Products Liability Litigation,* 624 F. Supp 1212 (S.D. Ohio 1985)], the judge offered the parties the opportunity to select either a "blue, blue ribbon jury" or a "blue ribbon jury". A double blue ribbon jury would consist of jurors who were educated in or had substantial knowledge of the fields from which the expert witnesses would be drawn. A single blue ribbon jury would consist of those persons on the jury panel that had the most extensive formal education. Those persons, one can presume, would be more likely to have taken advanced math and science courses and to be able to understand the evidence presented. The plaintiffs refused this offer and instead a jury was chosen that included at least one individual who had not attended high school (Lasagna & Shulman, 1993, p. 110).

Hindsight-bias, the circumstance in which persons make judgments regarding what should have been done based on their current knowledge of the outcomes (Fischoff, 1975), plays a significant role in jury decision-making (Worthington, Stallard, Price, & Goss, 2002; Casper, Benedict & Kelly, 1988; Casper, Benedict, & Perry, 1989; Christensen-Szalansk & Willham, 1991; Hastie, Schkade, & Payne, 1999; Hawkins & Hastie, 1990; Stallard & Worthington, 1998). Repeated studies have found that, especially in complex litigation involving scientific information, most jurors tend to use unsophisticated "cognitive shortcuts or heuristics" to make decisions (Worthington, Stallard, Price, & Goss, 2002). They reason backwards from what they now know or believe happened, e.g., that a plaintiff was injured, to determine what caused the injury and what the defendant could have and should have known and done to prevent the injury (Worthington, Stallard, Price, & Goss, 2002; Lowe, 1992 & 1993). This has two principal effects. First, jurors focus on the outcome (or the perceived outcome)—the injury—and filter evidence through this event. They emphasize the information that best explains to them how an injury occurred and use the selected data to make their judgment (Pennington & Hastie, 1981, 1991; Worthington, Stallard, Price, & Goss, 2002). Evidence that confuses the story or adds static to their understanding is de-emphasized, discounted, or even mentally discarded. Second, once they know (or believe) that an injury occurred, juries are more likely to hold that the defendant should have foreseen and prevented the injury. Thus they are more likely to award not only compensatory but punitive damages. When jurors know the sequence of a defendant's actions prior to an injury but do not yet know that an injury occurred, they are more likely to see the defendant as having acted responsibly. Once they learn of the injury that resulted, they are less likely to hold that the injury was foreseeable than jurors who are asked to judge a defendant's actions with full knowledge of injury claims (Hastie, Schkade, & Payne, 1999; Worthington, Stallard, Price, & Goss, 2002).

This limited understanding of statistics generates further difficulties concerning jurors' assessment of risk and their assessment of what the plaintiff should have understood regarding the risks associated with a procedure. There is extensive evidence that the average person has a limited ability to assess risk and that individuals interpret the same information regarding risk in widely different ways (Edwards, Elwyn, &

Mulley, 2002; Yamagishi, 1997; Lehman & Nisbett, 1990; Tversky & Kahnemann, 1981; Kovera, McAuliff, & Hebert, 1999). Thus in those cases in which there is scientific evidence to support the claim that a product did cause or contribute to a harm, jurors may be unable to assess whether a product poses such a remote risk to its users that the company might have been unable to know about it in advance or whether the manufacturer could have reasonably identified the risk and warned consumers. This issue can be critical not only to assigning liability but to determining punitive damages. If jurors fail to understand the mechanism of a particular adverse side-effect, they may attribute more wrong-doing to a manufacturer than may be merited, for example.

The fact that most healthcare involves risks, that all drugs and devices are likely to have side-effects and carry some risk, and that patients must engage a cost-benefit analysis to determine if the risks are "worth it" for them is something neither patients nor jurors may understand. First, they may not understand probability and may be ineffective at estimating risks (Nisbett & Ross, 1980; Tversky & Kahneman, 1982 in Worthington, Stallard, Price & Goss, 2002). Second, the idea of assuming risk and living with risk is not one many persons are happy to accept (Alcabes, 2003; Redelmeier, Rozin, & Kahnemann, 1993; Viscusi & Magat, 1987; Cates & Hinman, 1992). This can have implications for the informed consent process itself and for how jurors assess the responsibility a plaintiff has for bearing the consequences of assuming a risk of which he or she had been informed.

It is possible that even when they are told about a risk, patients may not understand the risk and thus may later allege that they were not fully informed such that someone else, e.g., a physician or manufacturer, is liable for their choice. People will often say that if they had realized a particular harm could befall them if they took a certain drug or underwent a certain procedure, that they never would have done it. They knew that the risk existed, but what they did not realize is that it was a real risk for them. They did not think that the harm would actually happen to them. This circumstance reflects the fact that the average person is not particularly adept at using statistical evidence or other information regarding risk to make decisions for him or herself. Individuals are not interested so much in the overall risks of a product. What they really want to know is whether or not something bad will happen to them; they seek certainties (Angell, 1996). In those cases in which they are told about risks but they do not realize that those risks are real for them, patients may allege that they were told about the risks in ways that minimized them. They may allege that the way in which they were told about the risk led them to dismiss the risk or to understand it as being less important or serious than it might be. Coupled with the way in which the benefits of a product are expressed in direct-to-consumer advertising, this could skew a patient's understanding of the risk-benefit ratio of a product. The dramatic increase in direct-to-consumer advertising in the pharmaceutical industry, for example, may help plaintiffs' attorneys to depict their clients as having been misinformed, thereby reducing their personal responsibility for their choices and increasing that of their physicians and/or the manufacturers in question. Thus even if they are told about a risk, plaintiffs may allege that they did not understand the risk, that the risk was not communicated effectively to them and so on.

A second scenario involves a manufacturer that knew of a risk, failed to do anything to minimize it and failed to warn consumers about it. The extent to which a manufacturer is liable in such cases was at issue in the now famous, or infamous, McDonalds coffee litigation.

In February of 1992, Liebeck, a passenger in a car driven by her grandson, purchased a cup of coffee from a drive-through McDonald's in Albuquerque, New Mexico (*Liebeck v. McDonald's Restaurant*). Upon receiving the order, the grandson pulled forward and stopped so that Liebeck could add sugar and cream to her coffee. Liebeck then placed the cup between her knees and began removing the plastic lid from the cup. In doing so, the coffee spilled into her lap. The sweatpants worn by Liebeck absorbed the coffee and held the scalding liquid next to her skin, causing third-degree burns over six percent of her body, including her inner thighs, perineum, buttocks, genital and groin areas. As a result of her injuries, Liebeck spent eight days in a hospital, undergoing treatment for these burns including skin grafting and debridement (removal of dead tissue). The burns left Liebeck scarred and disabled for over two years (Morgan, 1996). According to jury member Jack Elliott, this case was not simply about spilled coffee, rather about "callous disregard for the safety of the people" (Gerlin, 1994b). Liebeck informed McDonald's about her injuries and asked for $20,000 for compensation for her medical bills (which were estimated at $11,000). McDonald's responded with an offer for $800, which Liebeck refused (Gerlin, 1994a). McDonald's had several more opportunities to settle the case before trial, but refused several offers at $300,000 or less.

The jury considered the following facts. McDonald's, known for its control over franchises, required that coffee be brewed 195 to 205 degrees Fahrenheit and served between 180 and 190 degrees (Gerlin,

1994b). Coffee served at this temperature can cause third degree burns within three to seven seconds of exposure to the skin, whereas coffee served at 135 to 140 degrees (the general temperature of coffee served at home) may simply cause mild discomfort (Twiggs, 1997). Coffee served at 160 degrees requires at least twenty seconds of skin exposure to create third degree burns (Gerlin, 1994b).

McDonald's knew their coffee presented a danger to customers. A McDonalds quality assurance manager admitted during trial that "[our coffee] is not fit for human consumption because it would burn the mouth and throat" (Fact Sheet). During trial, McDonald's conceded that it had known about the risk of serious burns from its coffee for over ten years. From 1982 to 1992, McDonald's received over 700 reports of burns from their coffee (Morgan, 1996). McDonald's executive Christopher Appleton testified that McDonald's knew its coffee sometimes caused serious burns and admitted that customers were unaware of the extent of danger from coffee spills served at the company's required temperature and gave no explanation as to why there were no warnings on its cups (Morgan, 1996). Further, McDonald's stated that it had no intention of reducing the temperature of its coffee, saying "there are more serious dangers in restaurants" (Gerlin, 1994b).

The most damaging testimony came when Dr. P. Robert Knaff, a human factors engineer for McDonald's, told the jury that hot coffee burns were "statistically insignificant" when compared to the billion cups of coffee McDonald's sells annually (Gerlin, 1994b). To the jurors, this statement indicated that the burns suffered by Liebeck did not matter to McDonald's because they were uncommon (Gelin, 1994). Juror Betty Farnham commented, "There was a person behind every number and I don't think the corporation was attaching enough importance to that" (Gerlin, 1994b).

In returning a verdict, the jury awarded Liebeck $200,000 in compensatory damages for her medical costs and disability. This was reduced to $160,000 because the jury found that Liebeck was twenty percent at fault for spilling the coffee (*Liebeck v. McDonald's*). More notorious, however, was the jury's $2.7 million award in punitive damages, based on their finding that McDonald's had engaged in willful, reckless, malicious or wanton conduct (Morgan, 1996). Liebeck's attorney drew upon the jury's mounting disdain for the defendant by framing the case in terms of two days' worth of coffee sales profits to the McDonald's Corporation (approximately $2.7 million) (ATLA). Since punitive damages aim to punish a wrongdoer for engaging in the wrongful act and to discourage the wrongdoer and others from similar future action, the degree of punishment resulting from a judgment is proportionate to the wealth of the guilty party (Restatement). Thus, the jury could easily justify punishing McDonalds with an amount merely equal to two single days of coffee sales, regardless of how high that number may have been. The judge, however, announced that the punitive damages award was to be reduced to $480,000 (Morgan, 1997). Both sides appealed the decision, and after remittitur, the parties reached an out-of-court agreement for an undisclosed amount of money. Part of the settlement arrangement was that no one could release the details of the case, including the amount of damages finally agreed upon (Howard, 1994).

When a manufacturer knows of a risk and fails to minimize it and/or warn consumers about it, liability for the patient's choice may shift, at least to a significant extent, to the manufacturer. In the breast implant litigation, it was alleged that the manufacturers knew of the dangers of silicone breast implants and failed to disclose them or follow up on warnings they had of possible dangers (c.f., *Gladys J. Laas et al v. Dow Corning Corporation, et al, Harris County Texas and Jennifer H. Ladner v. Dow Corning Corporation et al,* Harris County Texas. Transcripts of closing arguments are available online at www.pbs.org/wgbh/pages/frontline/implants/).

Even though the causal connection between silicone and the ailments alleged by various plaintiffs has never been scientifically established, it is reasonable to think that the allegations of manufacturers having withheld information shaped the jurors' views of the defendants. This may be a result, at least in part, of the mistrust many Americans have in corporations.

A third scenario regarding risk and informed consent concerns a manufacturer that intentionally does not pursue certain kinds of tests in order to avoid identifying problems it would be obligated to disclose. Documents made available during the pretrial investigation of Bayer with regard to its no-longer-marketed cholesterol reducing drug, Baycol, suggest that this might in fact be the case at times. A note written by a Bayer official that was made available prior to the trial stated: "If the F.D.A. asks for bad news, we have to give, but if we don't have it, then we can't give it to them" (Berenson, 2003). The implication, no doubt, is that it may be best to remain ignorant of problems so as to not be obligated to divulge them. (Bayer voluntary withdrew Baycol from the market on August 9, 2001 after 31 people who had taken the drug died of rhabdomyolysis.)[4]

Finally, there may be cases in which a patient was not informed about a particular risk because it was not known. The liability issue here may turn on the question of whether the manufacturer could have and should have known about the risk. Could the manufacturer have done further testing on the product? How much more testing would likely have been required to identify the risk? Some risks may become evident only years after a patient undergoes a procedure or uses a product. For example, what initially appeared to be a breakthrough in the treatment of children with severe combined immunodeficiency syndrome (SCID) using gene therapy, turned out to be potentially connected to the development of leukemia in treated patients. But this was not learned until 30 months after the initial treatment (Hacein-Bey-Abin, et al., 2003). Or it may be so rare a risk that it is not until the product is widely used that the risk is identified. In those cases, someone with a reasonable understanding of the scientific method and statistics would observe that the manufacturer may not have reasonably been able to identify the risk and warn consumers about it. Such a circumstance might decrease the extent to which a jury awards a plaintiff punitive damages or even sees a defendant as liable. But jurors may not have the necessary understanding of statistics to make this assessment.

Even though someone with a reasonable understanding of science may understand and accept that certain risks could not have been known in advance because of the amount of time it would take for them to emerge, the law may not accept this time lag in part because of the hindsight-bias discussed earlier and in part because the cultures of science and the law collide over the concept of timeliness. Before we turn to the issue of the sometimes incompatible cultures of law and science, we would like to make one more comment regarding risk.

Litigation involving issues of risk, especially remote risk, establishes a threshold for product safety. This socially-constructed threshold can shape and affect the balance between the public policy goals of (1) promoting innovation in science and medicine and (2) bringing justice to injured parties. If juries set the level at maximum protection against any and all risks, regardless of how rare they are, the more costs are imposed on pharmaceutical and medical device manufacturers. Those costs may be seen as inordinate and as presenting an impediment to the development of treatments and devices that could lower risks of morbidity and mortality. Wherever one sets the threshold of acceptable safety and risk, one is committed to the view that harms to patients from drugs and devices that have met this threshold of safety must be accepted as unfortunate but not unfair. That is to say, they must not be seen as a basis for recovery at law.

Alternatively, some have argued that insofar as (1) there is some statistically predictable level of risk inherent in the use of drugs and devices and (2) overall it is beneficial to society that such products be available, a mechanism for compensating individual who are harmed by a product should be in place. Such "corrective justice" could be accomplished through products liability litigation or through a no-fault compensation system.[5] In either case, the goal would be to spread the costs of the risk embedded in using drugs and medical devices so that they are not borne solely by those who bear the consequences of said risk.

What in some cases appeals to be juror's disregard of scientific evidence may be the result, not of a poor understanding of science and statistics, but of a view that science is not reliable. Over time, scientific and medical opinion has changed on numerous issues, such as the use of rest and dietary restrictions to treat ulcers that were caused by bacteria (Cherry, 2002). Observing that scientists and physicians "change their minds" about what is good and bad for us, some might question whether we should "believe them" when they say a product is or appears to be safe. In due time they may change their minds, after all.

Finally, in some cases in which it may seem that a jury or judge has disregarded the scientific evidence, the underlying problem may be that the scientific evidence available cannot answer the question being asked by jurors and judges. The studies evaluating the causal relationship between silicone breast implants and connective tissue diseases are epidemiological studies. As discussed below with regard to alternative conceptions of causation (see Section E.), such studies are not meant to and cannot establish whether or not A causes B. Such studies only show correlations; they do not establish causality. Jurors and judges, who are assessing whether A caused B in a specific person or group of persons, may not find it appropriate, in assessing causation, to rely solely or primarily on data that is not meant to and cannot establish causality.

E. Culture Wars: Scientific and Legal Conceptions of Timeliness

The cultures of science and the law differ and sometimes clash in ways that result in what appear to be substantially skewed verdicts and settlements. One of the most significant of these culture clashes concerns time. A second concerns the way science and the law understand causation.[6]

The development of scientifically reliable knowledge regarding the effects of medical interventions requires the passage of time, sometimes a very long time. Thus one sense in which the law and science collide over time concerns the identification of risks and side-effects associated with drugs and devices, as noted above. To identify a rare side-effect of a drug or device might take years and may be accomplished only after a product is marketed and widely used. Clinical trials may involve thousands of individuals and yet may still miss those side-effects that are particularly rare. In deciding when to market a product, manufacturers and the FDA must make decisions regarding the overall costs and benefits of making a product available. If they wait too long, beneficial products may not be available to individuals who stand to benefit from them.

The long periods of time required to generate scientific evidence also contrast sharply with the circumstance that litigation operates on a fast track, *Bleak House* notwithstanding. Statutes of limitations require timely filing; discovery is deadline-driven (although extensions are expected); and settlement negotiations intensify as a trial date approaches or media coverage escalates. This intersection of contradictory notions of timeliness causes a time warp and associated distortions beyond inappropriately judging by hindsight. While scientists are still gathering and evaluating data and thus are not able to make judgments, the legal system requires that suits be filed, cases be heard, and juries render verdicts. During much of the breast implant litigation, for example, research was still being conducted to assess the correlation between silicone breast implants and the alleged ailments plaintiffs suffered (Hooper, Cecil, & Willging, 2001). The time-frame for science is much longer than the law permits. In both law and policy, choices must be made, sometimes without having all the information a scientist would require prior to making a choice (Foster, Bernstein, & Huber, 1993, p. 20).

F. Culture Wars: Scientific and Legal Conceptions of Causation

A second culture clash between science and the law involves the understanding of causation operative in each. Each field has built and in turn relies on different definitions of causation and proof. When scientists try to determine whether a particular product caused a harm, they generally rely greatly on epidemiologic data to assess the relationship, or lack thereof, between the product and harm in question. The importance of epidemiologic data has been affirmed by the courts. In the Bendectin case *Brock v. Merrell Dow Pharmaceuticals, Inc.*, the Fifth Circuit held epidemiological studies are "the most useful and conclusive type of evidence" and that "speculation unconfirmed by epidmiologic proof cannot form the basis for causation in a court of law" (quoted in Lasagna & Shulman, 1993, pp. 110-111). At the same time, the courts have recognized that there are differences between how epidemiologists understand causation and what constitute the sufficient conditions for proving causation in tort litigation. In *Ferebee v. Chevron Chemical Co.*, a products liability case over paraquat, an herbicide, the court held that "In a courtroom, the test for allowing a plaintiff to recover in a tort suit of this type is not scientific certainty but legal sufficiency" (quoted in Lasagna & Shulman, 1993, p. 111). It is difficult if not impossible to obtain scientific certainty. But litigation requires an end-point, a decision. The attempt to accommodate the dual conditions that scientific certainty is elusive or illusory and that law fixes liability at a particular point causes some inherent disjunction between science and the law.

There are four main categories of difference between the legal and scientific understandings of causation pertinent to products liability cases. First, scientists and the courts have different standards for the quantity of evidence necessary to make a declaration regarding causation. In the law, the requirement is that the preponderance of the evidence support a claim, meaning that the evidence must "render a fact more likely than not" (Lasagna & Shulman, 1993, p. 111). This standard is higher than mere chance, but it is not as high as the standard in science. Data that to scientists may be inconclusive may be to judges and juries strong enough to support a legal claim of cause.

Second, the focus of questions concerning causation and the goal in assessing causation is different in the law and in science. In the law, the goal is to assign liability for a particular harm that a particular claimant experienced. This is not the focus of epidemiological studies, and this is not a question epidemiologists can answer. Epidemiologists focus on risks, harms, diseases, and disorders in populations, not in particular persons (Dreyer, 1994). Epidemiological data will not be able to tell us, for example, whether a particular smoker developed lung cancer as a result of smoking or for some other reason or for some combination of reasons. The epidemiological data can, however, tell us that this person increased his risk of developing lung cancer by smoking. In the law this information about populations is used to determine the cause of particular instances of illness, injury, or harm.

Third, in the law, assessments of causation have a finality that they lack in science. Science typically is an open-ended endeavor in which cause and effect relationships can be studied over time. The goal in litigation is to make a decision, and there is a limited time frame for making the decision (Christoffel & Teret, 1991; Foster, Bernstein, & Huber, 1993, p. 20). In the courts, an answer of "yes" or "no" must ultimately be reached for questions of causality, while science is much slower to make such definitive pronouncements. In fact, epidemiologists rarely declare unequivocally that A causes B (Lasagna & Schulman, 1993, p. 112).

Finally, in the legal system assessments of causation often have an all-or-nothing character not shared by scientific assessments of causation. Epidemiologists generally recognize that one agent is rarely the sole cause of a harm. But the legal system does not necessarily build in the subtleties epidemiologists worry about (Rosenberg, 1984; Rothman, 1976, p. 589). Rosenberg (1984) argued for proportional liability and more nuanced standards of evidence to accommodate this conflict between science and the law. By setting up an all-or-nothing system, Rosenberg argues, some cases in which products contributed to a harm but were not the sole case may leave plaintiffs with no reward or with a reward that is too large. That is, the defendant may not be held sufficiently liable or may be held liable for more than it ought to be. If a product may have contributed to a harm but not been the sole cause of the harm, what are the other factors and can anyone be held liable for them? If no one else can be held liable and no one else will compensate the plaintiff, a jury might be inclined to require the defendant to disproportionately compensate the plaintiff. It is not unheard of for a jury to recognize that the scientific evidence does not support the plaintiff's claim but to award the plaintiff damages anyway (c.f., Bandow, 1998).

These differences reflect a clash of cultures between science and the law, yet in products liability litigation we expect the two to intersect.

G. The Influence of Outside Parties: The Media

No discussion of products liability would be complete without considering the role of the media. The media are not generally involved as parties in litigation. Yet they are extraordinarily influential in shaping public opinion. At the front end, the media can bring scientific and technical developments to the public's attention, sometimes making progress sound more rapid than it is, making new technologies sound more promising than they may be, and in general increasing the public's faith in science and medicine. If one considers, for example, some of the discussion of stem cell research in the popular press, one might think that the cure to many sources of morbidity, and mortality itself, lie just around the corner.

The media also can play a role in shaping public opinion regarding the "dark side" of science and medicine. When media attention to an issue is widespread prior to litigation, they can influence not only the public at large but those who will someday be expert witnesses and jurors. Although the jury selection process is intended to weed out those who already have a settled opinion, a strong bias, or a conflict of interest, it may not be possible to find a jury that is truly opinion-free and has never heard media reports on the issue or at least on related issues. The dangers of silicone breast implants are only one example. By telling horrific stories of individuals who are suffering or allegedly suffering as a result of a particular device or drug, it is sometimes difficult for the public to see the larger picture and to assess the extent to which the defendant is liable for the suffering.

The media are now playing another important role in products liability litigation. In addition to raising awareness of harms or alleged harms and perhaps skewing or biasing the opinions of future jurors by spreading information about alleged harms, users of products may suddenly "recognize" symptoms they have and associate them with a product they are using or have used. Through television, newspaper and radio advertising, plaintiffs' attorneys are communicating with those persons to generate client lists. Such attorneys first identify individuals who are extremely ill and they try their cases in favorable jurisdictions. If the first set of cases generates large verdicts, the corporate defendants are much more likely to settle future cases involving individuals who are also quite sick rather than go to trial. But a condition of settling later cases involving sick individuals is making payments to the long list of clients generated primarily through advertising, even though some or many of those individuals may not be sick at all (Berenson, 2003). Thus individuals who would have been unlikely to win a case are paid as part of the settlement.

Media also may inaccurately portray a system gone wild. The "McDonald's Coffee" lawsuit provides an example. In 1994, a jury awarded 81-year old Stella Liebeck $2.86 million for injuries she sustained from spilled McDonald's coffee. The media, hungry for attention-getting headlines, portrayed a tainted system of justice with headlines such as "Coffee Spill Burns Woman; Jury Awards $2.9 million" (Wall Street Journal, Aug. 19, 1994, at B3) and "Hot Cup of Coffee Costs $2.9 million" (The Orange County Reporter, Aug 19, 1994, at C1). However, both the media and those seeking to limit consumers' legal rights overlooked the facts of the case, described *supra,* which place the award to Mrs. Liebeck in a significantly different light. Media coverage of the ultimate reduction of the award by the trial judge, from $200,000 in compensatory damages to $160,000 and from $2.7 million in punitive damages to $480,000, was limited.

Although in the past the media have sometimes disregarded the scientific evidence and provided skewed information that shaped public opinion, the media can play an important role in better informing the public on matters of health and science and improving public understanding of the concepts involved, such as risk and causation. Responsible health and science reporting moves in this direction.

Notes

1. The authors would like to thank Vinita Ollapaly, Taylor Kerns, Barbara Hinze, and Jerome Schmelzer for their assistance with the preparation of this paper.
2. Prior to the 1976 Medical Device Amendment to the Food, Drug, and Cosmetic Act, medical devices, such as breast implants, were not regulated by the FDA. When they came under the FDA's purvey, makers of devices already on the market were not immediately required to submit data demonstrating the safety of their products. It was not until 1991 that the FDA asked makers of silicone breast implants to produce these data.
3. For a review and summary of a number of pertinent studies, see Sanchez-Guerrero, Schur, et al. (1994).
4. For further discussion of the Baycol litigation, see Langley (2004).
5. Catherine Wells, for example, has argued that tort law can be used to achieve corrective justice (Wells, 1990).
6. For further discussion of both issues, see Cheng (2003).

References

Alcabes, P. (2003, May 23). 'Epidemiologists need to shatter myth of risk-free life', *Chronicle of Higher Education,* B11-12.

American Medical Association. (2000). *Organizational Ethics in Health Care.* Chicago: American Medical Association.

Angell, M. (1996). 'Shattuck lecture—evaluating the health risks of breast implants: The interplay of medical science, the law, and public opinion', *New England Journal of Medicine,* 334(23), 1513-1518.

Aselton, P., Jick, H., Milunsky, A., Hunter, J., & Stergachis, A. (1985). 'First trimester drug use and congenital disorders', *Obstetrics and Gynecology,* 65, 451-455.

ATLA-TORT § 55:13

Bandow, D. (1998, November 30). 'Many torts later, the case against implants collapses', *Wall Street Journal,* Section A, p. 23, column 3.

Bekelman, J., Li, Y., & Gross, C.P. (2003). 'Scope and impact of financial conflicts of interest in biomedical research', *Journal American Medical Association,* 289, 454.

Berenson, A. (2003, May 18). 'Trial lawyers are now focusing on lawsuits against drug makers,' *New York Times,* 1.1.1

'Breast Implants on Trial'. (1996, February 27). *Frontline,* PBS.

Brown, M.N., Keeley, T.J., & Hiers, W.J. (1998). 'The epistemological role of expert witnesses and toxic torts', *American Business Law Journal,* 36, 1-72.

Buchanan, A. (2000). 'Trust in managed care organizations', *Kennedy Institute of Ethics Journal,* 10(3), 189-212.

Calabresi, G. & Bobbitt, P. (1978). *Tragic Choices.* New York: W. W. Norton and Company.

Capron, A.M. (1996). 'Daubert and the quest for value-free "scientific knowledge" in the courtroom', *University of Richmond Law Review,* 30(85), 86.

Casper, J.D., Benedict, K., & Kelly, J.R. (1988). 'Cognition, attitudes and decision-making in search and seizure cases', *Journal of Applied Social Psychology,* 18, 93-113.

Casper, J.D., Benedict, K., & Perry, J.L. (1989). 'Juror decision-making, attitudes, and the hindsight bias', *Law and Human Behavior,* 13, 291-310.

Cates, W. Jr, & Hinman, A.R. (1992). 'AIDS and absolutism—the demand for perfection in prevention', *New England Journal of Medicine,* 327(7), 492-94.

Caudill, D.S. & LaRue, L.H. (2003). 'Why judges applying the Daubert trilogy need to know about the social, institutional, and rhetorical—and not just the methodological —aspects of science', *Boston College Law Review,* 45(1), 1.

Cheng, E. (2003). 'Changing scientific evidence,' *Minnesota Law Review,* 88, 315.

Cherry, M.J. (2002). 'Medical fact and ulcer disease: A study in scientific controversy resolution', *History and Philosophy of the Life Sciences,* 24, 249-273.

Christensen-Szalanski, J.J. & Willham, C.F. (1991). 'The hindsight bias: A meta-analysis,' *Organizational Behavior and Human Decision Processes,* 48, 147-168.

Christoffel, T. & Teret, S.P. (1991). 'Epidemiology and the law: Courts and confidence intervals,' *American Journal of Public Health,* 18(12), 1661-1666.

Clarke, M. & Clayton, D.G. (1981). 'Safety of Debendox,' *The Lancet,* 1(8221), 659-660.

Cover, R.M. (1982). 'The Supreme Court, 1982 Term ___ Foreword: Nomos and narrative', *Harvard Law Review,* 97, 3.

Cowell, S.E. (2000). 'Pretrial mediation of complex scientific cases: A proposal to reduce jury and judicial confusion', *Chicago-Kent Law Review,* 75 (981), 984.

Cox, M.L. (2003). 'The Dalkon Shield saga,' *Journal of Family Planning and Reproductive Health Care,* 29(1), 8.

Donnai, D. & Harris, R. (1978). 'Unusual fetal malformations after antiemetics in early pregnancy,' *British Medical Journal,* 9(6114), 691-692.

Dorr-Goold, S. (2001). 'Trust and the ethics of health care institutions', *Hastings Center Report,* 31(6), 26-33.

Dreyer, N. (1994). 'An epidemiological view of causation: How it differs from the legal,' PBS Frontline: Breast Implants on Trial [Online]. Available at: www.pbs.org/wgbh/pages/frontline/implants/legal/defensejournal2.html

Eastman, H.A. (1995). 'Speaking truth to power: The language of civil rights litigators', *Yale Law Journal,* 104, 763-864.

Edwards, A., Elwyn, G., & Mulley, A. (2002). 'Explaining risks: Turning numerical data into meaningful pictures,' *British Medical Journal,* 324(7341), 827-830.

Elbroune, D., Mutch, L., Dauncy, M., et al. (1985). 'Debendox revisited,' *British Journal of Obstetrics and Gynecology,* 92, 780-786.

European Committee on Quality Assurance and Medical Devices in Plastic Surgery. (2003). *Consensus Declaration on Breast Implants* [Online]. Available at: www.secpre.org/pdf/equam.pdf.

Fact Sheet: *McDonald's Scalding Coffee Case.* [Online]. Available at: http://www.atla.org/DonsumerMediaResources/Tier3/press_room/FACTS/friv-

olous/McdonaldsCoffeecase.aspx
Feldman, H.L. (1995). 'Science and uncertainty in mass exposure litigation', *Texas Law Review,* 74(1), 16.
Fischoff, B. (1975). 'Hindsight foresight: The effect of outcome knowledge on judgment under uncertainty,' *Journal of Experimental Psychology,* 1, 288–299.
Fisher, J. E., Nelson, S.J., Allen, J.E., & Holzman, R.S. (1982). 'Congenital cystic adenomatoid malformation of the lung,' *American Journal of Disabilities in Children,* 136, 1071-1074.
Fleming, D. M., Knox, J.D., & Crombie, D.L. (1981). 'Debendox in early pregnancy and fetal malformation,' *British Medical Journal,* 283, 99-101.
Foster, K., Bernstein, D., & Huber, P. (2003). *Phantom Risk: Scientific Inference and the Law.* Cambridge: MIT Press.
Frey, A.L. & Orr, D.P. (2004). 'Litigating damages: Actual and punitive', 21 No. 2 GPSolo 30.
Friedman, M. (1979). 'The social responsibility of business', in: T.L. Beauchamp & N.E. Bowie (Eds.), *Ethical Theory and Business* (pp. 136-138). Englewood Cliffs, NJ: Prentice-Hall.
Friedman, M. (1967). *Legal Theory.* New York: Columbia University Press.
Frith, K. (1978). 'Fetal malformation after Debendox treatment in early pregnancy,' *British Medical Journal,* 9(6119), 925.
Gabriel, S.E., O'Fallon, W.M., Kurland, L.T., Beard, C.M., Woods, J.E., & Melton, L.J. (1994). 'Risk of connective-tissue diseases and other disorders after breast implantation', *New England Journal of Medicine,* 330, 1697-1702.
Gareen, I.F., Greenland, S., & Morgenstern, H. (2000). 'Intrauterine devices and pelvic inflammatory disease: Meta-analyses of published studies, 1974-1990,' *Epidemiology,* 11(5), 589-597.
Gerlin, A. (1994a, September 1). 'A matter of degree: How a jury decided McDonald's should pay a woman millions for a hot-coffee spill', *Wall Street Journal,* A1.
Gerlin, A. (1994b, September 14) 'McDonald's callousness was real issue, jurors say, in case of burned woman,' *Wall Street Journal,* A1.
Gibson, G. T., Colley, D.P., McMichael, A.J., & Harthshorne, J.M. (1981). 'Congenital anomalies in relation to the use of doxylamine/dicyclomine and other antenatal factors, an ongoing prospective study,' *Medical Journal of Australia,* 1(8), 410-413.
Golding, J., Vivian, S., & Baldwin, J.A. (1983). 'Maternal anti-nauseants and clefts of lip and palate,' *Human Toxicology,* 2, 63-73.
Golanski, A. (forthcoming). 'General causation at a crossroads in toxic tort cases', *Pennsylvania State Law Review,* 108, 479.
Gott, D.M. & Tinkler, J.J.B. (1994). *Silicone Implants and Connective Tissue Disease.* London: Medical Devices Agency.
Green, M.D. (1992). 'Expert Witnesses and Sufficiency of Evidence in Toxic Substances Litigation: The Legacy of Agent Orange and Bendectin Litigation', *Northwestern University Law Review,* 86, 643-645.
Grodofsky, M. P. & Wilmott, R.W. (1984). 'Possible association of use of Bendectin during early pregnancy and congenital lung hypoplasia', *New England Journal of Medicine,* 311, 732.
Hacein-Bey-Abina, S., von Kalle, C., Schmidt, M., Le Deist, F., Wulffraat, N., McIntyre, E., Radford, I., Villeval, J.L., Fraser, C., Cavazzana-Calvo, M., & Fischer, A. (2003). 'A serious adverse event after successful gene therapy for x-linked severe combined immunodeficiency,' *New England Journal of Medicine,* 348(3), 255-256.

Hart, H.M. & McNaughton, J.T. (1958). 'Evidence and inference in the law', *Daedalus*, Fall.

Hastie, R., Schkade, D.A., & Payne, J.W. (1999). 'Juror judgments in civil cases: Hindsight effects on judgments of liability for punitive damage,' *Law and Human Behavior*, 23, 597-64.

Hawkins, S.A. & Hastie, R. (1990). 'Hindsight: Biased judgments of past events after the outcomes are known,' *Psychological Bulletin*, 107, 311-327.

Hennekens, C.H., Lee, I.M., Cook, N., Hebert, P., Karlson, E., LaMotte, F., Manson, J.R., & Buring, J.E. (1996). 'Self-reported breast implants and connective-tissue diseases in female health professionals: A retrospective cohort study,' *Journal of the American Medical Association*, 275, 616-621

Henning, S.J. & Berman, D.A. (2003). 'A mold claims primer microbial contamination issues', Fall Brief, 33(22), 31. Cf.

Hersch, J. (2002). 'Breast implants: Regulation, litigation, and science.' In: W. K. Viscusi (Ed.), *Regulation Through Litigation* (pp. 142-182). Washington, DC: AEI-Brookings.

Hooper, L. L., Cecil, J.S., & Willging, T.E. (2001). 'Assessing causation in breast implant litigation: The role of science panels,' *Law and Contemporary Problems*, September.

Howard, T. (1994, December 12). 'McDonald's settles coffee suit in out-of-court agreement', *Nation's Restaurant News*, 1.

Illingworth, P. (2002). 'Trust: The scarcest of medical resources,' *The Journal of Medicine and Philosophy*, 27(1), 31-46.

Institute of Medicine. (2000). *Safety of Silicone Breast Implants*. Washington, DC: National Academies Press.

Jeffreis, J. A., Robboy, S.J., O'Brien, P.C., Bergstralh, E.J., Labarthe, D.R., Barnes, A.B., Noller, K.L., Hatab, P.A., Kaufman, R.H., & Townsend, D.E. (1984). 'Structural anomalies of the cervix and vagina in women enrolled in the Diethylstilbestrol Adenosis (DESAD) Project,' *American Journal of Obstetrics and Gynecology*, 148, 59-66.

Jick, H., Holmes, L.B., Hunter, J.R., Madsen, S., & Stergachis, A. (1981) 'First trimester drug use and congenital disorders,' *Journal of the American Medical Association*, 256, 343-346.

Kaplow, L. & Shavell, S. (2002). 'Fairness versus welfare', *Harvard Law Review*, 114, 961, 1319.

Kaufman, R.H., Adam, E., Binder, G.L., & Gerthoffer, E. (1980). 'Upper genital tract changes and pregnancy outcome in offspring exposed in utero to diethylstilbestrol,' *American Journal of Obstetrics and Gynecology*, 137(3), 299-308.

Kaufman, D. W., Watson, J., Rosenberg, L., Helmrich, S.P., Miller, D.R., Miettinen, O.S., Stolley, P.D., & Shapiro, S. (1983). 'The effect of different types of intrauterine devices on the risk of pelvic inflammatory disease,' *Journal of the American Medical Association*, 250(6), 759-762.

Kolata, G. & Meier, B. (1995, September 18). 'Implant lawsuits create a medical rush to cash in,' *The New York Times*, A1.

Kovera, M.B., McAuliff, B.D., & Hebert, K.S. (1999). 'Reasoning about scientific evidence: The effects of juror gender and evidence quality on juror decisions in hostile work environment case,' *Journal of Applied Psychology*, 84, 362-375.

Langley, M. (2004, May 3). 'Courtroom triage: Bayer, pressed to settle a flood of suits over drug, fights back,' *Wall Street Journal*, A1.

Lasagna, L. & Shulman, S. (1993). 'Bendectin and the language of causation,' in: K. Foster, D. Bernstein, & P. Huber (Eds.), *Phantom Risk: Scientific Inference and the Law* (pp. 101-122). Cambridge: MIT Press.

Lee, N.C., Rubin, G.L., Ory, H.W., & Burkman, R.T. (1983). 'Type of intrauterine device and the risk of pelvic inflammatory disease,' *Obstetrics and Gynecology*, 62(1), 1-6.

Lehman, D.R. & Nisbett, R.E. (1990). 'A longitudinal study of the effects of undergraduate training on reasoning', *Developmental Psychology*, 26, 952-960.

Liebeck v. McDonald's Restaurants. (1995). WL 360369 (N.M. Dist.).

Lowe, D.J. (1992/1993). 'An empirical examination of the hindsight bias phenomenon in evaluation of auditor decisions', Doctoral Dissertation, Arizona State University.

MacMahon, B. (1981). 'More on Bendectin,' *Journal of the American Medical Association*, 246, 371-372.

McCredi, J., Kricker, Elliott, J., & Forrest, J. (1984). 'The innocent bystander, doxylamine/dicyclomine/pyridoxine and congenital limb defects,' *Medical Journal of Australia, 140*, 525-527.

Mechanic, D. (1998). 'The Functions and Limitations of Trust in the Provision of Medical Care,' *Journal of Health Politics, Policy and Law*, 23, 661-686.

Mellor, S. (1978). 'Fetal malformation after debendox treatment in early pregnancy,' *British Medical Journal*, 1(6119), 1055-1056.

Menon, J.W. (1995). 'Adversarial medical and scientific testimony and lay jurors: A proposal for medical malpractice reform,' *American Journal of Law and Medicine*, 21, 281-300.

Menzies, C.J.G. (1978). 'Fetal malformation after debendox treatment in early pregnancy,' *British Medical Journal*, 1(6119), 925.

Michaelis, J., Michaelis, H., Gluck, E., & Koller, S. (1983). 'Prospective study of suspected associations between certain drugs administered during early pregnancy and congenital malformations', *Teratology*, 27, 57-64.

Milkovich, L. & van den Berg, B.J. (1976). 'An evaluation of the teratogenicity of certain antinauseant drugs,' *American Journal of Obstetrics and Gynecology*, 125, 244-248.

Morgan, S.R. (1996). 'Verdict against McDonald's is fully justified', *The National Law Journal*, 117(8), A20.

Nelson, M.M. & Forfar, J.O. (1971). 'Associations between drugs administered during pregnancy and congenital abnormalities of the fetus,' *British Medical Journal*, 1, 523-527.

Newman, N.M., Correy, J.F., & Dudgeon, G.I. (1977). 'A survey of congenital abnormalities and drugs in a private practice,' *Australia and New Zealand Journal of Obstetrics and Gynecology*, 17, 156-159.

Nisbett, R. & Ross, L. (1980). *Human Inference: Strategies and Shortcomings of Social Judgment*. Englewood Cliffs, NJ: Prentice Hall.

Paterson, D.C. (1969). 'Congenital deformities,' *Canadian Medical Association Journal*, 101, 175-176.

Paterson, D.C. (1977). 'Congential deformities associated with Bendectin,' *Canadian Medical Association Journal*, 116, 1348.

Pellegrino, E.D. (1991). 'Trust and distrust in professional ethics,' in E. D. Pellegrino, R. Veatch, & J. Langan (Eds.), *Ethics, Trust, and the Professions: Philosophical and Cultural Perspectives* (pp. 69-92). Washington, DC: Georgetown University Press.

Pennington, N. & Hastie, R. (1981). 'Juror decision-making models: The generalization gap,' *Psychological Bulletin*, 89, 246-287.

Pennington, N. & Hastie, R. (1991). 'A cognitive theory of juror decision making: The story model,' *Cardozo Law Review*, 13, 59-557.

Podlas, K. (2004). 'As seen on TV: The normative influence of syndi-court on contem-

porary litigiousness', *Villanova Sports & Entertainment Law Journal,* 11(1).
Potter, N. (1996). 'Discretionary power, lies, and broken trust: Justification and discomfort,' *Theoretical Medicine,* 17, 329-352.
Redelmeier, D.A., Rozin, P., & Kahneman, D. (1993). 'Understanding patients' decisions: Cognitive and emotional perspectives,' *Journal of the American Medical Association,* 270, 72-76.
RESTATEMENT (SECOND) OF TORTS § 908(a); § 908(e) (1979).
Rhodes, R. & Strain, J.J. (2000). 'Trust and transforming medical institutions,' *Cambridge Quarterly of Healthcare Ethics,* 9, 205-217.
Riley, S.E. (1996). 'The end of an ERA: Junk science departs products liability,' *Defense Counsel Journal,* 63, 502-508.
Rosenberg, D. (1984). 'The causal connection in mass exposure cases: "Public Law" vision of the tort system,' *Harvard Law Review,* 97, 849-929.
Rothman, K.J. (1976). 'Causes,' *American Journal of Epidemilogy,* 104, 587-592.
Rothman, K.J., Fyler, D.C., Goldblatt, A., & Kreidberg, M.B. (1979). 'Exogenous hormones and other drug exposures of children with congenital heart disease,' *American Journal of Epidemiology,* 109, 433-439.
Rubinson, R. (2004). 'Client counseling, medication, and alternative narratives of dispute resolution', *Clinical Law Review,* 10, 833-874.
Saks, M.J. (1992). 'Do we really know anything about the behavior of the tort litigation system—and why not?' *University of Pennsylvania Law Review,* 140(1147), 1268.
Sanchez-Guerrero, J., Schur, P.H., Sergent, J.J., & Liong, M.H. (1994). 'Silicone breast implants and rheumatic disease: Clinical, immunologic, and epidemiologic studies', *Journal of Arthritis and Rheumatology,* 37, 158-168.
Sanchez-Guerrero, J., Colditz, G.A., Karlson, E.W., Hunter, D.H., Speizer, F.E., & Liang, M.H. (1995). 'Silicone breast implants and the risk of connective tissue diseases and symptoms,' *New England Journal of Medicine,* 332, 1666-1670.
Senekjian, E.K., Potkul, R.K., Frey, K., & Gerbst, A.L. (1988). 'Infertility among daughters either exposed or not exposed to diethylstilbestrol,' *American Journal of Obstetrics and Gynecology,* 158, 493-498.
Sivin, I. (1993). 'Another look at the Dalkon Shield: Meta-analysis underscores its problems,' *Contraception,* 48(1), 1-12.
Smithells, R. & Sheppard, S. (1978). 'Teratogenicity testing in humans: A method demonstrating safety of Bendectin,' *Obstetrics and Gynecology Survey,* 33, 582-584.
Snowden, R. & Pearson, B. (1984). 'Pelvic infection: A comparison of the Dalkon Shield and three other intrauterine devices,' *British Medical Journal of Clinical Research Education,* 288, 1570-1573.
Stallard, M.J. & Worthington, D.L. (1998). 'Reducing the hindsight bias utilizing attorney arguments,' *Law and Human Behavior,* 22, 671-683.
Sternberg, E. (1999). *The Stakeholder Concept: A Mistaken Doctrine.* London: Foundation for Business Responsibilities.
Stewart, M.W. (2002). 'Clarifying the political and social context of corporate crime: A case study of breast implants,' *Amici,* fall, 6-9.
Tverseky, A. & Kahneman, D. (1981). 'The framing and decisions and the psychology of choice,' *Science,* 211, 453-458
Twiggs, H. (1997). 'How civil justice saved me from getting burned', Trial, 33, 9.
United States v. Kubrick. (1979). 444 U.S. 111, 117.
VanNunen, S.A., Gatenby, P.A., & Basten, A. (1982). 'Post-mammoplastly connective tissue disease,' *Arthritis and Rheumatology,* 25, 694-697.

Viscusi, W.K. & Magat, W.A. (1987) *Learning about Risk: Consumer and Worker Responses to Hazard Information*. Cambridge, MA: Harvard University Press.

Wagner, W.E. (2003). 'The "Bad Science" fiction: Reclaiming the debate over the role of science in public health and environmental regulation', *Law and Contemporary Problems*, 66, 63-112.

Wells, C.P. (1990). 'Tort law as corrective justice: A pragmatic justification for jury adjudication', *Michigan Law Review*, 88, 2348- 2360.

Werhane, P. (2000). 'Business ethics, stakeholder theory, and the ethics of healthcare organizations,' *Cambridge Quarterly of Healthcare Ethics*, 9, 169-181.

Worthington, D.L., Stallard, M.J., Price, J.M., & Goss, P.J. (2002). 'Hindsight bias, Daubert, and the silicone breast implant litigation,' *Psychology, Public Policy, and Law*, 8, 54.

Wright, C.A., Miller, A.R., & Kane, M.K. (2004). *Federal Practice & Procedure*. Chapter 5, Section 1778.

Yamagishi, K. (1997). 'When a 12.86% mortality is more dangerous than 24.14%: Implications for risk communication', *Applied Cognitive Psychology*, 11, 495-506.

Zaner, R.M. (1991). 'The phenomenon of trust and the patient-physician relationship,' in: E.D. Pellegrino, R. Veatch, & J. Langan (Eds.), *Ethics, Trust, and the Professions: Philosophical and Cultural Perspectives* (pp. 45-68). Washington, DC: Georgetown University Press.

Zierler, S. & Rothman, K.J. (1985). 'Congenital heart disease in relation to maternal use of Bendectin and other drugs in early pregnancy,' *New England Journal of Medicine*, 313, 347-352.

Contributors

Nicholas Capaldi is the Legendre-Soulé Distinguished Chair in Business Ethics at Loyola University New Orleans.

Pepe Lee Chang is Assistant Professor in the Department of Management at the University of Texas at San Antonio.

Andrew I. Cohen is Assistant Professor of Philosophy and Associate Director of the Jean Beer Blumenfeld Center for Ethics at Georgia State University.

H. Tristram Engelhardt, Jr., is Professor in the Department of Philosophy at Rice University, Professor Emeritus in the Department of Medicine at the Baylor College of Medicine. He is also the Editor of *The Journal of Medicine and Philosophy* and the Founding and Senior Editor of *Christian Bioethics.*

Richard A. Epstein is James Parker Hall Distinguished Service Professor of Law at the University of Chicago School of Law and the Peter and Kirsten Bedford Senior Fellow at the Hoover Institution, Stanford University.

Jeremy Garrett is Assistant Professor in the Department of Philosophy at California State University, Sacramento. He is also Managing Editor of *The Journal of Medicine and Philosophy.*

John C. Goodman is founder and president of the National Center for Policy Analysis, a nonprofit public policy institute with offices in Dallas, Texas, and Washington, D.C. Goodman received a Ph.D. in economics from Columbia University and has taught at a number of colleges and universities.

John R. Graham is Director of Health Care Studies at the Pacific Research Institute. He earned a BA (Hons) from the Royal Military College of

Canada and a MBA from the London Business School.

Ana S. Iltis is Associate Professor of Health Care Ethics and Ph.D. Program Director in the Center for Health Care Ethics at Saint Louis University. She is co-editor-in-chief of the *Journal of Law, Medicine & Ethics* as well as Associate Editor of *The Journal of Medicine and Philosophy.*

Sandra H. Johnson holds the Tenet Chair in Health Law and Ethics at Saint Louis University with appointments as Professor of Law in the Center for Health Law Studies at the University's School of Law and Professor of Health Care Ethics in the Center for Health Care Ethics. She is co-editor-in-chief of the *Journal of Law, Medicine & Ethics.*

Michael A. Rie, M.D., is Associate Professor of Anesthesiology and Director of the Anesthesiology Intensivist Service at the University of Kentucky College of Medicine.

James Stacy Taylor is Assistant Professor of Philosophy at The College of New Jersey. His main work is on autonomy theory, the metaphysics of death, and applied ethics. He is the editor of *Personal Autonomy: New essays* (Cambridge University Press, 2005), and the author of *Stakes and Kidneys: Why markets in human body parts are morally imperative* (Ashgate, 2005).

Index

Conflicts and Trends®: Studies in Values and Policies

Series Editor: H. Tristram Engelhardt, Jr.

Global Bioethics: The Collapse of Consensus

Edited by H. Tristram Engelhardt

2006, xii + 396pp. ISBN 978-0-9764041-3-2